Lidia's

CELEBRATE LIKE AN ITALIAN

Lidia's
CELEBRATE LIKE AN ITALIAN

LIDIA MATTICCHIO BASTIANICH
AND TANYA BASTIANICH MANUALI

Photographs by Steve Giralt

Alfred A. Knopf   New York   2017

THIS IS A BORZOI BOOK PUBLISHED BY ALFRED A. KNOPF

Copyright © 2017 by Tutti a Tavola, LLC

www.aaknopf.com

Knopf, Borzoi Books, and the colophon are registered trademarks of Penguin Random House LLC.

Library of Congress Cataloging-in-Publication Data
Names: Bastianich, Lidia, author. | Manuali, Tanya Bastianich, author. |
Giralt, Steve, photographer.
Title: Lidia's celebrate like an Italian : 220 foolproof recipes that make
every meal a party / Lidia Matticchio Bastianich and Tanya Bastianich
Manuali ; photographs by Steve Giralt.
Description: First edition. | New York : Alfred A. Knopf, [2017] | Includes index.
Identifiers: LCCN 2017010180 | ISBN 9780385349482 (hardcover : alk. paper) |
ISBN 9780385349499 (ebook)
Subjects: LCSH: Cooking, Italian. | LCGFT: Cookbooks.
Classification: LCC TX723 .B31566 2017 | DDC 641.5945—dc23
LC record available at https://lccn.loc.gov/2017010180

Interior photography by Steve Giralt
Jacket photographs by Steve Giralt
Jacket design by Kelly Blair

Manufactured in the United States of America
First Edition

THIS BOOK IS DEDICATED TO YOU, THE READER.

*The special moments in life are those shared with family and friends
around a table, celebrating with food and love.
So, please, have many grand and delicious moments.*

A SEAT AT THE TABLE OPENS A WINDOW TO THE HEART.

—Tanya Bastianich Manuali

Contents

Aperitivi

Appetizers

Salads

Soups

Vegetables and Sides

Polenta, Risotto, and Pasta

Fish and Seafood

Poultry and Meat

Desserts

Preface

This book is written with the intent and desire to share with the reader and home cook all my knowledge of, experience in, and enthusiasm for cooking and entertaining. It is a delight and an act of love to cook for family and friends on a daily basis, but my hope is that this book will help everyone turn that love into a great celebration, be it a wedding or just a relaxed get-together. I chose these particular recipes because they are delicious and easy to make, and they serve and fit any celebration you might be planning. I give you suggestions about how to make your party successful and how to set it up, and even how to start it off with interesting and delicious Italian-style drinks, alcoholic and nonalcoholic. Do you want to host a gathering serving only butlered appetizers, or do you envision a grand buffet? Is it an elegant dinner or a casual pizza party that you have in mind? I have plenty of suggestions to share with you: from how best to set the table to how to serve the recipes you choose. There are even suggestions for how to throw the ultimate warm and loving Italian wedding that you have dreamed of (and I provide recipes for your caterer, so you can relax and just enjoy the blessed event). My daughter, Tanya, and I have made sure that all the food selections and entertaining advice work for every age group, since everyone, at every age, should be celebrating life. This book was written with the hope that there will be much entertainment in all of your lives. By sharing these recipes and all the suggestions in this book, I now feel that I will always be present at your events and able to give you celebratory good wishes.

Acknowledgments

The making of a book is always a huge collaborative effort. Tanya and I have a wonderful team of people helping and supporting us when we work on our books. Amy Stevenson, always with us in the kitchen and a dear friend, is invaluable as we cook, measure, and write the days away; she's an extreme professional and a huge asset. We have enjoyed our many hours with Amy, watching her children grow along with us and listening to Grandma's stories. We also get a lot of work done together. A big thank-you to Peter Gethers and Tom Pold for pushing us to work harder and write better; it was a pleasure working on the book with both of you. Thank you to Jenna Brickley for her utmost professionalism and organization; it is much appreciated. A heartfelt thank-you to Paul Bogaards, for years of friendship and support and for always being enthusiastic about our books. You are a believer, and we love that. To our Knopf promotional mavens, Jordan Rodman and Sara Eagle, we are so thankful that you get us out there for everyone else to enjoy. Thank you, Kristen Bearse, Kelly Blair, and Carol Carson, for designing it—inside and out—and making it all look so good. It's a tough job to pull it all together, and thank goodness we have you to do it for us. Penelope Bouklas, we thank you for your style and attention to every detail of every utensil, linen, and plate. You made it all so easy. And for capturing it all with a wonderful eye, thank you to Steve Giralt. Your work in photography is gorgeous, and you are an absolute pleasure to work with.

Thank you also to our office and restaurant staff, who provide us with support so we can be creative and make books. Thank you to the American Public Television team for the fabulous work done in the distribution of the show. And thanks to the wonderful team at WGBH in Boston—Laurie Donnelly, Anna Adams, Bara Levin, and Matthew Midura. Your support has always been a strength and is greatly appreciated. A heartfelt thank-you to the sponsors of the show, Cento, Loacker, Rovagnati, Regione Calabria, and Il Consorzio di Grana Padano; it has been wonderful working with you. Thank you also to Juliska for the gorgeous tableware and linens, and to the wonderful showroom consultants at Clarke, who provide the gorgeous kitchen in which the show is filmed.

My eternal gratitude goes to my family. It is through them that I found the strength, the drive, the passion, the love, and the prose and recipes for this book. All the festivities, cooking, and entertaining described in these pages have happened within our family at some point.

My mother, Erminia, age ninety-seven, has much *esperienza vitae,* or experience of life, as she says, and she was and still is always willing to share and celebrate with us. My brother Franco's and my graduations, then our marriages and the births of our children, have all been acknowledged with family celebrations, as have christenings, communions, engagements, and then the marriages of the next generation. Grandma, thank you for cooking, setting up, and celebrating every milestone in our family's life. This book is a recollection of those celebrations.

Introduction

I love to entertain; it is my way of sharing the best of me, my affection and love, my way of saying I want to nurture you. When you eat my food, I want you to become part of my life, of my family, of my world. Food communicates how we feel so well, and when the food is both delectable and well presented, any event becomes a celebration.

I get a thrill from serving people good food and seeing the group share and interact in the moment, so when I designed my kitchen I kept in mind how I like to entertain. I prefer not to have my guests in a far-off dining room. I like them at a big casual table right in front of me as I cook on my island. I use the granite top of my island as an antipasto buffet space. Soup, pasta, and main courses are served to guests seated at the table, and then it is back to the island for a buffet-style serving of desserts. This is pretty much the standard at my house, and my regular guests already know the system. Only when it is not the usual crowd of family and friends, possibly someone special from Europe, do I serve my food a bit more formally and dress the table up with a fancier tablecloth and cloth napkins.

Italians love to celebrate life, family, and friends, and for us, this is best done through food, with the addition of some good wine, music, and some space to socialize and dance. Entertaining Italian style is not only about what to eat but also about that welcoming feeling, the setting, and the mood, *la festa*. So how does one organize such a party, dinner, wedding, or gathering?

Depending on what type of event you are planning—whether an intimate gathering or a larger sit-down dinner, a family-style meal, a buffet, a barbecue, or a cocktail party with tasty hors d'oeuvres, this book will help you pull it off with real Italian style and flavor. An Italian celebration can be structured many ways, but a good guideline to follow is to begin with an *aperitivo,* or pre-meal *stuzzichini* (tasty bites or hors d'oeuvres) and fruity bubbly cocktails, or, if you are planning a big *festa,* a buffet with salads, cured meats, and frittate. Serving the antipasto as a buffet, with lots of selections, is my favorite way to start off holiday meals and large family gatherings. A buffet gives everybody an opportunity to mingle, choose the food they like, go back for seconds, and then sit down together as I serve the main course at the table, which is usually family-style, with platters of seasonal favorites. After the main meal, it is back to the buffet for dessert.

In this book, I will give you ideas and suggest different possibilities to help you create your own style of Italian entertaining. Maybe you like to start with passed *stuzzichini* and then go straight to a sit-down meal served family style. Or perhaps the affair you are planning is more formal in nature, and you will serve three full courses, each individually plated for your guests—*che eleganza*! Whatever your style of entertaining, the recipes in this book will render it easy and delicious, and I am sure that many of them will become part of your everyday cooking as well, making every day a party.

Stuzzichini are an elegant addition to any party. *Stuzzicare* means "to pick on," and *stuzzichini* are small bite-sized portions. In this book, some recipes are meant to be served only as *stuzzichini;* others are part of a meal, which if cut into bite-sized pieces become *stuzzichini* and can be passed around to guests as they sip some prosecco or an Aperol Spritz (page 10).

Italian recipes lend themselves well to being served on a buffet table. From salads to marinated vegetables, hot or chilled soups, frittate, pasta, fish, and meat, there are plenty of recipes in this book appropriate for an Italian buffet of *abbondanza,* truly plentiful. Or pick a few and create an elegant sit-down meal. Everyone loves a barbecue, and grilling with an Italian flair is extra fun, particularly when a good grill is flanked by excellent Italian side dishes of salads, marinated vegetables, pastas, and cured vegetables: that's when the *festa* really begins. Of course, the easiest way to handle a big crowd at a sit-down dinner is by serving food family style, one of my favorite ways, for which there are an abundance of recipes in this book.

In these pages, you will find favorite Italian apéritifs to open a meal, as well as luscious Italian desserts and coffees to close it. There are special instructions on how to prepare, cook, and serve food for a crowd, plus seasonal recipes, from hot soups for the cooler days to chilled versions for the summer. It is important to know when and what is best to serve hot or at room temperature; getting all these details right makes for a very memorable party, and you will find them in this book.

Entertaining comes in many forms, from big celebrations that highlight life's important moments, such as weddings, to just having a few friends over to break bread. Every time food is served, it is something of a special moment for me. First off, I love to feed people, and it gives me great satisfaction. I always pay attention to the details and plan what foods would go well together, even if it is just for my immediate family on a plain old Sunday afternoon. I hope this book will help you figure out how best to entertain in a way that suits your food, style, and home, and that my suggestions for formal meals or buffet-style service will give you the opportunity to try new ways of entertaining. Most important, never forget that entertaining is about bringing people together, and there is no better way to do that than by sharing food, good conversation, and a few laughs as well.

Enjoy. *Buona festa!*

Lidia's

CELEBRATE LIKE AN ITALIAN

Planning a Party? Where to Start

The first thing to decide when planning an event is what type of party you want to throw. A major determining factor is the number of guests you are expecting and what kind of space you have available; the significance of the event and the budget are also important deciding elements. Will it be a family-style dinner, or a seated and plated meal? Or is it something more casual, with buffet service or perhaps an outdoor barbecue? You also need to take into consideration the time you have to prepare for the event, and whether or not you will have help making and serving the food and drinks. And do not forget the clean-up part; make sure you have planned for some help or allotted enough time for yourself. Make a list of the equipment, plates, utensils, and glasses needed. Do you have enough? Will you need to rent some, or will you use disposable versions? Do you have enough platters, glasses, silverware, and so on to make everything look fabulous?

Choose your table decorations wisely. I like to go back to nature and pick flowers, branches, and herbs from my garden to decorate the tables and the space. Also, you should make a rough plan or rendering of the space available and place the tables, chairs, and service stations appropriately. Do you have enough tables and chairs, or will you need to rent some of those as well? Do not crowd the buffet dishes all on one side, but distribute them evenly around, so people will not be crowded into one area of service.

If you're entertaining on a larger scale, you must figure out the right quantities of food and beverage so that everyone has enough. You do not want to run out, but you do not want to go overboard, either—having too much just makes extra work and wastes food. You can really think it through carefully, down to deciding an approximate amount of *stuzzichini* per head or planning for a half-bottle of wine per person.

When it comes time to serve the food for a buffet, do not put it all out at one time. Divide it, and keep some aside to refresh the *stuzzichini* or buffet table if that is what you have chosen to do.

Once you have determined most of the above elements, you can begin to plan your menu. I find it best to vary the dishes to keep things manageable. If you are going to be serving an entrée that takes time to prepare and is a bit more costly, then maybe decide on a less expensive vegetable-based antipasto that can be made ahead of time to start. You should also consider planning your dishes based on the cooking method, so you do not end up with an oven or stove that is too crowded or unmanageable. Divide the menu by serving some salads or cold foods that can be prepared in advance, and some side dishes that can be served at room temperature or reheated fast.

If you are going to be garnishing your dishes, use items that are complementary to the recipes, such as produce or herbs you used to cook. It is also a good idea to have some "user-friendly" dishes: even if you are an adventurous cook and eater, not all of your guests may be as out there as you. Always mix some guaranteed crowd pleasers—salads and pasta are safe bets—in with your more ambitious dishes, so no one goes hungry and everyone leaves satisfied and happy.

And never forget the grand finale, dessert. Italian desserts are much less complicated and certainly less sweet than American ones. Beautiful fruit in season; *dolce al cucchiaio*, a dessert that is creamy and soft and usually eaten with a spoon, which can be prepared a day in advance; or some biscotti, *cioccolatini,* and good espresso are all you need to triumph in the end. For that extra Italian touch, bring out the amaro, a bitter after-dinner drink, and the grappa. The more you plan ahead, the more effortless your Italian-style meal will be.

Aperitivi

Aperol Spritz 10

Aperol Veneziano 10

Campari and Soda 11

Campari Americano 11

Fragolì Prosecco 12

Fragolì Daiquiri 12

Negroni 14

Vodka all'Aceto Cocktail 14

Pear Bellini 15

Amaro Bellini 15

Limoncello Martini 16

Boulevardier 16

An Italian in Manhattan 17

The Panache 17

Vin Brûlé 19

Sgroppino 19

Prosecco Punch 20

Blackberry Basil Spritzer 20

Grapefruit Fennel Spritzer 21

Cherry Almond Spritzer 21

Spiced Fruit Compote 22

Bomba Calabrese Bloody Mary 23

An opener to festivities, an *aperitivo,* can be a cocktail made with hard liquors such as gin or vodka, or a service of sparkling wines, such as champagne or prosecco. More often than not, at the beginning of an Italian dinner party or cocktail party an *aperitivo* is made with softer, gentler liquors, such as Aperol or Campari, to which prosecco, wine, juices, or amaro can be added. These are drinks meant to "open the appetite," or wake up your palate, and prepare you for the meal to come. But to invite someone for an *aperitivo* in Italy could simply be a social invitation to get together without a meal to follow. The tradition of going out for an *aperitivo* prior to eating is still quite strong in Italy, and some bars serve elaborate finger foods during the *aperitivo* time slot prior to dinner, usually starting somewhere around 7:00 p.m. And, more often than not, these elaborate *aperitivo* settings, which are usually short, can turn into the perfect Italian all-night cocktail party. To pull this off at home, put together some drinks from this chapter along with a nice selection of food from the appetizers chapter and *ecco là,* you are all set for an Italian-style cocktail party to celebrate important events like a birthday, graduation, or retirement. To make it really Italian, put on some Pavarotti, Bocelli, or Lucio Battisti to set the mood. You should also complement your cocktails with the bounty of the season. Dress your *aperitivo* with spring herbs such as mint and basil, especially if you will be entertaining on a terrace outside. Or get into the citrus family with lemons, tangerines, blood oranges, and bergamot for the holiday season.

APEROL SPRITZ

A spritz is a light drink in which club soda or seltzer water is added to a liqueur or wine or a combination of both. Light in taste and alcohol, and quite refreshing, it is also easy to scale up and serve in larger quantities in a pitcher. You can stir together the Aperol and white wine and chill them ahead of time, but add the club soda at the last minute. The orange-flavored element is essential, so if you do make a batch of it make sure you add orange slices to the pitcher.

Makes 1 cocktail

Ice cubes
2 ounces Aperol
1 cup dry white wine, chilled
Club soda, chilled
Orange slice, for garnish

Fill a white wine glass halfway with ice. Add the Aperol and white wine, and stir. Pour in club soda (up to ½ cup) to top off the glass.

Garnish the side of the glass with the orange slice, and serve.

APEROL VENEZIANO

This is a very refreshing and festive apéritif. The club soda makes it lighter in alcohol, but it is also delicious with just Aperol and prosecco. Do not forget the orange slice.

Makes 1 cocktail

Ice cubes
2 ounces Aperol
1 cup chilled prosecco
Club soda, chilled
Orange slice, for garnish

Fill a white wine glass halfway with ice. Add the Aperol and prosecco, and stir. Pour in club soda (up to ¼ cup) to top off the glass.

Garnish the side of the glass with an orange slice, and serve.

CAMPARI AND SODA

I like to serve this refreshing apéritif in a tall highball glass, with some ice cubes and an orange slice or an orange or lemon peel.

Makes 1 cocktail

Ice cubes
3 ounces Campari
¾ cup club soda, chilled
Orange slice, or orange or lemon peel, for garnish

Fill a highball glass with ice cubes. Add the Campari, and top with the chilled club soda. Stir.

Garnish the side of the glass with an orange slice, and serve each drink with a stirrer so your guests can mix the drink well.

CAMPARI AMERICANO

The recipe here is for the original Americano, but I sometimes like serving it in a highball glass with more club soda added.

Makes 1 cocktail

Ice cubes
2 ounces Campari
1 ounce Cinzano Rosso vermouth
Club soda, chilled, to taste
Strip of orange peel, for garnish

Fill a rocks glass or an Old Fashioned glass with ice cubes. Add the Campari and Cinzano Rosso. Top with a splash of club soda, and stir.

Twist the orange peel over the top of the glass, drop it in, and serve.

FRAGOLÌ PROSECCO

Fragolì is a sweet liqueur made with alcohol-infused wild strawberries. It can also be mixed with ginger ale instead of prosecco for a less alcoholic but much sweeter version of this drink. And it is good poured over vanilla ice cream for a quick dessert. It is bright red and sweet, with an intense strawberry flavor. Other flavorful fruit liqueurs can be substituted, such as peach liqueur, banana liqueur, or limoncello.

Makes 1 cocktail

1 ounce Fragolì (strawberry liqueur)
Prosecco, chilled
2 small strawberries, halved

Pour the Fragolì into a champagne flute, and fill the flute with prosecco. Stir.

Thread the strawberries onto a plastic pick, place in the drink, and serve.

FRAGOLÌ DAIQUIRI

To give a new, fruity twist to a standard daiquiri, try adding Fragolì, fresh strawberries, and, to balance the sweetness, some simple syrup. To make simple syrup, combine equal parts sugar and water, and bring to a simmer to dissolve the sugar. Cool completely, and chill. Simple syrup will keep in the refrigerator for a week or so, tightly covered, and can be used in a number of cocktails or to sweeten iced tea or iced coffee.

Makes 1 cocktail

1 tablespoon fresh lime juice
1 ounce chilled simple syrup (see headnote)
2 medium strawberries, stemmed and chopped, plus
  2 whole strawberries halved for garnish
4 fresh basil leaves
2 ounces Fragolì (strawberry liqueur)
About 6 ounces prosecco, chilled

Chill a highball glass in the freezer for at least 15 minutes.

In the highball glass, combine the lime juice, simple syrup, chopped strawberries, and basil. With a muddler (or use the back of a spoon), crush and press the berries to make a chunky purée and bruise the basil leaves. Remove the basil and discard.

Add the Fragolì, and pour in prosecco to fill the glass. Thread the halved strawberries on a plastic pick, place this in the drink, and serve.

NEGRONI

This is a classic Negroni. If you don't have a cocktail shaker, you can also just stir all of the ingredients together in the glass. A Negroni can be served on the rocks, as in this recipe, but it also makes for a very elegant drink when served straight up in a chilled martini glass.

Makes 1 cocktail

Ice cubes
1 ounce gin
1 ounce Campari
1 ounce Cinzano Rosso vermouth
Strip of orange peel, for garnish

Chill a rocks glass or an Old Fashioned glass in the freezer for at least 15 minutes.

In a cocktail shaker filled with ice, combine the gin, Campari, and Cinzano Rosso. Shake to combine. Pour over fresh ice in the chilled glass.

Twist the orange peel over the top of the glass, drop it in, and serve.

VODKA ALL'ACETO COCKTAIL

On its own, the vinegar syrup makes a refreshing nonalcoholic drink—just add more club soda. With vodka, it's a perfect summer cocktail.

Makes 6 cocktails

VINEGAR SYRUP
2 cups red wine vinegar
½ cup honey

DRINK
Ice cubes
Vodka
Club soda, chilled

In a small saucepan, combine the vinegar and honey. Bring to a boil, and cook until reduced to a syrup that coats the back of a spoon, about 15 minutes. You should have about ¾ cup syrup. (This is enough for three or four drinks.) Let the syrup cool completely.

For each drink, fill a highball glass with ice cubes. Add 2 tablespoons syrup and 1 ounce vodka, and stir. Add club soda to fill the glass, about 1 cup, and stir again.

PEAR BELLINI

The recipe for the pear purée makes about 1½ cups, enough for about eight cocktails, but if you have any left over it will keep in the refrigerator for several days, or can be frozen. The purée can also be made with peaches or apricots.

Makes purée for 8 Bellinis

PEAR PURÉE
3 ripe medium Bartlett pears, peeled, cored, and chopped
3 tablespoons sugar
1 tablespoon lemon juice

BELLINI
Prosecco, chilled
Strip of candied ginger, for garnish

In a medium saucepan, combine the pears, sugar, lemon juice, and 2 cups water. Simmer until the pears are very tender, about 20 minutes. When it is cooled, purée the mixture in a blender, then chill.

For each Bellini, pour 1 ounce purée into a champagne flute and fill the flute with prosecco. Stir, drop in a piece of candied ginger, and serve.

AMARO BELLINI

A Bellini is usually a somewhat fruity, bubbly, sweet apéritif, but here I give it a bitter twist with some amaro, a bitter liqueur usually served as a digestif at the end of a meal.

Makes 1 cocktail

2 sugar cubes
About 2 teaspoons amaro, to soak the cubes
Prosecco, chilled
Strip of orange peel, for garnish

Drop the sugar cubes into a champagne flute, and pour amaro over them to soak them. Let sit a few minutes.

Fill the flute with prosecco. Twist the orange peel over the flute, drop it in, and serve.

LIMONCELLO MARTINI

If you are a martini drinker, there is nothing like a dry straight-up martini with an olive, but today martinis are found in many different renditions. I do like the apple martini, but for a more Italian drink, here is a limoncello martini with a daiquiri presentation.

Makes 1 cocktail

Kosher salt, for rimming the glass
½ lemon
Ice cubes
1½ ounces limoncello
1½ ounces vodka
4 fresh basil leaves

Spread a layer of salt in a saucer. Rub the rim of a martini glass with the cut side of the lemon half. Lightly dip the rim of the glass in the salt, to coat.

Fill a cocktail shaker with ice. Pour in the limoncello and vodka, roughly tear the basil leaves, and add. Shake vigorously.

Strain the mixture through the shaker into the prepared glass, and serve.

BOULEVARDIER

This cocktail swaps rye (or bourbon, if you prefer) for the gin in a traditional Negroni, making it an ideal choice in cooler months.

Makes 1 cocktail

Ice cubes
1 ounce rye or bourbon
1 ounce Campari
1 ounce Cinzano Rosso vermouth
Strip of orange peel, for garnish

Chill a rocks glass or an Old Fashioned glass in the freezer for at least 15 minutes.

In a cocktail shaker filled with ice, combine the rye, Campari, and Cinzano Rosso. Shake to combine. Strain into the chilled glass.

Twist the orange peel over the top of the glass, drop it in, and serve.

AN ITALIAN IN MANHATTAN

This is an Italian take on the classic Manhattan, substituting your favorite Italian amaro (a family of bitter liqueurs) for the bitters in the classic version, and amarena cherries for the maraschinos.

Makes 1 cocktail

Ice cubes
2 ounces whiskey
1 ounce Cinzano Rosso vermouth
½ ounce Averna (or other Italian amaro)
2 amarena cherries in syrup, drained

Chill a rocks or martini glass in the freezer for at least 15 minutes.

In a cocktail shaker with a few ice cubes, combine the whiskey, sweet vermouth, and Averna. Stir with a cocktail stirrer to combine. Strain into the chilled glass, drop in the cherries, and serve.

THE PANACHE

This Italian version of the shandy is a perfect low-alcohol refresher in the hot summer months. In Italy, you'll also see these made with beer and Sprite, but I like the slightly less sweet and more effervescent Limonata. The most important aspect of this drink is that your glasses, beer, and soda all be ice cold!

Makes 2

One 12-ounce bottle Italian lager beer, such as Peroni, chilled
One 12-ounce can Italian lemon soda, such as Limonata, chilled

Put two pint or other tall drinking glasses in the freezer 30 minutes before serving.

Divide the beer between the glasses. When the beer settles, pour in the soda, give each glass a brief stir, and serve.

VIN BRÛLÉ

Vin brûlé is a version of mulled wine enjoyed in Piemonte, in northwestern Italy. It's a perfect choice for holiday entertaining, because you can double or even triple the recipe and leave it over very low heat, ladling it out as your guests come in from the cold. To really take off the chill, add a dash of brandy to the cup when serving. Most recipes call for only the citrus zest, but I add the juice as well—why waste it?

Serves 6 or more

2 oranges
1 cinnamon stick
1 teaspoon allspice berries
6 whole cloves
Two 750ml bottles dry red wine (it's okay to use something inexpensive here)
¾ to 1 cup sugar
Thin slices of orange, for serving
Brandy (optional)

Remove the peel from the oranges with a vegetable peeler. Set the peel in a square of cheesecloth with the cinnamon, allspice, and cloves, and tie to enclose.

Put the sachet in a large Dutch oven, and add the wine and ¾ cup sugar. Bring to a bare simmer over low heat. Taste, and add the remaining sugar, to your taste. Simmer 5 minutes, then reduce heat to the lowest setting and simmer for an additional 5 to 10 minutes. To serve, drop an orange slice and a splash of brandy (if using) into a coffee mug or teacup, and ladle in the *vin brûlé.*

SGROPPINO

This slushy cocktail originally came from Venice; it's just the right start to a brunch in the hot summer months, or a delightful finish to a dinner party (drink your dessert!). It's usually made with vodka, but I sometimes like to vary it by using limoncello instead. You can make several of these at one time if you have a crowd, doubling or quadrupling the amounts in a large measuring cup or pitcher, but serve right away, so they stay nice and slushy.

Makes 1 cocktail

4 ounces prosecco, chilled
½ cup lemon sorbetto
1 ounce vodka or limoncello

Put a wineglass in the freezer to chill for 15 minutes.

In a spouted measuring cup, stir together the prosecco, sorbetto, and vodka or limoncello until smooth and slushy. Pour into the wineglass, and serve right away.

PROSECCO PUNCH

This is a lovely colorful punch for big spring or summer gatherings, such as showers and graduation parties. You can vary the fruit, substituting other stone fruits or berries, based on what is in season.

Serves about 20

2 cups Aperol
1 cup citrus vodka
1 pint raspberries
2 oranges, quartered and thinly sliced
3 peaches or nectarines, pitted, quartered, and thinly sliced
1 liter citrus-flavored seltzer, chilled
Two 750ml bottles prosecco, chilled
1 ice block or mold

In a large bowl, combine the Aperol, vodka, raspberries, oranges, and peaches or nectarines. Chill 1 to 2 hours, to let the flavors mingle.

When you're ready to serve, dump the fruit mixture into a large punch bowl, and add the seltzer and prosecco. Add the ice, and serve.

BLACKBERRY BASIL SPRITZER

You can use between 2 and 4 tablespoons of the syrup base here for each drink, depending on how sweet you'd like it to be.

Serves 2 to 4

¾ cup sugar
1 pint blackberries
4 small stalks fresh basil, plus more for garnish
Seltzer, chilled
Ice cubes

In a small saucepan, combine the sugar, blackberries, basil, and 1 cup water. Bring to a simmer and reduce until syrupy, about 15 minutes. (Watch carefully so it doesn't burn.) Strain and cool.

To serve, pour 2 to 4 tablespoons syrup into each serving glass, and add 1 cup chilled seltzer to each. Stir, and fill the glasses with ice. Garnish each with a basil sprig, and serve.

GRAPEFRUIT FENNEL SPRITZER

Serves 2 to 4

3 large red grapefruits
¾ cup sugar
2 tablespoons fennel seeds
Seltzer, chilled
Ice cubes

With a vegetable peeler, remove the peel from one grapefruit. Squeeze enough juice from the grapefruits to yield 2 cups.

In a small saucepan, combine the peel, juice, sugar, and fennel seeds, and simmer until syrupy, about 18 minutes. Strain and cool.

To serve, pour 2 to 4 tablespoons syrup into each serving glass, and add 1 cup chilled seltzer. Stir, and fill the glasses with ice. Serve.

CHERRY ALMOND SPRITZER

Serves 2 to 4

2 cups tart cherry juice
½ cup sugar
½ teaspoon pure almond extract
Seltzer, chilled
Ice cubes

In a small saucepan, combine the cherry juice and sugar, and simmer until syrupy, about 18 minutes. Stir in the almond extract, and cool.

To serve, pour 2 to 4 tablespoons syrup into each serving glass, and add 1 cup chilled seltzer to each. Stir, and fill the glasses with ice. Serve.

SPICED FRUIT COMPOTE

Don't throw away the fruit used in the compote. It makes a wonderful breakfast with oatmeal or plain yogurt.

Serves 8 to 10

3 whole cloves
3 pounds apples, cored and cut into wedges
1 cinnamon stick
1 medium orange
1 medium lemon
8 ounces mixed dried fruit, such as prunes, figs, apricot, and pears
½ cup sugar, plus more to taste

Stick the cloves into three of the apple wedges. In a medium Dutch oven, combine all the apples and 2 quarts cold water. Add the cinnamon stick. With a vegetable peeler, remove the peel from half of the orange and half of the lemon, and add peel to the pot. Squeeze juice from the entire orange and lemon into the pot, and add the dried fruit and sugar.

Bring to a simmer, cover, and gently simmer the compote until reduced by about a third, about 30 minutes.

Strain through a sieve, pressing on the cooked fruit to extract any remaining juices. Taste, and add more sugar if desired. Serve hot as a tea on cold day, or chilled on warmer days.

BOMBA CALABRESE BLOODY MARY

Calabrians like spice, and I use Bomba Calabrese, their red pepper paste, to make this hot Bloody Mary.

Makes 4 to 6 drinks

MIX

1 quart tomato juice
2 teaspoons grated fresh horseradish
1 teaspoon Calabrese peperoncini paste
2 teaspoons Worcestershire
Juice of ½ lime, freshly squeezed
Juice of ½ lemon, freshly squeezed
Pinch sea salt
Pinch freshly grated black pepper
Pinch celery powder

DRINK

6 to 8 ounces Bloody Mary mix
1½ to 2 ounces vodka

Blend all mix ingredients well. Adjust the peperoncini paste, lemon juice, salt, and pepper to taste, and set in the refrigerator to blend the flavors for a few hours or overnight.

To make the drink, combine 6 to 8 ounces of the mix with 1½ to 2 ounces of vodka and stir well.

Serve straight or over some ice cubes.

Decorate with a celery stalk with leaves, a few slices of English cucumber, a sprig of basil or thyme . . . as you like it.

Appetizers

The beauty of all the appetizer recipes included here is that they fit whatever style of entertaining you choose. They can be finger foods, passed around at a cocktail party, or be plated as a delectable buffet for a self-service party where people mingle and socialize. Or you can use them as delicious appetizers for your sit-down dinner.

For a family-style dinner, choices from this section can be set on platters and placed in the middle of the table for everyone to choose from or pick up the plate and pass around. The smaller appetizers, such as the stuffed mushrooms (opposite) or pizzette (page 70), work wonderfully for a cocktail party with only passed finger foods. As another passed snack, you could make small bruschette (pages 58–64) and have people pick them up off a tray. To truly impress, pass around swordfish skewers (page 87) and fried mozzarella skewers (page 81), or serve some stewed summer vegetables Sicilian style on a spoon (page 39). For a self-serve cocktail party—for example, if you're in charge of an office party—then you might try bite-sized *stuzzichini* on trays strategically placed around the party space, and also add a couple of dips, such as the carrot and chickpea dip (page 37) and the dip of baked goat cheese, fava, and artichoke (page 40) served with some Italian flatbreads, grissini, and savory fried bread. One important thing to keep in mind is to diversify your choices; make sure to have some things that are vegetarian, pescatarian, and gluten-free. And of course, if you really want to go all-out, you could make a whole dinner party out of appetizers, also known in my circle of friends as heavy appetizers—not in weight, but in abundance. For these types of gatherings, I like to put out small plates and forks and set up the appetizers buffet style. People love to pick; this usually means piling a plate high with a little bit of everything, which is a big part of the fun. Guests can try many different items and feel they have had a full meal. Here I often serve the stuffed vegetables (page 30), some skewers, arancini (page 78), lamb meatballs (page 97), pizzette, and so on down the line, always trying to keep a good balance between vegetables, starches, and proteins. If you choose this kind of service, always plate only half of each item to start with: if you put it all out at once, it will start to look messy once your guests begin to pick. Then, when you bring out the fresh plates with seconds, the buffet is refreshed.

STUFFED MUSHROOMS

Funghi Ripieni

This recipe is simple to multiply if you have a large number of guests. The mushrooms can be served warm or at room temperature, and are easily made ahead of time. They can be stuffed and frozen a few days to a week before, sealed tightly with plastic wrap before freezing, then defrosted and baked when needed. This recipe is delicious even without the chopped walnuts, if you are concerned about nut-intolerant guests. Stuffed mushrooms are an Italian American favorite, and we used to serve them back in the early 1970s in my first restaurant in Queens. We often put two or three on the table as a small starter. You can serve them on a platter in a buffet, or pass them around at a cocktail party as hors d'oeuvres.

Makes 24

24 medium white or cremini mushrooms, or a mix
¼ cup extra-virgin olive oil, plus more for brushing
4 tablespoons unsalted butter
4 cups loosely packed baby spinach
1 bunch scallions, white and green parts, chopped (about 1 cup)
2 teaspoons kosher salt
½ cup chopped toasted walnuts
⅓ cup fine dried bread crumbs
⅓ cup grated Grana Padano
¼ cup dry white wine
½ cup chicken stock (page 148)
2 tablespoons chopped fresh Italian parsley

Preheat oven to 400 degrees. Remove stems from mushrooms and finely chop the stems.

In a large skillet over medium heat, melt 2 tablespoons of the butter in 2 tablespoons of the olive oil. When the butter is melted, add the stems and cook until they begin to wilt, about 4 minutes. Add the spinach, scallions, and 1 teaspoon salt. Cook until vegetables are wilted and no liquid from the spinach remains in the pan, about 4 minutes. Spread on your cutting board to cool slightly, then chop and put into a large bowl.

Mix in the walnuts, bread crumbs, and grated cheese. In a separate large bowl, toss the mushroom caps with the remaining 2 tablespoons oil and remaining 1 teaspoon salt. Brush a rimmed sheet pan with olive oil. Divide the filling among the mushrooms. Pour the wine and stock into the pan. Cut the remaining butter into cubes, and add to the liquid in the pan. Tent the pan with foil, taking care not to touch the mushrooms. Bake, covered, until the mushrooms are softened and release their juices, about 15 minutes. Uncover, and bake until the tops are crisp and golden, about 10 minutes more. Put the mushrooms on a platter. Pour the juices into a skillet, and reduce to whatever consistency you like. Stir in the parsley, and pour the juices around the mushrooms.

BAKED STUFFED VEGETABLES

Verdure Farcite al Forno

If you want to serve these hot (though they are also marvelous at room temperature), the vegetables can be stuffed earlier in the day and refrigerated. Add about 5 to 10 minutes to the total baking time if you're baking from the refrigerator. I often make these when I entertain my own family; served with a protein, such as meatloaf, they complete a good family dinner. These are also a great option as a main course for any vegetarian guests you might have. You get the following pieces of each vegetable once prepped: peppers, sixteen total; eggplant, eight total; yellow squash, twelve total; zucchini, twelve total; red onion, eight total.

Serves 10 or more as an antipasto

6 cups cubed day-old bread
1½ cups vegetable or chicken stock
8 baby bell peppers, assorted colors, halved and seeded
2 small eggplants
2 small yellow squash
2 small zucchini (about 6 ounces each)
2 small red onions (about 4 ounces each)
2 large eggs, beaten
1 bunch scallions, chopped (about 1 cup)
2 tablespoons chopped fresh Italian parsley
2 tablespoons chopped fresh thyme
2½ cups grated Grana Padano
8 ounces fresh mozzarella, diced
¼ cup extra-virgin olive oil
2 teaspoons kosher salt

Preheat oven to 400 degrees. Line two sheet pans with parchment paper. Put the bread cubes in a large bowl, and pour the stock over them. Let sit, tossing occasionally, until the stock is absorbed and the bread is soaked through, about 10 minutes. Squeeze out and discard any excess stock.

In the meantime, prep the vegetables. Trim the stems of the eggplants, cut each crosswise into four rounds, scoop out the flesh, and chop to make 1 cup.

Cut the yellow squash in thirds crosswise, then halve them, scooping out the center to make "boats"; discard the scooped-out flesh. Prepare the zucchini the same way as the yellow squash. Cut halved crosswise the onions, then remove the inner rings; onions should look like cups, using some of the scooped center pieces to patch the bottom of the onion cups before stuffing them.

Add the eggs, scallions, parsley, thyme, 2 cups of the grated cheese, and the mozzarella to the bread, and toss well to make a cohesive stuffing.

In another large bowl, toss the vegetables with the olive oil and salt. Stuff the vegetables with the filling, putting all of the eggplants and onions on one sheet pan, the zucchini, squash, and peppers on the other. Sprinkle the tops with the remaining ½ cup grated cheese. Tent the pans with foil (making sure it doesn't touch the filling), and bake, rotating the pans halfway through from top to bottom, until the vegetables are tender, about 30 minutes. Uncover, and bake until the tops are brown and crispy, about 15 to 20 minutes more.

Stuzzichini

Italians do not snack much. Generally, they eat only at mealtimes, nothing in between. So most bite-sized Italian snacks are consumed during an *aperitivo* or as *stuzzichini.* These snacks are usually accompanied by a light alcoholic beverage, often with bubbles, such as prosecco, a Bellini (page 15), or an Aperol Spritz (page 10), or a non-alcoholic choice such as Crodino, or a simple fruit juice with some sparkling water mixed in.

The *aperitivo,* before a meal, typically includes a mixture of nuts, olives, and chips, in Italian known as *salatini,* or salted items, and some more hearty snacks, such as mini-bruschette (pages 58–64), small pizzette (page 70), maybe stuffed button mushrooms (page 29) or mini-arancini (page 78). The items eaten during an *aperitivo* are small. The more abundant *stuzzichini* served as hors d'oeuvres are always a bit bigger in size, but still easy to pick up with your fingers and slip into your mouth. These can also be served on small skewers or in utensils that contain only one bite of food.

I find grilled polenta, topped in various ways (page 67), is an interesting alternative or a complement to toasted bread with toppings, like bruschette. I am a huge fan of baking savory crostate (pages 75–76) and cutting them into bite-sized squares. Not only is this delicious, but it is super-easy to make, stays warm in the oven, and is quick to plate and garnish. Everyone loves mini-meatballs with dipping sauce (page 97) at a cocktail party; I make not only a meat version, but also monkfish meatballs (page 89) with a dipping sauce, for which crowds go wild.

I mix up my *stuzzichini* by preparing items that are a bit more elaborate as well as those that are really simple and can be made ahead of time, like pitted prunes stuffed with roasted almonds, a perfect accompaniment to a cool glass of prosecco. To vary things a bit and make easier and more flavorful *stuzzichini,* Italians use *affettati* such as prosciutto, salami, a variety of different cheeses and cured vegetables (like olives and artichokes) and cured fish (like anchovies, tuna, and sardines). All are cut into small portions and usually served on serving toothpicks or in little spoons.

STUFFED ARTICHOKES

Carciofi Imbottiti

You can also make this with baby artichokes; you will need sixteen to use up all of the filling, and be sure to reduce the cooking time by about 15 minutes total. Either way, this recipe is wonderful served hot, with the juices spooned over, or at room temperature. The anchovies add complexity in flavor, but if you are concerned about picky guests, they can easily be left out. I often serve these in more casual entertaining.

A stuffed artichoke is also a great beginning to a meal as an antipasto. One artichoke per person is ideal. I like to serve it in a soup bowl with an underplate. Center the stuffed artichoke in the soup bowl and spoon some sauce around it. Your guests can pluck and enjoy leaf by leaf with the stuffing. And once they have scraped the inner part of the artichoke leaves, they can deposit them on the underplate and work their way around until they get to the heart.

Although I greatly enjoy the finger-licking fun of pulling off the leaves to scrape and suck off the stuffing and juices from each one, this can be a bit messy, so I like to give each guest a wet towelette.

Serves 8, or more if you halve them
for an antipasto buffet

ARTICHOKES

1 lemon, zested and halved
8 medium artichokes (about 8 ounces each)
¾ cup fine dried bread crumbs
½ cup grated pecorino
2 hard-boiled eggs, finely chopped
2 tablespoons chopped capers
2 tablespoons chopped fresh Italian parsley
1 tablespoon chopped fresh thyme
3 anchovy fillets, finely chopped
¼ cup extra-virgin olive oil

PAN SAUCE

2 cups dry white wine
1 cup chicken stock (page 148)
4 cloves garlic, sliced
1 lemon, thinly sliced
2 tablespoons chopped fresh Italian parsley

3 sprigs fresh thyme
1 teaspoon kosher salt
¼ teaspoon crushed red pepper flakes
¼ cup extra-virgin olive oil

Preheat oven to 400 degrees. For the artichokes, squeeze the juice from one lemon into a large bowl of cold water, and add the squeezed-out halves.

To prep the artichokes, trim the stems from the artichokes, peel the stems, and add them to the water. Snap any tough outer leaves from each artichoke and discard. Using a paring knife, trim any tough parts from the base of the artichoke and discard. With a serrated knife, cut off the top third of the artichoke and discard. Push the leaves open to expose the fuzzy purple choke, and scrape it out with a small spoon. Plunge the artichoke into the lemon water. Repeat with the remaining artichokes.

Remove the artichoke stems from water. Finely chop them and combine in a large bowl with the bread crumbs, grated cheese, eggs, capers, parsley, thyme, grated lemon zest, and anchovies. Drizzle with the olive oil, and toss to coat everything with the oil.

Drain and dry the artichokes well. To stuff, spread the leaves of an artichoke open and fill the center with ½ teaspoon of filling. Working outward, sprinkle and pack the stuffing into the rows of leaves as you spread them open using 2 to 3 teaspoons per artichoke. Put the artichoke in a 9-by-13-inch baking dish, and repeat with the remaining artichokes.

For the sauce, add the wine and stock and scatter the garlic, lemon slices, parsley, thyme, salt, red pepper flakes, and 2 tablespoons of the olive oil around the artichokes in the baking dish. Drizzle the remaining 2 tablespoons oil over the tops of the stuffed artichokes. Tent with foil (making sure it doesn't touch the crumbs), and bake until the artichokes are cooked through, about 40 minutes. Uncover, and bake until crumbs are golden brown and crisp and the sauce has reduced, about 20 minutes more.

ROASTED OLIVES WITH ORANGE AND ROSEMARY

Olive al Forno con Agrumi e Rosmarino

Big green Castelvetrano olives are delicious prepared this way, but any meaty olive will do well. Just change the baking time according to the size. These olives are perfect to accompany an aperitivo.

Serves 8

2 oranges
1 pound large green olives with pits (such as Castelvetrano)
3 tablespoons extra-virgin olive oil
3 sprigs fresh rosemary
2 sprigs fresh thyme
3 cloves garlic, thinly sliced
2 pinches crushed red pepper flakes
¼ teaspoon fennel powder

Preheat oven to 400 degrees. Grate the zest of one orange, remove the zest of the second orange with a vegetable peeler, and then juice both oranges. In a 9-by-13-inch glass or ceramic baking dish, toss together the olives, olive oil, 2 sprigs rosemary, the thyme, the zest removed with a peeler, orange juice, garlic, and 1 pinch crushed red pepper. Bake, tossing every 10 minutes, until olives are slightly shriveled and juices have reduced to a glaze, about 30 minutes.

While the olives are still hot, break the remaining sprig of rosemary over the top. Sprinkle with the finely grated orange zest, the fennel powder, and one more pinch crushed red pepper. Toss, and serve while still hot.

PROSCIUTTO DI PARMA "PURSES"

Fagottini di Prosciutto di Parma e Grana Padano

I was first served a similar dish by my friend Carlo at Galloni Prosciutto in Langhirano, near Parma. He took thin slices of prosciutto, stuffed them with Robiola, and tied them closed with a chive. A mouthful of flavor. Here I cook them and use an aged cheese, which is more tasty than a fresh cheese. Cook the "purses" just long enough to brown them. Overcooking will make them salty, and since Prosciutto di Parma is an air-cured product, it doesn't need to be cooked to be rendered edible. When buying the prosciutto, ask for slices from the widest part of the ham, measuring about 8 by 4 inches.

Makes 20 purses

20 sturdy fresh chives, each at least 5 inches long
10 thin slices Prosciutto di Parma, each
approximately 8 by 4 inches
½ cup grated Grana Padano
2 tablespoons unsalted butter
Ripe fresh figs, quartered, or ½-inch cubes of ripe
cantaloupe or honeydew melon, for serving

Bring a large skillet of water to a boil, and add the chives. Stir, separating the chives gently, just until they turn bright green, about 5 seconds. Transfer them with a slotted spoon to a bowl of cold water, and let stand a few seconds to stop the cooking. Remove the chives, and drain them on paper towels.

Cut the prosciutto slices in half crosswise to make pieces that measure approximately 4 by 4 inches. Place 1 teaspoon grated cheese in the center of each square. Gather the edges of the prosciutto over the cheese to form a "purse" with a rounded bottom and a ruffled top. Pinch the prosciutto firmly where it is gathered, and tie around this "neck" with a length of chive. Continue with remaining prosciutto slices, cheese, and chives.

In a large nonstick skillet, melt 1 tablespoon of the butter over low heat. Add half of the purses, and cook, shaking the skillet very gently, until the undersides are golden brown, about 3 to 4 minutes. Add the remaining 1 tablespoon butter, and cook the remaining purses in the same manner. Serve hot with fresh figs or ripe melon pieces.

CARROT AND CHICKPEA DIP

Intingolo di Carote e Ceci

This dip can be made a day ahead; just be sure to let it come to room temperature before serving. It freezes well, so, if you have some left over, cover with plastic wrap pressed against the dip, seal the container, and freeze. This way, the flavors will stay fresh and not get that freezer taste. It is perfect served with some vegetable sticks, or crackers, or used as an alternative spread on sandwiches.

Serves 8 or more

1 pound carrots, cut into 2-inch chunks
4 cloves garlic, crushed and peeled
2 fresh bay leaves
Two 15½-ounce cans chickpeas, rinsed and drained
Zest and juice of 1 lemon
1 teaspoon kosher salt, plus more to taste
⅛ teaspoon cayenne pepper
½ to ¾ cup extra-virgin olive oil
Flatbread, grissini, or crudités, for serving

In a medium saucepan, cover the carrots, garlic, and bay leaves with water by 2 inches. Bring to a simmer, cover, and cook until the carrots are very tender, about 20 to 25 minutes. Drain, reserving the cooking liquid. Discard the bay leaves.

In a food processor, combine the carrots, garlic, chickpeas, lemon zest and juice, salt, and cayenne. Process to make a smooth paste. With the motor running, add the olive oil in a slow, steady stream to ensure a smooth and creamy dip, a total time of 7 to 10 minutes. Add a little cooking water to adjust to a spreadable consistency. Serve with flatbread, crudités, or grissini, or a combination of some or all of these.

STEWED SUMMER VEGETABLES SICILIAN STYLE

Caponata

Caponata can last several days in the refrigerator and is even better after marinating for 24 hours. It is best eaten at room temperature, so remove it from the refrigerator about 2 hours before serving. Caponata is usually served as part of an antipasto assortment, although it makes a wonderful summer contorno, *or side dish, to serve with grilled meats or fish. It also makes a great topping for crostini; just chop it up into smaller pieces before spreading it on grilled bread. It's certainly perfect for summer entertaining.*

Serves 6 to 8

1 medium red bell pepper, cored, seeded, and cut into 1-inch squares
½ cup vegetable oil
1 medium eggplant, cut into 1-inch cubes
¼ cup extra-virgin olive oil
1 medium zucchini (about 6 ounces), cut into ½-inch cubes
1 medium onion, chopped
2 stalks celery, chopped
½ cup golden raisins
¼ cup pitted green olives, coarsely chopped
1 tablespoon toasted pine nuts
1 tablespoon drained capers in brine
1 teaspoon kosher salt, plus more to taste
Pinch crushed red pepper flakes
2 fresh medium tomatoes, peeled, seeded, and diced
¼ cup white wine vinegar
2 tablespoons sugar
1 tablespoon chopped fresh mint leaves

Bring a medium saucepan of salted water to a boil. Add the red pepper, and cook 1 minute. Drain well and pat dry.

Heat the vegetable oil in a large skillet over medium heat. Add the eggplant cubes and fry, stirring and turning them so they cook evenly, until the eggplant is golden brown on all sides, about 4 to 5 minutes. Remove the eggplant with a slotted spoon, and drain on a paper-towel-lined plate.

Heat the olive oil in a second large skillet. Add the zucchini, and cook, stirring occasionally, until golden, about 5 minutes. Remove with a slotted spoon, and add to the eggplant. Add the onion and celery to the olive oil remaining in the second pan, and cook until the vegetables are wilted, about 5 minutes. Stir in the raisins, green olives, pine nuts, capers, and blanched bell pepper. Season with the salt and red pepper flakes, and continue cooking, stirring, until the vegetables are soft but not mushy, about 10 minutes. Add the diced tomatoes, and cook until they are softened, about 5 minutes.

While the vegetables are cooking, make the sugar-mint syrup. Bring the vinegar to a boil in a small saucepan. Add the sugar and the mint, reduce the heat to low, and simmer until thick and syrupy, about 5 minutes.

Pour the syrup into the skillet of vegetables, and cook until the vegetables are very soft and juicy but not broken up—you should be able to see the shape of each vegetable—about 3 to 4 minutes. Finally, stir in the eggplant and zucchini and cook 1 to 2 minutes to combine the flavors. This can be served warm, at room temperature, or cold from the fridge.

BAKED GOAT CHEESE, FAVA, AND ARTICHOKE DIP

Intingolo di Fave, Carciofi, e Caprino al Forno

To make this dip any time of year, use frozen peeled favas and thaw under running water. If using fresh favas, remember that 2 pounds in the pod will equal about 1 cup of beans, once shelled and peeled. This dip can be assembled ahead of time, but bake it at the last minute. It is fabulous served warm, but also good at room temperature.

Serves 8

One 10-ounce log goat cheese, at room temperature
One 8-ounce package cream cheese, at room temperature
Zest of 1 lemon, plus 2 tablespoons juice
½ teaspoon kosher salt
1 cup coarsely chopped drained marinated artichoke hearts
1 cup fresh fava beans, shelled, blanched, and peeled (frozen favas are okay to use)
1 bunch scallions, white and green parts, chopped (about 1 cup)
¼ cup panko bread crumbs
¼ cup grated Grana Padano
Crackers or toasted baguette slices, for serving

When using fresh fava beans, after shelling from the pods, blanch for 5 minutes in boiling water, rinse in cold water, and remove skin from each bean.

Preheat oven to 375 degrees. In a food processor, combine the goat cheese, cream cheese, lemon zest and juice, and salt. Process until very smooth, scraping down the work bowl several times in between pulses.

Add the artichokes, favas, and scallions, and pulse several times, just to break them up a bit; you want them to remain quite chunky.

Scrape the mixture into a 2-quart gratin or other shallow baking dish. Sprinkle with the panko and the grated cheese. Place on a baking sheet (to catch any drips), and bake until the top is golden brown and the edges are bubbly, about 25 to 30 minutes.

Serve with a basket of toasted breads or crackers.

Sports Party

Watching soccer in Italy—or, here in the United States, football—involves a whole bunch of food and libations. Oftentimes, chips, dips, and prepackaged snacks are on the menu. I propose an alternative: use your oven and get out your grill. You can bake a crostata with mushrooms and onion (page 76) as much as a day or two in advance, and just cut it up and set it in the oven to reheat instead of serving chips. Or make some cannellini and pancetta bruschetta (page 62) and herb frittata roll-ups (page 51) to serve at room temperature. Include some raw vegetables to munch on, but instead of a thick ranch dressing, make some carrot and chickpea dip (page 37) or a dip of baked goat cheese, fava, and artichoke (page 40). You could put out a cheese platter with crackers, but I also like to include some toasted prosciutto and fig bruschetta (page 61), or bruschetta topped with kale (page 64) or sliced beef (page 58), along with some Prosciutto di Parma purses with Grana Padano and walnuts (page 36). And who doesn't love Italian deviled eggs (page 49)? If you like cheesy, gooey snacks, then, the day before the game, make some polenta, let it sit in a mold, then slice to quarter-inch thickness, grill or top with your favorite cheese or sautéed mushrooms, and serve. Throw in some arancini (page 78) and pizzette (page 70) and you have a winning party for sure. Your friends and family will want to watch weekend sports only at your place.

MARINATED MUSHROOMS

Funghi Marinati

These mushrooms will keep about a week in the fridge, so you can make a large batch and use them in various ways—on a sandwich or in a salad, as part of an antipasto spread, or as a nibble with cocktails. They are great served at a party together with other cured or pickled vegetables or a giardiniera (recipe follows).

When you are pickling or jarring vegetables, it is always recommended to sterilize the jars before using them.

Makes about 1½ quarts

1½ cups white wine vinegar

2 sprigs fresh rosemary

2 fresh bay leaves

2 teaspoons kosher salt

¼ teaspoon crushed red pepper flakes

1 pound small white button mushrooms (the smaller the better; bite-sized is best), cleaned and trimmed, halved if larger than button-sized

2 cloves garlic, crushed and peeled

Peel of 1 orange, removed with a vegetable peeler

Extra-virgin olive oil, for tossing

2 tablespoons chopped fresh Italian parsley

In a large saucepan, combine the vinegar, 1 cup water, the rosemary, bay leaves, salt, and red pepper flakes. Bring to a boil, add the mushrooms, and adjust the heat to a low simmer. Cover, and cook until the mushrooms are tender, about 5 minutes.

Remove the pot from the heat, add the garlic and orange peel, and let cool completely in the cooking liquid.

Pack the mushrooms and their seasonings into a sterilized jar or crock, and pour over them the cooking liquid to cover. Seal the jar, and refrigerate at least 24 hours or up to a week, to let the flavors develop.

To serve, drain off the liquid, and place the mushrooms in a serving bowl. Drizzle with olive oil to coat, add the parsley, toss well, and serve.

SPICY GIARDINIERA

Giardiniera Piccante

Start this at least 24 hours before you want to serve it to allow the pickling process to penetrate all of the vegetables. It will keep for several weeks in the refrigerator, and is good served on an antipasto table, or tossed in a green salad or with tomatoes. I also like to chop it up and use it as a condiment for heroes or other sandwiches. A little giardiniera juice also adds a kick to a Bloody Mary, and you can use the vegetables whole as a garnish if you wish.

Makes 3 quarts

1 medium cauliflower, cut into 1-inch florets

1 large red bell pepper, halved crosswise, seeded, and cut into ½-inch-thick strips

3 large carrots, cut into 2-by-½-inch-thick sticks

3 stalks celery, cut crosswise into ½-inch pieces on the bias

1 small red onion, sliced ½ inch thick

2 jalapeño peppers, seeded and slivered lengthwise

4 fresh bay leaves

4 cloves garlic, crushed and peeled

⅓ cup coarse sea or kosher salt

3 cups cider vinegar

3 tablespoons sugar

1 tablespoon mustard seeds

1 teaspoon celery seeds

1 teaspoon fennel seeds

In a very large glass or ceramic bowl, toss together the cauliflower, bell pepper, carrots, celery, red onion, jalapeños, bay leaves, and garlic. Sprinkle with the coarse salt, and toss well. Cover, and refrigerate overnight.

The next day, drain and rinse the vegetables very well. Pack them tightly into three sterilized quart jars, distributing the bay leaves and garlic equally among the jars.

In a medium saucepan, combine the cider vinegar, 3 cups water, the sugar, mustard seeds, celery seeds, and fennel seeds. Bring to a simmer, and simmer 1 minute. Slowly pour the liquid over the vegetables in the jars, distributing the spices evenly among the jars. Carefully tap the jars on the counter to remove any air bubbles, screw the lids on, and let cool completely. Refrigerate until ready to serve—at least 24 hours and up to 2 weeks.

STEWED SAVORY PEPPERS

Peperonata

This can be served warm or at room temperature, as part of an antipasto buffet or as a side dish. Serve lots of grilled or toasted bread alongside; if you have some peperonata left over, it makes a great frittata filling.

Serves 8 or more

¼ cup extra-virgin olive oil

4 anchovy fillets, chopped

2 medium onions, sliced ½ inch thick

6 small (or 4 large) bell peppers (red, yellow, and orange), cut into 1-inch strips

1 teaspoon kosher salt

½ cup pitted oil-cured black olives

¼ cup drained capers in brine

¼ teaspoon crushed red pepper flakes

One 28-ounce can whole San Marzano tomatoes, crushed by hand

Grilled or toasted country bread, for serving

Heat the olive oil in a large straight-sided skillet over medium heat. When the oil is hot, add the anchovies. Cook and stir until they dissolve into the oil, about 1 to 2 minutes. Add the onions, and cook until they begin to wilt, about 4 minutes.

Add the peppers, and season with the salt. Add the olives, capers, and red pepper flakes, and get everything sizzling; then add the tomatoes, slosh out the can with 1 cup water, and add that to the pan. Cover, and cook until the peppers begin to droop, about 10 minutes.

Uncover, and cook until the peppers and onions are tender and the sauce is thick and flavorful, about 10 to 15 minutes more. Serve with a basket of grilled or toasted bread on the side.

MEATLESS MEATBALLS WITH CHEESE AND QUINOA

Polpettine al Formaggio e Quinoa

These meatballs can also be baked on parchment-lined sheet pans in a 400-degree oven until crisp, about 20 minutes. Though they are wonderful served with the suggested sauce, they can also be served baked until crispy, with a drizzle of balsamic reduction. They are versatile, and can be served as bite-sized snacks at a cocktail party or on a platter in a buffet. The main problem in my house is that everyone who walks by the pot snags one, so there are usually very few left by the time the party begins.

Makes about 36 small meatballs, serving 8 or more as an appetizer

SAUCE

¼ cup extra-virgin olive oil
1 medium onion, chopped
One 28-ounce can whole San Marzano tomatoes, crushed by hand
2 fresh bay leaves
¼ teaspoon crushed red pepper flakes
½ teaspoon kosher salt

MEATBALLS

Vegetable oil, for frying
8 large eggs
1 medium zucchini (6 to 8 ounces), grated on the coarse holes of a box grater and squeezed dry
1 cup cooked quinoa
¼ cup chopped fresh Italian parsley
1 tablespoon chopped fresh thyme
½ teaspoon kosher salt, plus more to taste
2 cups grated Grana Padano
2 cups panko bread crumbs, plus more as needed

For the sauce, in a medium Dutch oven, heat the olive oil over medium heat. When the oil is hot, add the onion, and cook until it begins to soften, about 5 to 6 minutes. Add the tomatoes, bay leaves, red pepper flakes, and salt. Slosh out the tomato can with 3 cups water, and add that to the pot. Bring to a simmer, and cook until slightly thickened, about 15 minutes. (This sauce should be a little more watery than most if you are serving the meatballs in it, because they will absorb a lot of the liquid.)

For the meatballs, in a large straight-sided skillet, heat 2 inches of vegetable oil to 365 degrees. In a large bowl, beat the eggs. Stir in the zucchini, quinoa, parsley, thyme, and salt until well mixed. Stir in the grated cheese and panko. The mixture will seem wet; let it sit for 5 minutes so the crumbs absorb the liquid. If it is still very wet, add a little more panko, until you can roll the mixture into soft balls.

Roll heaping tablespoons of the mixture (or use a small ice-cream scoop) to make about thirty-six meatballs. Fry, in batches, until crisp and golden all over, about 4 minutes per batch, making sure the oil returns to 365 degrees between batches. Drain on paper towels, and season with salt.

Remove bay leaves from sauce when ready to serve. Serve the meatballs warmed in the sauce, or with the sauce on the side for dipping (in which case you can reduce it a bit more to thicken it).

ITALIAN DEVILED EGGS
Uova Farcite

My Italian version of this American favorite leaves out the mayo and replaces it with bright flavors reminiscent of salsa verde. They can (and should, because they taste better after the flavors blend for an hour or two) be made earlier in the day and kept in the refrigerator until you're ready to serve. The filling can easily be mixed by hand or in a mini-processor.

Makes 24 halves

12 large hard-boiled eggs
2 tablespoons Dijon mustard
2 tablespoons white wine vinegar
¼ teaspoon kosher salt
¼ cup extra-virgin olive oil
¼ cup finely chopped cornichons
¼ cup finely diced zucchini
¼ cup finely chopped roasted red bell peppers
2 tablespoons chopped drained capers in brine
2 tablespoons chopped fresh Italian parsley, plus more for garnish

Halve the eggs lengthwise, and remove the yolks. Put the yolks in a mini–food processor (or in a bowl, if you're working by hand), and add the mustard, vinegar, and salt. Process to a paste. With the machine running, add the olive oil in a stream to make a very smooth mixture.

Scrape the mixture into a medium bowl, and add the cornichons, zucchini, roasted peppers, capers, and parsley. Mix well to combine.

Stuff or pipe the mixture into the egg whites. Sprinkle with chopped parsley.

HERB FRITTATA ROLL-UPS
Involtini di Frittata

These are actually easier to slice if rolled a few hours ahead and left to set in the refrigerator. Slice cold, and let return to room temperature before serving. They're perfect for cocktail parties or a buffet brunch; stick a toothpick in each roll, and pass them around.

Makes 20 pieces

PESTO

1 cup loosely packed fresh basil leaves
1 cup loosely packed fresh Italian parsley leaves
2 tablespoons extra-virgin olive oil
¼ teaspoon kosher salt
3 tablespoons mayonnaise

FRITTATE

6 large eggs
⅓ cup milk
½ cup finely chopped scallions (white and green parts)
1 tablespoon chopped fresh thyme
¼ teaspoon kosher salt
2 tablespoons extra-virgin olive oil

For the pesto, in a mini–food processor combine the basil, parsley, olive oil, and salt, and process to make a smooth paste. Scrape into a small bowl, and stir in the mayonnaise. Refrigerate while you make the frittate.

For the frittate, in a large bowl, whisk the eggs, milk, scallions, thyme, and salt until smooth.

Heat a large (12-inch) nonstick skillet over medium heat, and add 1 tablespoon of the olive oil. When the oil is hot, add half of the egg mixture, and quickly swirl the pan to make an even layer. Cook until the bottom is set, about 1 to 2 minutes, then flip (using a wide spatula if it needs coaxing). Cook until the underside is light golden and the frittata is cooked through, 1 to 2 minutes more. Remove to a plate. Repeat with the remaining oil and egg mixture. Let the frittate cool.

To assemble, spread half of the pesto on each frittata, spreading it almost all the way to the edges. Roll each frittata into a tight cylinder. Cut each rolled frittata into ten pieces.

Brunch Italian Style

When I think of an Italian brunch, the first dish that springs to mind is a bountiful frittata. I've included a recipe for a simple herb frittata (page 51), as well as a zucchini frittata (opposite), but you can make any variation you like. Try using just vegetables, or adding some crumbled sausage, or some chunks of country bread to add crunchiness, or even adding leftover pasta from the day before—a family favorite at my house. No matter what you add, you can't have an Italian brunch without a frittata.

I think brunch is best served buffet style, especially if you have a crowd, so everyone can pick what they like and go back for seconds. I really like offering an even mix of breakfast foods and more savory fare. My brunches always include a good crostata, such as the mushrooms and onion crostata or the kale and squash crostata included here (pages 76, 75), cut into squares to make it easy for my guests to pop one in their mouths and then put a few on their plates. I also like some bruschette, usually one with vegetables, such as the kale bruschetta (page 64), and one with meat, such as the sliced beef bruschetta (page 58). Some pizette (page 70), and we are well on the way to a good brunch. A platter of prosciutto, cold cuts, cheeses, and cured vegetables is always welcome at an Italian brunch spread, and of course a variety of breads, bread sticks, and taralli (bite-sized toasted rounds that can be found in Italian bakeries or specialty sections of grocery stores) is essential.

There also have to be some simple, seasonal refreshing salads and vegetables, and, for the younger crowd (or for those in an older crowd who have a sweet tooth, like my mother, the *nonna* of the family), I always include some fried bread (page 98) sprinkled with cinnamon and sugar, and offer toppings for it such as jam and sweetened mascarpone. All of this deliciousness is best washed down with a Bellini (or two) (page 15).

FRITTATA WITH ZUCCHINI AND POTATOES

Frittata con Zucchine e Patate

A frittata can be served warm or at room temperature. It's an ideal brunch or breakfast entrée when cut into wedges, but you can also serve it as an hors d'oeuvre, cut into bite-sized squares. Other vegetables, such as peppers or asparagus, can be added or substituted, according to what's in season.

Serves 6 as a breakfast or brunch entrée, more as an appetizer

¼ cup extra-virgin olive oil

1 pound russet potatoes, peeled and cut into ½-inch chunks

1 pound medium zucchini, sliced into ¼-inch-thick half-moons

1¼ teaspoons kosher salt

1 bunch scallions, white and green parts, chopped (about 1 cup)

10 large eggs

½ cup grated Grana Padano

⅓ cup milk

Preheat oven to 375 degrees. In a large ovenproof nonstick skillet, heat the olive oil over medium heat. When the oil is hot, add the potatoes and cook until browned on the edges, about 5 minutes. Add the zucchini, and season with 1 teaspoon of the salt. Cook, stirring occasionally, until potatoes and zucchini are well browned and tender, about 7 to 8 minutes. Add the scallions, and cook just until wilted, about 1 to 2 minutes.

Meanwhile, in a large bowl, whisk together the eggs, grated cheese, milk, and remaining ¼ teaspoon salt until smooth.

When the zucchini and potatoes are tender, reduce the heat to medium low, and pour the egg mixture into the skillet. Cook, moving the skillet around to expose all parts of it to the flame and create a bottom crust on the frittata, about 3 to 4 minutes. Bake until the frittata is set all the way through (insert a knife in the center to check) and the top is golden brown, about 20 to 25 minutes. Remove, and let cool 10 minutes.

To unmold, slide the frittata onto a cutting board and cut if serving it warm. It is also delicious at room temperature.

SPINACH FLAN WITH FRESH TOMATO COULIS

Flan di Spinaci con Coulis di Pomodoro Crudo

This flan is best when warm, and can be served as an appetizer or as an entrée for lunch or brunch. If it is the main focus of your meal, I would suggest serving it with some crispy bread choices and a salad. Easy to make and totally delectable, it is always a favorite at my parties.

Serves 6

FLAN

Unsalted butter, for the ramekins
1 teaspoon kosher salt, plus more for the cooking water
1½ pounds leaf spinach, stemmed
4 large eggs
¼ teaspoon freshly ground black pepper
Pinch freshly grated nutmeg
⅓ cup chopped chives
4 fresh sage leaves
⅓ cup grated Grana Padano
2 cups heavy cream

COULIS

2 cups peeled and seeded fresh tomatoes cut into ¼-inch cubes
2 tablespoons extra-virgin olive oil
Kosher salt, to taste
Freshly ground black pepper, to taste

For the flan, preheat oven to 275 degrees. Butter six 8-ounce ramekins or disposable aluminum cups. Bring a large pot of salted water to a boil. Bring a kettle of water to boil as well.

Add the spinach to the boiling pot of salted water, and cook until tender, about 3 to 4 minutes. Drain thoroughly. Rinse under cold water until cool enough to handle. With your hands, squeeze out as much water as possible.

In a small bowl, whisk the eggs, ¼ teaspoon salt, pepper, and nutmeg until blended. Combine the squeezed spinach, chives, and sage in a food processor, and process until coarsely chopped. Add the egg mixture and grated cheese, and process until the mixture is smooth. Add the cream, and process until thoroughly incorporated, about 30 seconds.

Set the ramekins in a baking pan. Divide the mixture among the prepared baking ramekins. Place the baking pan with the filled ramekins on the middle rack of the oven, and pour in enough hot water from the kettle to come halfway up the sides of the baking dishes. Bake until the centers are firm to the touch, about 1 hour.

While the flans are baking, make the coulis. In a blender, pulse the tomatoes at low speed until finely chopped. With the blender motor running, slowly add the olive oil and blend until smooth. Pass through a sieve, and season to taste with salt and pepper.

Let the flans cool in the water 10 minutes. Run a thin-bladed knife around the sides of the dishes, and invert the flans onto serving plates. Spoon the tomato coulis around them, and serve immediately.

INDIVIDUAL EGGPLANT CUSTARDS

Flan di Melanzane

This is one of my favorite versions of flan; best served warm with some marinara sauce (page 234) or with fresh tomato coulis (preceding recipe), it makes a great appetizer or lunch dish. I think these are a perfect starter for a romantic dinner for two—the consistency is very sensual.

Serves 6

Unsalted butter, softened, for lining the ramekins
Fine dried bread crumbs, for lining the ramekins
2 medium Italian eggplants, halved lengthwise (about 2 pounds total)
3 tablespoons extra-virgin olive oil
¾ teaspoon kosher salt
8 sprigs fresh thyme
2 whole heads garlic
2 cups ½-inch cubes day-old bread
1 cup milk
4 large eggs, beaten
¼ teaspoon freshly grated nutmeg
1 cup plus 2 tablespoons grated Grana Padano
1½ cups marinara sauce (page 234), for serving

Preheat oven to 375 degrees. Grease six 5-ounce or larger ramekins with softened butter. Sprinkle with bread crumbs, and turn to coat, tapping out the excess.

Brush the eggplants all over with 2 tablespoons of the olive oil, and season the cut sides with ¼ teaspoon salt. Place the sprigs of thyme on a baking sheet, and arrange the eggplants, cut side down, over them. Prick the eggplants in several places with a fork. Drizzle the garlic with the remaining tablespoon of oil, and wrap in foil. Roast the eggplants until the cut sides are browned, about 20 minutes, then flip and roast until very tender, about 15 to 20 minutes

more. Roast the garlic until the cloves are completely softened, about 30 minutes. Let all cool.

When the eggplants are cooled, pick out and discard any large clumps of seeds and scrape the flesh from their peel, discarding the peel. Squeeze the roasted garlic cloves from their peels onto the eggplants. Chop the eggplant flesh and garlic, and let drain in a colander for about 15 minutes. You should have about 1 to 1½ cups eggplant flesh.

Reduce oven temperature to 350 degrees. In a medium bowl, soak the bread cubes in the milk until softened, about 10 minutes. Squeeze the excess milk out, and put the bread in a large bowl. Add the drained eggplant flesh, the eggs, remaining ½ teaspoon salt, and the nutmeg. Stir in 1 cup grated cheese. Divide the custard among the ramekins, and sprinkle with the remaining 2 tablespoons grated cheese. Bake on a baking sheet (to catch any drips) until the tops are golden brown and the custard is set, about 35 minutes. Let cool slightly on a rack. Meanwhile, warm the marinara. To unmold, run a paring knife around the edges of the ramekins. Spoon a dollop of marinara onto each plate, and turn out a custard on top. Serve immediately.

RICE FRITTATA

Frittata di Riso

This dish can be served warm or at room temperature. As with most frittate, you can stir in leftover vegetables and meat; if you don't have peas on hand, try another combination you like. It is a fabulous buffet dish—cut it into slices, and let your guests serve themselves—or it can be a superb appetizer, slices of frittata topped with some dressed salad.

Serves 8 as an entrée, more as an hors d'oeuvre

1 tablespoon unsalted butter, softened, plus
    2 tablespoons cut into bits
2 tablespoons bread crumbs
5 cups milk
1½ cups Arborio rice
2 teaspoons kosher salt
8 large eggs, separated
½ cup diced ham
½ cup frozen peas, thawed
¾ cup grated Grana Padano
½ cup grated Gruyère
1 bunch scallions, white and green parts, chopped
    (about 1 cup)
2 tablespoons extra-virgin olive oil

Preheat oven to 350 degrees. Grease a large nonstick skillet with the softened butter, and sprinkle in bread crumbs to coat the bottom and sides, tapping out the excess. In a medium saucepan, combine 4 cups of the milk, the rice, and 1 teaspoon of the salt. Bring to a simmer, and cook until rice is barely al dente and the mixture is custardy, about 10 minutes. Stir in the 2 tablespoons cut-up butter and the remaining cup milk.

Whisk the egg yolks in a large bowl with the remaining teaspoon salt. Slowly pour in the rice mixture, continuing to whisk until all is incorporated. Stir in the ham, peas, ½ cup of the grated Grana Padano, the Gruyère, and the scallions.

In another bowl, whisk the egg whites at medium speed with an electric mixer until foamy, then raise the speed to high and whip to soft peaks. Stir a third of the whites into the yolk mixture to lighten it, then gently fold in the rest of the whites.

Brush a 10-inch springform pan with 2 tablespoons of extra-virgin olive oil. Pour the mixture into the prepared pan, and sprinkle with the remaining ¼ cup grated Grana Padano. Bake until set and browned on top, about 40 to 45 minutes. Let cool on a rack for 15 minutes before unmolding.

The Versatility of Bruschetta

You could have a party serving only bruschette and still please everyone. Toasted or grilled bread with toppings, in their simplest form bruschette are thickly cut country bread toasted until crisp and golden, then rubbed with a raw garlic clove and brushed with extra-virgin olive oil, or—as they call it in Tuscany—*fett'unta*. Pure joy.

Bruschette can be simply topped with chopped tomatoes, extra-virgin olive oil, salt, and basil. They can be topped with chicken liver pâté, as is traditional in Tuscany, or draped with a thin slice of cured lard or prosciutto. I give you in this chapter some of my favorite toppings: bruschetta with dinosaur kale (page 64), beef and arugula bruschetta (page 58), bruschetta with prosciutto and figs (page 61), and cannellini and pancetta bruschetta (page 62).

Any way you slice the bread for bruschette, they are a vehicle for you to express your creativity. The gamut of toppings ranges from fish, to vegetables, to cured meats, fruits, and combinations of any of these. So be creative, but I suggest you keep it fresh, in season, and simple.

BEEF AND ARUGULA BRUSCHETTA

Bruschetta con Tagliata di Rucola

For an elegant starter, make this with thinly sliced cold beef tenderloin (page 318) and your own homemade giardiniera (page 45). For a super-quick version, use sliced rare roast beef and giardiniera from a good deli.

Makes 16, serving 8 as a first course, more as part of an antipasto buffet

Sixteen ½-inch-thick slices hearty country bread

2 cups drained giardiniera, plus 2 tablespoons of the brine

2 tablespoons extra-virgin olive oil

2 cups loosely packed baby arugula, coarsely chopped

Kosher salt, to taste

1 pound beef tenderloin, cooked rare to medium, thinly sliced (or 1 pound thinly sliced rare roast beef from the deli)

Lightly toast or grill the bread on both sides. In a large bowl, toss together the giardiniera, brine, and olive oil. Add the arugula, and toss gently. Taste, and season with salt if necessary.

Layer the beef on the bread. Top with the giardiniera mixture, and drizzle with any juices left in the bowl. Serve immediately.

BRUSCHETTA WITH PROSCIUTTO AND FIGS

Bruschetta con Prosciutto e Fichi

If you have any leftover balsamic reduction, it is good drizzled over cooked vegetables or chunks of Grana Padano.

Makes 6

1 cup balsamic vinegar

2 teaspoons honey

1 fresh bay leaf

6 thick slices country bread, grilled or toasted on both sides, still warm

Extra-virgin olive oil, for drizzling

Kosher salt

6 ripe figs, thickly sliced

12 thin slices prosciutto

Combine the vinegar, honey, and bay leaf in a small saucepan. Bring to a boil, and cook until thick and syrupy and reduced to ⅓ cup, about 5 to 6 minutes. Let cool. Discard bay leaf.

Drizzle the warm bread with olive oil, and season with salt. Lay the fig slices over the bread. Drape the prosciutto over the figs. Drizzle with balsamic reduction. Serve.

CANNELLINI AND PANCETTA BRUSCHETTA

Bruschetta con Cannellini e Pancetta

The beans can be made a day ahead; just warm them up before serving. This recipe might give more beans than you need, but they will keep for several days and also freeze well. Stir them into soup, or serve as a side dish next to a big grilled steak. In a pinch, canned cannellini can be used. Drain them and sauté them with the oil and parsley for a few minutes, until warm.

Makes 16

1 pound dried cannellini beans, soaked overnight

1 large carrot, finely chopped

1 large stalk celery, finely chopped

2 fresh bay leaves

¼ cup extra-virgin olive oil, plus more for drizzling

1 teaspoon kosher salt

¼ cup chopped fresh Italian parsley

16 thin slices pancetta

16 slices country bread, about 3 inches long each, grilled or toasted

Drain the soaked cannellini, and put in a pot with water to cover by 2 inches. Add the carrot, celery, bay leaves, and 2 tablespoons of the olive oil. Cover, bring to a simmer, and cook until the beans are tender, about 1 hour.

Uncover the beans, and simmer to reduce the cooking liquid down so it just covers the beans, about 5 minutes. Remove from the heat, season with the salt, and let cool until just warm.

Drain the beans, and toss with the remaining 2 tablespoons olive oil and the parsley.

Meanwhile, lay the pancetta in a nonstick skillet (you may have to do this in batches), and cook over medium heat until crisp. Drain on paper towels.

To serve, mound some of the warm beans on the bread slices on a platter. Drizzle with a little more olive oil. Break the pancetta into shards, and set them on top of the beans.

BRUSCHETTA WITH DINOSAUR KALE

Bruschetta con Cavolo Nero

Dinosaur kale, also called black kale, has darker, crinklier, almost scaly leaves. If you can't find it, use regular kale instead. Do not be afraid do overcook it. A crunchy piece of bread with sautéed kale reminds me of the first time I ever ate kale, at an open-air table at a vineyard in the Tuscan countryside. All the flavors and the smell of the country air come rushing back to me with each mouthful.

Makes 6

3 tablespoons extra-virgin olive oil

2 cloves garlic, crushed and peeled

6 slices thick bacon, julienned

½ medium onion, thinly sliced

1 small bunch dinosaur kale, stemmed and cut into
¼-inch-thick shreds (about 8 ounces)

½ teaspoon kosher salt

Pinch crushed red pepper flakes

6 thick slices country bread, about 5 inches wide,
grilled or toasted on both sides

In a large skillet, heat the olive oil over medium heat. Add the garlic and bacon, and cook until bacon renders its fat, about 3 minutes. Add the onion, and cook until it's wilted, about 3 minutes. Add the kale, and season with the salt and red pepper flakes. Reduce the heat to low, and continue cooking the kale, stirring often, until it is very tender, about 20 minutes. If the kale begins to stick, add a tablespoon or so of water and continue cooking.

Remove the crushed garlic cloves, and divide the kale evenly among the bread slices. Serve immediately.

BAKED EGGS WITH POTATOES AND CREAM

Uova e Patate al Forno

This is a fantastic breakfast or brunch dish if you have overnight guests, made even more festive if you have some white truffles to shave on top.

Serves 6

¼ cup extra-virgin olive oil
2 large russet potatoes (about 12 ounces), unpeeled, thinly sliced
1 medium onion, thinly sliced
½ teaspoon kosher salt
2 tablespoons unsalted butter, softened
1 cup heavy cream
½ cup milk
6 large eggs
3 tablespoons grated Grana Padano
4 slices white country bread
2 ounces fresh Alba truffles (optional)

Preheat oven to 375 degrees. Bring a kettle of water to boil. In a medium nonstick skillet, heat 2 tablespoons of the oil over medium-high heat. Add half of the potatoes and fry, turning frequently to brown evenly, until crisp, about 4 minutes. Drain on paper towels and repeat with the remaining olive oil and potatoes. To the oil left in the pan after the last batch of potatoes are fried and removed, add the onion, and cook, stirring occasionally, over medium heat until softened, about 5 minutes. Season potatoes with ¼ teaspoon salt.

Divide the butter among six 6-ounce ramekins, and smear to coat the bottom and sides of the dish. Layer the potatoes and onion in the ramekins.

In a spouted measuring cup, mix together the cream, milk, and remaining ¼ teaspoon salt. Pour this over the potatoes and onions. Carefully break an egg into each ramekin, and sprinkle with some of the grated cheese.

Place the ramekins in a deep roasting pan, and pour water from the kettle to come halfway up the sides. Cover the pan with foil, and bake until the whites of the eggs just begin to set, about 15 minutes. Uncover, and bake until yolks are set to your liking, about 10 to 15 minutes more.

While the eggs bake, cut the bread slices into three sticks each, and toast until crisp. Serve each ramekin on a plate with toast sticks for dipping.

If serving with Alba truffles, use a truffle shaver to shave thin slices on each egg.

POTATO AND EGG FRICO

Frico di Patate con Uova

From the Friuli region in Italy, frico is a traditional dish in which potatoes and cheese are baked together. My rendition makes a hearty breakfast or, served topped with salad, a great lunch. Cut in slices, it can be passed around at a cocktail party. It is a favorite breakfast dish when I have my family visiting.

Serves 6

1½ pounds russet potatoes (about 4 small potatoes)
¼ cup extra-virgin olive oil
1 large onion, sliced
¼ cup drained chopped pickled peperoncini
1 teaspoon kosher salt
4 cups shredded Asiago
¼ cup fine-grind polenta or cornmeal
6 large eggs

Put the potatoes in a large saucepan with water to cover, and simmer until a knife just pierces the potatoes or they're about halfway cooked, about 10 to 12 minutes. Drain, cool, peel, and slice ½ inch thick.

Heat a 12-inch nonstick skillet over medium heat, and add the olive oil. When the oil is hot, add the onion, potatoes, and peperoncini, and cook until browned, about 8 to 10 minutes. Season with the salt, and scrape onto a plate.

In a large bowl, toss together the Asiago and polenta. Wipe the skillet clean, and return it to medium heat. Sprinkle half of the cheese mixture in an even layer in the pan, and top with ¾ of the potato mixture, spreading evenly. Make six depressions in the potato mixture, and break an egg into each. Spoon remaining potato mixture gently over each egg. Sprinkle over this the rest of the cheese mixture to cover evenly.

Cook, moving the pan around the flame, so each part of the bottom browns evenly. You will know the frico is ready to flip when it slides in the pan. If necessary, loosen the sides with a knife to help it along. Gently invert the frico into another 12-inch nonstick skillet or slide the frico onto a 12-inch plate and invert in same skillet. Continue to cook until the bottom is browned and the eggs are set, about 4 to 5 minutes for yolks that are still runny.

GRILLED OR BROILED POLENTA
Polenta alla Griglia

Polenta is a cornmeal porridge, much used throughout Italy, especially in the northern regions, where it is served as a hot accompaniment to meats, fish, and vegetables. But once it is chilled, it solidifies and can be cut into pieces and grilled, broiled, or fried.

Serves 4 to 6

2 tablespoons extra-virgin olive oil, plus more for brushing
1 fresh bay leaf
2 teaspoons kosher salt
1 cup coarsely ground polenta
½ cup grated Grana Padano

Put 4 cups cold water in a saucepan, and stir in the 2 tablespoons olive oil, the bay leaf, and salt. Set the pan over medium-low heat, and whisk in the polenta in a slow, steady stream until all is incorporated.

Continue to cook and stir, switching to a wooden spoon, as polenta is gently bubbling. Cook until it is thick and glossy and pulls away from the sides of the pan, about 25 minutes (depending on how coarse the polenta is).

Take the finished polenta from the heat. Remove bay leaves, then stir in the grated cheese. Quickly spread into a parchment-lined sheet pan, and evenly spread with an offset spatula. Let cool completely, then chill in the refrigerator.

TO GRILL: Cut chilled polenta into squares, triangles, or rectangles. Preheat a grill or grill pan over medium-high heat. Brush the grill and the polenta with olive oil. Set the polenta on the grill, and let cook without moving until a crust forms (the polenta will be easier to move when the crust has formed), about 3 minutes. Flip, and cook the other side in the same manner.

TO BROIL: Preheat broiler. Cut chilled polenta into squares, triangles, or rectangles. Arrange polenta on a greased sheet pan, add toppings, and broil until brown and bubbly on top, anywhere from 1 to 4 minutes, depending on the strength of your broiler.

Whether grilled or broiled, polenta is delicious when topped with stewed summer vegetables Sicilian style (page 39), stewed savory peppers (page 46), monkfish meatballs in tomato sauce (page 89), fried banana peppers (page 88), asparagus gratin (page 154), skillet escarole gratin (page 164), and mushrooms and celery (page 169). Grilled or broiled polenta is also good as a side dish with stewed fish and braised meats like stuffed calamari (page 242), monkfish in tomato sauce with green olives and capers (page 255), mixed seafood stew (page 264), chicken breast and livers with marsala (page 272), braised beef rolls stuffed with barley (page 312), and lamb and fennel stew (page 321).

Pizza Party

I don't think there is anything more versatile in the Italian repertoire than pizza. The dough alone can be baked, grilled, or fried and used as a bread to eat with cold cuts. Pizza can be made with just one cheese, or a variety of different cheeses. Or for vegetarians perhaps just red sauce and no cheese, or topped with your favorite vegetables.

If you are planning a child's birthday, think pizza and bruschetta; the fun is in letting the children top their own bruschetta and pizza. Pizzette with four toppings (recipe follows) and bruschetta with simple chopped tomato or with sliced beef (page 58) are great, but feel free to change the topping on the bruschetta.

In making pizzas, most of the work will be in preparing the dough, the sauce, and the different toppings and customizing them to the tastes of your children and their friends. Have everything prepped and cut to the right size, and the cheese shredded, before your guests arrive. Cut the pizza dough into portions, so each child has his or her own. Set up a workstation on your table or counter, set out a plastic cutting board and a small bowl of flour so that each child can roll out and top his own little pizza, and then help to bake them. Have an extra batch of dough made, and use that to make pizzas for your other guests while the kids make their own. Depending on the age of the children, you never know if they will sneeze into their dough or drop it on the floor—so be sure to have extra on hand. I suggest each child make two pizza rounds; keep the second one aside for dessert. Toppings should include grated mozzarella, sliced pepperoni salami, bell pepper slices, tomato sauce, sliced onions, crumbled sautéed sausage, and anything else you think your group might like. While the pizzas are baking, toast up or grill the bread slices (cut in advance) on a cast-iron skillet, and allow the children to top them with chopped tomato, onion, basil, mozzarella cubes, ham, or chopped greens, all dressed with salt and olive oil. The children can munch on the bruschetta while waiting for the pizza.

Dessert is also served pizza style. Later on, bake the second pizza rounds; once they have cooled a bit, have the children spread on Nutella, jam, peanut butter and jelly, melted chocolate, or fresh fruits such as sliced strawberries and banana.

Yes, kids love pizza, but the affinity for pizza does not seem to fade with age, and a pizza party for adults is always welcome. For those adult parties, a pizza oven is always best, but pizza can be made in a home oven or on a grill as well.

But what is fun, as with the kids, is to get everyone involved. Have someone stretch the pizza dough (page 70) and put it on a peel or pizza stone, and set up a selection of toppings your guests can use to top their pizzas the way they want. For adults the selection of toppings should include some tomato sauce and fresh basil as well as four or five different cheese options; I suggest shredded or sliced mozzarella, Gorgonzola, Italian Fontina, Robiola, and some Grana Padano. Have some thin slices of prosciutto crudo (salt-cured prosciutto), prosciutto cotto (ham), and salami available, as well as olives and capers. A bowl of fresh arugula salad to sprinkle on top after baking adds some freshness to any pizza. And do not forget anchovy fillets for that sought-after adult flavor.

INDIVIDUAL PIZZETTE WITH FOUR TOPPINGS

Pizzette Gustose

Makes 16

DOUGH

1¼ cups warm water (about 100 degrees)
1 packet active dry yeast (2¼ teaspoons)
Pinch sugar
2 tablespoons extra-virgin olive oil, plus more for the bowl and brushing
1½ teaspoons kosher salt
3 cups all-purpose flour, plus more for rolling and shaping

Sprinkle the yeast and pinch of sugar over the water. Let sit until bubbly, about 5 minutes. Stir in the olive oil and salt.

Pour the yeast mixture into the bowl of an electric mixer fitted with the paddle attachment. Add 3 cups of flour, and mix at low speed until the dough just comes together.

Switch to the dough hook, and knead at medium to medium-high speed until the dough clears the sides of the bowl and is soft, smooth, and springy, about 5 minutes. (Add a little more water initially if the dough is dry or looks tough, or more flour if it doesn't form a ball at all.)

Oil a large bowl, add the dough, and turn to coat. Cover with a kitchen towel, and let rise until doubled, about 1½ hours.

Preheat oven to 450 degrees. Once the dough has risen, punch it down and divide into four pieces. Cut each piece into four more pieces, to make sixteen total. Form these into balls, then stretch into circles about 3 to 4 inches in diameter. Rest them on parchment-lined sheet pans. Let the circles rise, uncovered, for 15 minutes.

Lightly brush the circles with olive oil, and top with the toppings of your choice (see below). Bake, rotating the pans from top to bottom halfway through, until the pizzette are puffed and the bottom crust is golden, about 10 minutes.

TOPPINGS

Onion and Cheese

4 tablespoons extra-virgin olive oil
2 medium onions, thinly sliced
½ teaspoon kosher salt
½ cup grated Grana Padano

Heat a medium skillet over medium heat. Add the olive oil. When the oil is hot, add the onions, and season with the salt. Cook, stirring often, until the onions are just golden and wilted but still have a slight crunch, about 8 to 10 minutes. Let cool. Spread the onions on the pizzette, sprinkle with the grated cheese, and bake as directed above.

Chicken and Mushroom

3 tablespoons extra-virgin olive oil
One 6-ounce boneless, skinless chicken breast
1 small leek, white and light-green parts, halved lengthwise and thinly sliced
8 ounces mixed mushrooms (white, cremini, shiitake, oyster, etc.), thinly sliced
½ teaspoon kosher salt
¼ cup grated Grana Padano

In a medium nonstick skillet, heat 2 tablespoons olive oil over medium-high heat. When the oil is hot, add the chicken and brown on both sides, about 2 minutes per side. Remove, let cool slightly (it won't be cooked all the way; that's okay), and cut into small pieces.

In the same skillet, heat the remaining tablespoon of olive oil over medium heat. Add the leek and mushrooms. Cover, and cook until the mushrooms give up their liquid, about 3 minutes. Uncover, and increase the heat to boil away the liquid. Add back the chicken, season with salt, and cook until chicken is no longer pink, about 2 minutes. Cool. Spread the chicken mixture on the pizzette, sprinkle with the grated cheese, and bake as directed.

Pear and Gorgonzola

2 medium Bosc pears, medium-ripe
4 ounces Gorgonzola

Core and thinly slice (but don't peel) the pears. Arrange over the pizzette, and crumble the Gorgonzola on top. Bake as directed.

Tomato and Pecorino

½ cup grated pecorino
2 ripe plum tomatoes, thinly sliced crosswise
1 to 2 teaspoons dried oregano, preferably Sicilian on the branch

Sprinkle half of the pecorino on the pizzette. Top each with one or two slices of tomato. Sprinkle with the remaining pecorino and the oregano, and bake as directed.

PIZZA ROLLS WITH BROCCOLI RABE AND SAUSAGE OR RICOTTA AND LEEKS

Scaccia (Rotolini di Pizza Ripieni di Broccoli di Rape e Salsicce oppure Ricotta e Porri)

This is a perfect preparation for picnics, buffets, and snacks; it is best when served warm, but also makes a good room-temperature snack at a picnic. Along with a tossed salad, it is a fantastic lunch or brunch. Either of these fillings makes enough for the whole batch of dough, so, if you want to make both and are feeding a crowd, make a double batch of dough.

Makes 2, each about 8 slices

1 recipe pizza dough (page 70)

SAUSAGE AND BROCCOLI RABE

3 tablespoons extra-virgin olive oil
3 cloves garlic, crushed and peeled
1 pound sweet Italian sausage, removed from
   casings
¼ teaspoon crushed red pepper flakes
1 bunch broccoli rabe, stems peeled, coarsely
   chopped (about 1 pound)
½ teaspoon kosher salt

RICOTTA AND LEEKS

3 tablespoons extra-virgin olive oil
2 medium onions, sliced ¼ inch thick
1 bunch leeks (about 24 ounces), white and light-
   green parts, sliced into ½-inch-thick half-moons
1 teaspoon kosher salt
¼ teaspoon crushed red pepper flakes
1½ cups fresh ricotta
½ cup grated Grana Padano
1 large egg, beaten
¼ cup chopped fresh Italian parsley

Make the pizza dough. While it rises, make the fillings.

For the sausage filling, add the olive oil to a large skillet over medium heat. When the oil is hot, add the garlic and let sizzle a minute. Add the sausage, and cook, crumbling with a wooden spoon, until no longer pink, about 4 minutes.

Season with the red pepper flakes, and add the broccoli rabe. Toss to coat in the oil, and season with the salt. Cover, and cook until broccoli rabe is very tender, about 15 to 17 minutes, stirring occasionally. Uncover, and increase the heat if necessary, to reduce away any excess liquid in the skillet. Let cool completely. Remove garlic.

For the ricotta filling, add the olive oil to a large skillet over medium heat. When the oil is hot, add the onions and leeks, and season with the salt and crushed red pepper. Cook, stirring occasionally, until the onions and leeks are softened, about 10 to 12 minutes. Let cool.

In a bowl, stir together the ricotta, grated cheese, egg, and parsley.

To make the scaccia, preheat oven to 400 degrees. Divide the dough into two equal pieces. On floured parchment, roll one piece into a 10-by-14-inch rectangle with the long side nearest you. Spread half of the filling (for the leek-and-ricotta scaccia, do a layer of onions and leeks, then a layer of ricotta) on the lower half of the rectangle, leaving about 2 inches of space on the bottom and 3 on the top and 2 inches on each end. Fold the ends over, then the bottom to form a lip. Fold the top edge over, and crimp all around. Fold the crimped ends under to form a neat package. Slide the parchment onto a baking sheet, and repeat with the remaining piece of dough and filling, sliding it onto a second baking sheet.

Brush both lightly with olive oil, and cut four or five slits in the top with a sharp paring knife. Bake, rotating the pans from top to bottom halfway through baking time, until the crust is golden and the filling can be seen bubbling through the vents, about 35 to 40 minutes.

CROSTATA WITH KALE, BUTTERNUT SQUASH, AND RICOTTA

Crostata di Cavolo Nero, Zucca, e Ricotta

You can make this crostata, or tart, earlier in the day and serve at room temperature. It makes for a lovely first course or lunch with a side of dressed greens—and is just as good cut into bite-sized squares as part of a buffet. You can wrap leftovers in foil and freeze them; thaw and reheat before serving.

Serves 10 to 12 as a first course, more as an hors d'œuvre

DOUGH

2 cups all-purpose flour, plus more for rolling
1 teaspoon kosher salt
½ cup extra-virgin olive oil

FILLING

Unsalted butter, softened, for the sheet pan
1 pound peeled butternut squash, grated on the
    coarse holes of a box grater
½ cup Arborio or other short-grain rice
1 teaspoon kosher salt, plus more for cooking water
1 bunch kale, stemmed and chopped (about 8 cups)
1½ pounds fresh ricotta (about 2½ cups)
2 cups grated Grana Padano
2 bunches scallions, white and green parts, chopped
    (about 2 cups)
3 large eggs, beaten
1½ cups milk
½ cup heavy cream
½ cup golden raisins (optional)

For the dough, in a food processor, combine the flour and salt and pulse to mix. In a spouted measuring cup, whisk together the olive oil and ⅓ cup cold water. With the machine running, pour in the liquids and process until a soft dough forms on the blade, about 30 seconds. If the dough is still crumbly,

add a bit more water. If it is too wet, add a bit more flour. Dump the dough on a floured countertop, and knead until it just comes together. Wrap in plastic wrap, and let rest at room temperature for 30 minutes (or refrigerate, if making a day ahead).

Preheat oven to 375 degrees. Butter a rimmed half-sheet pan. For the filling, in a large bowl, stir together the grated squash and rice and let sit at room temperature for 1 hour, so the rice absorbs some of the liquid from the squash.

Meanwhile, bring a large pot of salted water to boil and add the kale. Simmer until just tender, about 10 minutes. Rinse, drain, cool, and squeeze very dry and finely chop the kale.

Add to the bowl, along with the ricotta, grated cheese, scallions, eggs, milk, cream, raisins (if using), and 1 teaspoon salt. Mix well.

On a floured work surface, roll the dough to a rectangle 2 inches longer and wider than the sheet pan. Center the dough in the pan, and press to fit. Pour and spread the filling into the crust, and fold the edges of the crust back over to create the sides of the crostata. Bake until the crust is deep golden brown and the filling is set, about 50 minutes. Cool on a rack before cutting into squares.

CROSTATA WITH MUSHROOMS AND ONION

Crostata con Funghi e Cipolla

This makes a nice first course cut into larger squares with simply dressed greens on the side. Cut it into smaller squares or triangles to pass, or to include in a buffet. My grandson Lorenzo has perfected this recipe, and it is hard to keep any on the plate when all the grandkids are over.

Serves 8 as a first course, more as part of an antipasto buffet

¼ cup extra-virgin olive oil

1 pound russet potatoes, peeled and sliced ¼ inch thick

1 teaspoon kosher salt

2 tablespoons unsalted butter

1 small onion, thinly sliced

1 pound mixed mushrooms (white, cremini, shiitake, oyster, etc.), thinly sliced

1 tablespoon fresh thyme leaves, chopped

1 cup heavy cream

2 sheets frozen puff pastry, thawed in the refrigerator

All-purpose flour, for rolling

1 cup grated Italian Fontina

½ cup grated Grana Padano

Preheat oven to 400 degrees. Heat the oil in a large nonstick skillet over medium-high heat. When the oil is hot, add the potatoes, and cook, tossing frequently, until they are crisp and golden (but they don't need to be entirely cooked through at this point), about 7 minutes. Drain on paper towels and season with ½ teaspoon of the salt.

Wipe the skillet clean. Over medium heat, melt the butter. When it is melted, add the onion and cook until it begins to wilt, about 3 to 4 minutes. Add the mushrooms, and season with the thyme and remaining salt. Cover, and cook until the mushrooms have given up their juices, about 2 to 3 min-

utes. Uncover, and increase the heat to reduce the liquid away, about 2 to 3 minutes more. Add the cream, and boil until reduced by half, about 2 minutes. Pour the mixture into a bowl, add the potatoes, and toss to combine. Let cool.

Line a flat sheet pan with parchment. Unroll the puff pastry, lightly flour both sides, and line the two pieces up side by side on the parchment. Roll to fuse the two pastry sheets together, all the way to the edges of the cookie sheet.

In a medium bowl, toss together the Fontina and Grana Padano. Spread the filling over the puff pastry, leaving a 1-to-2-inch border. Fold the edges of the pastry over to form a crust. Sprinkle the exposed part of the filling with the cheese mixture. Bake until pastry is crisp and golden and cheese is brown and bubbly, about 30 minutes. Slide off the cookie sheet and onto a cooling rack. Cool at least 15 minutes before cutting into squares to serve.

CHEDDAR FRICO WITH DITALINI

Frico di Formaggio Cheddar con Ditalini

Feel free to change the vegetables in the ditalini filling, according to the season or what you have in the fridge. Mushrooms, asparagus, and broccoli are all good. Just cut them into small pieces, and make sure they are cooked well with the onions before tossing in with the ditalini. The frico can be cut into wedges and served on a platter, or as a finger food. If the latter, make sure to have napkins nearby.

Serves 6 to 8

Kosher salt
2 cups ditalini
2 tablespoons extra-virgin olive oil
1 medium onion, finely chopped
4 ounces ham or prosciutto, diced
1 tablespoon tomato paste
1 cup frozen peas, defrosted
1 cup grated Grana Padano
4 cups shredded yellow cheddar cheese (12 ounces)
¼ cup fine-grind polenta or cornmeal

Bring a large saucepan of salted water to boil. Cook the ditalini until still quite al dente. Drain, and pat dry.

In a large (12-inch) nonstick skillet, heat the olive oil over medium heat. Add the onion and ham, and cook until onion is softened, about 5 to 6 minutes. Clear a space in the pan, and add the tomato paste. Cook and stir the tomato paste in that spot until it is toasted and darkens a shade or two, about 1 minute. Add the peas and the pasta and ½ cup water, and simmer a minute. Stir in the grated Grana Padano. Scrape into a large bowl, and wipe the skillet clean.

In another large bowl, toss the cheddar with the polenta. Reheat the skillet over medium heat, and sprinkle in an even layer of half of the cheddar cheese mixture. Top with the ham, ditalini, and cheese mixture in an even layer. Sprinkle the remaining cheddar mixture over to cover. Cook, moving the skillet over the burner to brown the crust evenly, until the bottom is set and nicely brown, about 6 to 8 minutes. Flip the frico (either into another skillet or onto a plate, then slide back into the skillet), and brown the other side in the same way. Invert onto a round platter or board. Let cool a few minutes before cutting into wedges to serve.

RICE BALLS STUFFED WITH SAUSAGE RAGÙ

Arancini di Riso con Salsicce

The rice balls can be completely assembled ahead of time. They are best when fried at the last minute, though you can also fry them in advance and reheat in a 350-degree oven. This recipe makes a small amount of ragù to go inside the rice balls, but double the recipe to make a larger batch if you want to save some to use as a pasta sauce.

Makes about 20

RAGÙ

2 tablespoons extra-virgin olive oil
2 links sweet Italian sausage, removed from casings
4 ounces chicken livers, cleaned and finely chopped
¼ cup finely chopped carrot
¼ cup finely chopped onion
¼ cup finely chopped celery
1 tablespoon tomato paste
½ cup dry white wine
1 cup canned whole San Marzano tomatoes, crushed by hand
½ teaspoon kosher salt
⅓ cup frozen peas, thawed

RICE

4 cups chicken stock (page 148)
2 tablespoons extra-virgin olive oil
2 cups Arborio or other short-grain rice
½ teaspoon kosher salt
2 large eggs
1 cup grated Grana Padano

COATING AND FRYING

Twenty ½-inch cubes fresh mozzarella (from about 4 ounces cheese)
1 cup all-purpose flour
2½ cups fine dried bread crumbs

3 large eggs
Kosher salt, for seasoning
Vegetable oil, for frying

For the ragù, heat the oil in a medium saucepan over medium heat. When the oil is hot, add the sausage. Cook, crumbling with a wooden spoon, until the sausage is no longer pink, about 4 to 5 minutes. Then add the chicken livers, and cook until they're no longer pink, about 3 minutes. Add the carrot, onion, and celery and ¼ cup water. Simmer the water away to soften the vegetables a bit, then clear a space in the pan and add the tomato paste. Cook and stir the tomato paste in that spot until it is toasted and darkens a shade or two, a minute or two, before stirring it into the vegetables. Add the wine, bring to a simmer, and add the tomatoes and salt. Simmer, uncovered, until very thick and flavorful, about 15 minutes. Let cool completely. Stir in the peas.

For the rice, bring the stock to a simmer in a large saucepan. Add the olive oil, rice, and salt. Simmer, uncovered, until the rice is al dente, about 12 to 13 minutes. Scrape onto a sheet pan to cool. Once it's cool, put the rice in a large bowl and beat in the eggs and grated cheese.

To form the rice balls, make a mound of rice in your palm and roll into a small ball, 1½ inches in

(recipe continues)

diameter. Make a depression in the ball with your thumb, and fill it with a piece of mozzarella and some ragù. Re-form the rice around the filling to seal it in.

Once you've filled all of the rice balls (you should get about twenty), place them on a parchment-lined sheet pan. Spread the flour in a shallow bowl and the bread crumbs in another, and beat the eggs in a third bowl. Season the contents of each bowl with a pinch of salt. Dredge the rice balls in flour, coating evenly, then in egg, then in bread crumbs, and rest them back on the lined sheet pan.

When you are ready to fry, heat 2 inches deep of vegetable oil in a medium Dutch oven to 365 degrees. Fry the rice balls in batches as many fit in pan without crowding, until crisp and golden brown all over, about 4 minutes per batch. Drain on paper towels, sprinkle with salt, and serve.

FRIED MOZZARELLA SANDWICH SKEWERS

Mozzarella in Carrozza

You can assemble the skewers and make the sauce ahead of time, but fry these as close to serving as you can, keeping them in a warm oven while you finish frying. Sauce the skewers just before serving.

Serves 8

SKEWERS

16 slices whole-wheat bread, lightly toasted

1½ pounds mozzarella di bufala, or any freshly made mozzarella, sliced ¼ inch thick

Vegetable oil, for frying

4 large eggs

¼ cup milk

1 teaspoon kosher salt

Pinch freshly ground black pepper

All-purpose flour, for dredging

SAUCE

5 tablespoons extra-virgin olive oil

4 cloves garlic, crushed and peeled

8 anchovy fillets, chopped

3 tablespoons drained capers in brine

Juice of 1 small lemon

⅓ cup dry white wine

¼ cup chicken stock (page 148) or water

2 tablespoons chopped fresh Italian parsley

Preheat oven to 200 degrees or its lowest setting. Using eight slices of bread, make eight layers (sandwiches), alternating bread and mozzarella. Cut and fit the mozzarella slices to cover the bread slices. The cheese shouldn't overhang the bread slices. Repeat with remaining bread and cheese. Each tall sandwich will be cut into four squares. Place a sturdy wooden skewer through the center of each imaginary square, piercing through to the cutting board. Hold the tall sandwich pierced with the four skewers firmly and, with a serrated knife, saw off the outside crust of the bread on all four sides, then cut the tall sandwich into four squares, with a skewer at the center of each square, forming four long rectangular sandwiches. Press gently as you cut, to make nice compact sandwiches. Repeat with the other stack. You now have eight multilayered sandwiches, each on a skewer.

Pour enough vegetable oil into a wide, deep skillet to fill it by 1½ inches. Heat over medium heat until the oil registers 350 degrees on a deep-frying thermometer. Line a baking sheet with a double thickness of paper towels, and set aside. Meanwhile, in a shallow wide bowl, whisk the eggs, milk, salt, and pepper until thoroughly blended. Spread the flour on a plate.

When the oil comes to temperature, dredge each skewered stack in the flour, being sure to coat all sides lightly but well. Working with half the floured skewers at a time, dip each in the egg mixture to coat on all sides. Don't soak the bread in the egg—just coat it thoroughly. Let some of the excess egg drip back into the bowl, and gently slip the stacks into the oil. Fry, turning as necessary with tongs, until golden brown on all sides, about 4 minutes. Drain the sandwiches on the paper towels, and place in the warm oven. Repeat with the remaining sandwiches.

For the sauce, heat the olive oil and garlic in a

(recipe continues)

small skillet over medium heat. Cook, shaking the pan occasionally, until the garlic is golden, about 2 to 3 minutes. Stir in the anchovies and capers, and cook until anchovies dissolve, about 2 minutes. Pour in the lemon juice and white wine. Bring the ingredients to a vigorous boil, add the stock, and boil until the sauce is lightly thickened, about 3 minutes. Stir in the parsley, and remove from the heat.

Arrange the hot mozzarella sandwiches on a warm platter or plates, and remove or leave the skewers. Spoon the sauce over and around the sandwiches, and serve.

MUSSELS WITH ZUCCHINI SALSA VERDE

Cozze alla Salsa Verde di Zucchine

The zucchini salsa verde is a wonderfully versatile condiment. Try it on roasted beef tender-loin, grilled chicken, or roasted vegetables, such as eggplant. It is also good as a dressing for boiled potatoes. These mussels are perfect for guests to slurp down at a cocktail party, but have a plate handy for the empty shells.

Serves 6 to 8

2 tablespoons extra-virgin olive oil

2 cloves garlic, sliced

2 sprigs fresh thyme

2 pounds mussels, scrubbed and debearded if necessary

½ cup dry white wine

1 medium zucchini (about 6 ounces)

1 large hard-boiled egg, finely chopped

¼ cup finely chopped cornichons

¼ cup finely chopped red onion

¼ cup finely chopped roasted red bell peppers

¼ cup chopped fresh chives

½ teaspoon kosher salt, plus more to taste

3 tablespoons red wine vinegar

1 tablespoon Dijon mustard

3 tablespoons extra-virgin olive oil

Put the olive oil in a medium Dutch oven over medium heat. When the oil is hot, add the garlic and thyme and let sizzle for a minute. Add the mussels and wine, bring to a simmer, and cover. Cook until the mussels are done, about 4 to 5 minutes; discard any that haven't opened. Drain the mussels and let cool.

Slice the green sides from the zucchini in 4 planks, down to the seedy core. Finely dice the green parts; discard the core. In a medium bowl, combine the diced zucchini, egg, cornichons, red onion, roasted peppers, and chives. Season with the salt, and toss. In a small bowl, whisk together the vinegar and mustard. Whisk in the olive oil to make a smooth dressing, and pour over the zucchini mixture. Toss well, season with more salt if necessary, and let sit at room temperature while you return to the mussels.

Remove from each mussel the half-shell it's not attached to, and discard these shells. Arrange the shells with the meat still in them on a serving tray. Top each with a little of the zucchini mixture. Serve slightly chilled or at room temperature.

SWORDFISH SKEWERS GLAZED WITH SWEET AND SOUR SAUCE

Spiedini di Pesce Spada all'Agrodolce

Swordfish is marvelous this way, but you can substitute other firm fish, such as tuna or grouper; just be mindful as each fish has a different cooking time. I had these for the first time at an outdoor grigliata *near the sea in Trapani, Sicily.*

Serves 6 to 8

1 cup balsamic vinegar, preferably aged at least
   6 years
18 red or white pearl onions
2 pounds skinless swordfish, cut into 1-inch cubes
   (about 30 pieces)
1 teaspoon kosher salt
Freshly ground black pepper, to taste
¼ cup extra-virgin olive oil
12 fresh bay leaves

Preheat an outdoor grill or an indoor grill pan to medium-high heat. Soak eight long wooden skewers in water for 15 minutes (or use metal skewers). Bring the balsamic vinegar to a boil in a small saucepan. Lower the heat to a gentle boil, and cook until the vinegar is reduced to about ⅓ cup, about 5 to 6 minutes. Set aside.

Drop the pearl onions into a medium saucepan of boiling water, and cook until softened but still quite firm, about 4 minutes. Drain, and let stand until cool enough to handle. Slip off the skins, leaving the roots intact and the onions whole.

In a large bowl, toss the swordfish cubes and onions with the olive oil. Season lightly with salt and pepper, and toss again.

Thread the fish, onions, and bay leaves onto the skewers, dividing the ingredients evenly among the skewers and alternating them as you like. Grill the skewers until the swordfish is just cooked through, about 2 minutes on each side (4 minutes total). Serve with a drizzle of the balsamic reduction, and pass remaining reduction separately.

FRIED BANANA PEPPERS

Peperoni Fritti

Banana peppers are a long, thin-skinned, mildly spicy variety of pepper that, because of their skin and fairly meaty texture, are perfect for frying. To serve them as a room-temperature salad, prepare them as described below. If you'd rather serve them hot, arrange the peeled peppers and their juices in a baking dish, sprinkle the bread crumbs over them, and bake in a hot oven until the crumbs are lightly browned. This recipe is delicious as an appetizer, part of a buffet table, or as a side dish. I love using any leftovers to stuff sandwiches.

Serves 6

¼ cup extra-virgin olive oil
6 banana or cubanelle peppers (about 5 inches long), or other long, thin-fleshed, mildly spicy peppers
6 cloves garlic, crushed and peeled
Kosher salt, to taste
¼ cup fine dried bread crumbs

Heat the olive oil in a large heavy skillet over medium heat. Arrange the whole peppers in a single layer in the skillet. Scatter the garlic cloves around the peppers. Place a smaller skillet over the peppers to weight them. As the peppers soften, the weight of the skillet will help them cook and brown evenly.

Fry the peppers and garlic, turning as necessary, until the peppers are evenly browned and blistered on all sides and the garlic is golden brown, about 10 minutes for the peppers, less for the garlic. Remove and reserve the garlic cloves as they brown.

Remove the skillet from the heat, and transfer the peppers to a baking pan to cool. Reserve the oil and any juices from the pan. Pull out and discard the cores and seeds from the peppers, draining the juice from inside them and adding it to the juices in the baking pan. Pull off as much of the skins from the peppers as possible, and tear each pepper lengthwise into four strips. Arrange the pepper strips in a serving dish as you work. Add the oil from the skillet and the reserved garlic, if you wish, to the juices in the baking pan, and season to taste with salt. Sprinkle the pepper strips with a light coat of bread crumbs, and toss to mix. Let stand at room temperature 30 minutes to 1 hour before serving.

MONKFISH MEATBALLS IN TOMATO SAUCE

Polpette di Rana Pescatrice in Sugo di Pomodoro

It is a good idea to do a test run, rolling up and frying one of these fish balls, before forming the whole batch. That way, you can check the seasoning and add a little salt and pepper if you like before you cook them all. Cooking a little sample first is a good thing to keep in mind when you're making other meatballs, too.

Serves 8

1½ pounds monkfish fillets

2 cups 1-inch cubes crustless day-old Italian bread

1 large egg, beaten

⅓ cup chopped fresh Italian parsley

⅓ cup drained capers, chopped

1 teaspoon kosher salt, plus more to taste

¼ teaspoon freshly ground black pepper, plus more to taste

All-purpose flour, for dredging

Vegetable oil, for frying

⅓ cup extra-virgin olive oil

1 small onion, chopped

One 28-ounce can whole San Marzano tomatoes, crushed by hand

2 fresh bay leaves

½ cup golden raisins

½ cup toasted pine nuts

Trim any skin and the gray membrane from the monkfish fillets. Cut the fillets into 1-inch chunks, and chill them thoroughly. Pass the fish through a meat grinder fitted with a disk with holes about ¼ inch in diameter. (Alternatively, you may grind the fish, half of it at a time, using quick on/off pulses in a food processor fitted with a metal blade. Either way, the fish should resemble ground beef after grinding.)

Toss the bread into a mixing bowl, and pour enough cold water over it to cover completely. Let soak until completely saturated. Drain the bread well, and squeeze it between your hands to remove as much water as possible.

Crumble the bread into a mixing bowl, and add the egg, parsley, capers, 1 teaspoon salt, and ¼ teaspoon pepper. Stir in the ground monkfish until incorporated. Using 1 tablespoon of the fish mixture for each, form balls by rolling the mixture between your palms. Spread some flour on a plate, and dredge the balls lightly in flour to coat all sides.

Heat ½ inch vegetable oil over medium heat in a skillet, and add as many fish balls as will fit without touching. Fry, turning as necessary, until they're golden all over, about 5 minutes. Remove with a slotted spoon, and drain on a paper-towel-lined baking sheet, and finish frying.

Pour off the oil from the pan, pour in the olive oil, and heat over medium heat. Stir in the onion, and cook, stirring, until wilted, about 4 minutes. Add the tomatoes; slosh out the can with 1 cup of water, and add that to the pan, along with the bay leaves. Season to taste with salt and pepper. Bring to a boil, then lower the heat so the sauce is at a simmer. Cook until slightly thickened, about 15 minutes.

Stir in the raisins and pine nuts, and nestle the fish balls into the sauce, shaking the pan gently until they are covered with sauce. Simmer 20 minutes, shaking the pan occasionally. Remove the bay leaves and let the fish balls rest in the sauce off the heat for 10 minutes before serving.

CRISPY SHRIMP

Gamberi Croccanti

Everybody loves crispy fried shrimp. They are best when fried at the last minute, but if you're feeding a crowd, after the shrimp are fried spread them on a sheet pan and keep them in a 325-degree oven. Hold for no longer than 10 minutes in the hot oven; otherwise, the shrimp will get tough. These are a huge crowd pleaser at my house, so I rarely have this problem.

Serves 4 to 6

Vegetable oil, for frying
1 cup all-purpose flour, plus more for dredging
½ teaspoon baking powder
½ teaspoon kosher salt, plus more to taste
1 cup club soda, chilled, plus more as needed
2 tablespoons finely chopped pickled peperoncini
1 pound large shrimp, peeled and deveined
Fresh lemon slices, for serving

Heat 2 inches of vegetable oil in a medium Dutch oven to 365 degrees.

In a large bowl, whisk together the flour, baking powder, and salt. Whisk in the club soda to make a smooth batter. (The batter should be as thick as pancake batter; if it's too thick, whisk in a little more club soda.) Whisk in the peperoncini.

Spread some flour on a plate. Lightly dredge the shrimp in the flour, tapping off the excess. Dip the shrimp in the batter in batches, so they're not touching in the pan, and fry until crisp and golden, about 3 to 4 minutes per batch. Season all with salt, and serve right away with slices of lemon.

SPICY STUFFED CLAMS

Vongole Ripiene

Ask your fishmonger to shuck the clams for you, leaving them on the half-shell, and tell him to reserve ½ cup of the clam juice. Then all you have to do when you get home is stuff and bake them. These are best served hot out of the oven, but you can lower the temperature and keep them warm for a limited time before serving (no more than 15 minutes, or the clams will get dry and tough) if needed. If you're not a fan of spicy peppers, you can substitute roasted red peppers or sweet pickled peppers for the hot ones. I warn my eager guests to go slowly: straight out of the oven, the clams can be quite hot if eaten too quickly.

Serves 4 as an appetizer, or more as part of an antipasto buffet

24 littleneck clams, shucked, plus ½ cup clam juice
1 cup panko bread crumbs
½ cup finely chopped scallions
¼ cup grated Grana Padano
2 hot pickled cherry peppers, seeded and finely chopped, plus 2 tablespoons brine from the jar
1 tablespoon chopped fresh Italian parsley
¼ teaspoon kosher salt
¼ cup extra-virgin olive oil
¾ cup dry white wine

Preheat oven to 425 degrees. Set the clams on a rimmed sheet pan.

In a medium bowl, combine the panko, scallions, grated cheese, pickled cherry peppers, parsley, and salt, and toss with a fork. Drizzle with 2 tablespoons oil, and toss again to make a moist stuffing.

Press some stuffing over each clam, dividing evenly and leaving a couple tablespoons filling in the bowl.

Stir the reserved stuffing and the pepper brine into the white wine, and pour this into the bottom of the pan. Add ½ cup of the reserved clam juice. Drizzle the clams with the remaining 2 tablespoons olive oil. Bake until filling is crisp and golden, about 15 to 18 minutes. Serve hot or at room temperature.

Cured Meats, Cheese, and Pickled Vegetables

One of the easiest ways to entertain is to prepare a spread of charcuterie, cheeses, and cured and jarred vegetables, served with different condiments and a variety of breads. Because it is so simple, the quality of the product is on display, so buying the best will ensure the success of your event. Here are some suggestions.

Charcuterie

PROSCIUTTO: Italian air-cured pork hindquarter. Make sure it is from Parma or San Daniele. Have it thinly sliced, and make sure it is packed in single layers, with a piece of wax paper between them. Buy it as close to the event as possible, or, even better, the same day.

MORTADELLA: Known as Italian bologna, a sausage of finely ground pork product with pork-fat squares. Buy an imported variety. I like the one with pistachios in it, thinly sliced. With mortadella, it is okay if the slices are piled on top of each other, because they separate easily.

CAPOCOLLO: Dried cured pork sausage made of the meat from the neck to the fourth or fifth rib: It comes in both sweet and hot varieties. Have it thinly sliced and packed with wax paper between layers.

BRESAOLA: Air-dried salted beef from the top round, cut so it is leaner than other cured meats. Should be cut into thin slices and packaged with wax paper in between layers.

SPECK: Smoked, air-cured pork hindquarter. Have it sliced like prosciutto.

CACCIATORINI: A small, dry link sausage usually consisting of equal parts pork and beef. Buy this whole; when ready to serve, peel skin off and cut it into slices with a knife, not too thin.

All of the cold cuts just mentioned look good spread on plates or on wooden serving boards. Place a variety on the serving platter with mixed olives or Tuscan green peperoncini nearby.

FRUIT *MOSTARDA*: A fruit condiment made with apples, pears, or apricots and a syrup flavored with mustard—or the chutney of your choice. Goes great next to the cheeses.

PICKLED VEGETABLES: Marinated artichokes, mushrooms, eggplants, sun-dried tomatoes, giardiniera, and roasted peppers are good close to the cured meats.

OLIVES: Cerignola are big, meaty, brined green olives; Gaeta are cured small black olives. Sicilian olives are dried and packed in oil.

FISH: Anchovies, fillet of mackerel in olive oil, sardines in olive oil, tuna. Drain the oil from the fish, and plate the anchovies on a separate small plate. On top of the mackerel and sardines, put some thinly sliced purple onions and toss the drained tuna in olive oil with some cooked cannellini beans, celery leaves, and a splash of wine vinegar and olive oil.

CHEESES: A chunk of Grana Padano, a piece of Gorgonzola, a piece of pecorino (medium-aged), a piece of Taleggio, and a piece of Montasio. Put all the cheeses on a large cutting board, and have cheese knives nearby so your guests can serve themselves. Set out a jar of good honey, which can be drizzled on the cheese, and some almonds, walnuts, and hazelnuts in bowls next to the cheeses.

On a separate plate, present mozzarella with a drizzle of olive oil and shreds of basil leaves.

You can serve this cheese spread on its own, but I like to add a tossed green salad and a salad of tomato, onion, and basil. To crown the event, your selection of breads is very important, so diversify: offer crispy baguettes, multigrain bread, bread sticks, crackers, and fried dough. Fill decorative bread baskets, and fit them on each side of the display.

Fresh fruit is always welcome with the cheese; make sure it is seasonal and ripe. My favorites are pears, peaches, apples, and grapes.

Set on the table a good bottle of virgin olive oil and a bottle of balsamic vinegar—Tradizionale is the best—for those who like an extra drizzle.

LAMB MEATBALLS WITH LEMON SAUCE

Polpette d'Agnello al Limone

The meatballs can be formed ahead of time, but bake them and make the quick sauce at the last minute before serving.

Makes about 48 small meatballs, serving 8 as an appetizer

MEATBALLS

2 cups cubes day-old bread, coarsely chopped in
   food processor into crumbs
½ cup plain Greek yogurt
1¼ pounds lean ground lamb
Grated zest of 1 lemon
¼ cup toasted pine nuts, coarsely chopped
¼ cup chopped fresh Italian parsley
¼ cup grated Grana Padano
2 large eggs
1 teaspoon kosher salt

SAUCE

2 large eggs
½ cup chicken stock (page 148)
Juice of 1 lemon
½ teaspoon kosher salt

Preheat oven to 375 degrees. For the meatballs, mash the bread crumbs and yogurt together in a large bowl. Add the lamb, lemon zest, pine nuts, parsley, and grated cheese. In a small bowl, beat the eggs with the salt, and pour this over the meat mixture. Mix well with your hands to combine.

Line a baking sheet with parchment. Roll the meat mixture into forty-eight 1-inch meatballs, and line them up on the baking sheet so they don't touch one another. Bake until meatballs are cooked through, about 20 minutes.

For the sauce, in a small saucepan, whisk together the eggs, chicken stock, lemon juice, and salt. Set the saucepan over low heat, and cook, stirring constantly, until the mixture thickens and coats the back of a spoon, about 5 minutes. Strain the sauce into a small serving bowl. Set the bowl on a platter, and surround the sauce with the meatballs; serve with toothpicks for spearing the meatballs.

FRIED BREAD

Pane Fritto

There are endless uses for these little breads. After they are fried, you can split and stuff them with cheese, meats, or cooked vegetables, or top them with thin slices of prosciutto or salami. They are also good on their own, with a sprinkle of salt or grated cheese. For a sweet ending to a meal, I love eating them drizzled with honey or just sprinkled with sugar.

Makes about 36 rounds

1½ cups milk
1 packet active dry yeast (2¼ teaspoons)
2 teaspoons sugar
2 tablespoons extra-virgin olive oil
1 large egg, beaten
2 teaspoons kosher salt, plus more for sprinkling
4 to 4½ cups all-purpose flour, plus more as needed for shaping
Vegetable oil, for frying

In a small saucepan (or in a spouted measuring cup in the microwave), heat the milk until just warm to the touch (about 100 degrees on an instant-read thermometer). Stir in the yeast and sugar until dissolved, then let sit until bubbly, about 2 minutes. Whisk in the oil, egg, and salt.

Put 3½ cups of the flour in an electric mixer fitted with the paddle attachment. Pour in the yeast mixture, and mix at low speed to make a shaggy dough (adding more flour, as necessary, to make the dough hold together).

Switch to a dough hook, and knead at medium speed until the dough is smooth and elastic and cleans the sides of the bowl, about 5 minutes. Put the dough in an oiled bowl, turn to coat, and cover with plastic wrap. Let rise until doubled in size, about 1 hour.

Divide the dough into two pieces with floured hands. Flour your work surface, and roll one piece to an approximate 10-by-18-inch rectangle. With a 2-inch round cutter dipped in flour, cut as many rounds as you can get, and set them on parchment-lined baking sheets. Repeat with the remaining piece of dough. You can combine and reroll the scraps once more, though these rounds will not puff quite as much as the others.

Heat about 2 inches of oil in a medium skillet to 360 degrees (the tip of a bread round will sizzle on contact when the oil is ready). Fry the breads in batches until golden and puffed on both sides, about 3 to 4 minutes total. Drain on paper towels, and keep warm on a sheet pan in a low oven until all the breads are fried. Season with salt.

BREAD STICKS

Grissini

Grissini—thin bread sticks—are welcome on any table. They can be served with a cured-meats platter, set standing up straight at the ends of a buffet, or served in the bread basket at a sit-down dinner. Don't work the dough too much as you pat and roll, or the grissini will be tough. They can be made earlier in the day, but are also delicious served hot from the oven.

Makes about 40

¾ cup warm water (about 100 degrees)
1 packet active dry yeast (2¼ teaspoons)
1 teaspoon sugar
2 cups all-purpose flour, plus more as needed
2 tablespoons extra-virgin olive oil, plus more for
   brushing
1½ teaspoons kosher salt
Grated Grana Padano, cayenne, sesame seeds,
   poppy seeds, and flaky sea salt, for garnish

In a spouted measuring cup, combine the warm water, yeast, and sugar. Let sit until bubbly, about 5 minutes.

In the bowl of an electric mixer fitted with the paddle attachment, mix to combine flour, extra-virgin olive oil, and salt. Pour in the yeast mixture, and mix with the paddle at low speed until the dough comes together.

Switch to the dough hook, and knead at medium speed until the dough is soft and springy and cleans the sides of the bowl, about 5 minutes. Put the dough in an oiled bowl, and cover with plastic wrap. Let rise in a warm place until doubled in size, about 1 hour.

Preheat oven to 400 degrees. Line two sheet pans with parchment paper. Cut the dough into four equal pieces. Working with one piece at a time, pat the piece with floured hands into a square. Gently roll the dough (with an unfloured rolling pin) into a square or rectangle about ½ inch thick. With a pizza cutter, cut into ten strips. Stretch the strips as you move them to the baking sheet so the grissini are about the thickness of a pencil. Repeat with the remaining pieces of dough.

For topping, mix the grated cheese with a pinch or two of cayenne. The other toppings can be used as is. Lightly brush the grissini with olive oil, and sprinkle with the topping(s) of your choice. Let the grissini rise for 15 minutes, then bake until golden and crisp, about 10 to 12 minutes, rotating the pans from top to bottom halfway through the baking time.

Salads

When celebrating in the spring or summer—or if you're hosting vegetarian, pescatarian, or gluten-free friends—consider a salad party to make the most of the bounty of the season. You should feel free to throw in an extra ingredient or two to any of the salads included here, to make the dish more your own or to meet the preferences of your guests. I like to set up a long buffet with several big bowls of different types of salad—something with leafy greens, a string-bean salad, a carrot salad, something with beans, a salad with fish, and a salad with cheese in it—all accompanied by lovely breads and grissini.

If you have meat eaters in your group, then you can also include a chicken salad, or serve large platters of sliced prosciutto and mortadella, always an excellent accompaniment for any of the salad recipes included here. Or grill some large T-bone steaks and make three salads to be placed in large bowls on your dining-room table. I would probably go with an asparagus and leeks in lemon vinaigrette salad (page 104), an arugula with porcini mushrooms and shavings of Grana Padano salad (page 114), and a leek, walnut, and Gorgonzola salad (page 115), some of my favorites.

Salads are always welcomed at a buffet table, but do not dress them ahead of time. Wait until just before the party begins, and always split them into two bowls—dressing and serving one, so that when the first is finished you can dress and serve the second bowl.

ASPARAGUS AND LEEKS IN LEMON VINAIGRETTE

Asparagi e Porri al Limone

I like serving this salad while the vegetables are still warm, but it is also delicious chilled, especially if you are hosting a buffet or a picnic. The important thing is to dress it just before serving, since the lemon juice will change the color of the vegetables.

Serves 4 to 6

1 teaspoon kosher salt, plus more for the cooking water

2 bunches medium-thick asparagus, trimmed, lower third of stalks peeled (about 2 pounds)

1 bunch medium leeks, white and light-green parts, halved lengthwise

Juice of 1 large lemon

¼ cup extra-virgin olive oil

4 hard-boiled eggs, coarsely chopped

Bring a large pot of salted water to boil. Cut the peeled asparagus into thirds crosswise. Cut the leeks in thirds crosswise as well. Add the asparagus and leeks to the boiling water, and cook until tender, about 5 to 7 minutes, depending on their thickness. Drain, and plunge into an ice bath to stop the cooking and set the color. Drain and pat very dry.

Put the asparagus and leeks in a serving bowl. Drizzle with the lemon juice and olive oil, and season with the salt. Toss well. Mound the asparagus and leeks on a serving platter, and scatter the hard-boiled eggs over the top.

CARROT AND ORANGE SALAD

Insalata di Carote ed Arance

This bright salad is a great way to add color to a winter menu, and also ideal for buffets and summer picnics. It can be made ahead and is easily doubled for a larger crowd. For more complexity, try adding some pitted cured black olives.

Serves 4 to 6

4 large navel oranges
2 large carrots, julienned by hand or on a
 mandoline
½ cup halved pitted oil-cured black olives
2 tablespoons extra-virgin olive oil
1 tablespoon white wine vinegar
½ teaspoon kosher salt
Freshly ground black pepper

Strip the bottom from an orange so it sits flat. With a sharp knife, shave off the peel and pith to expose the flesh. Holding the orange in your hand, cut out the individual segments, and put them in a large bowl. Once you have cut out all of the segments, squeeze the remaining juice from the membranes into the bowl. Repeat with the three remaining oranges.

Add the carrot and olives to the bowl, and toss. Drizzle with the oil and vinegar, and season with the salt and lots of black pepper. Toss, and chill until ready to serve.

SALAD OF WARM GREENS WITH BACON AND MUSHROOMS

Insalata Tiepida con Pancetta e Funghi

You can use a combination of baby greens to make this salad; just be sure they are hearty enough to stand up to the warm dressing. Baby arugula, spinach, kale, and romaine all work well. Since this is a warm salad, tossing it at the last minute before serving is best. The dressing, bacon, and mushrooms can be prepared in advance, but make sure they are warm when you're tossing them into the salad. I think this is a perfect salad for a romantic lunch; there is something warm and fuzzy about a warm, savory salad.

Serves 4 to 6

3 tablespoons extra-virgin olive oil, plus more as needed

4 ounces thickly sliced bacon, coarsely chopped

8 ounces white mushrooms, sliced

½ teaspoon kosher salt, plus more to taste

1 tablespoon grainy Dijon mustard

3 tablespoons red wine vinegar

Freshly ground black pepper

5 cups loosely packed baby arugula

5 cups loosely packed baby spinach

Add 1 tablespoon of the oil and the bacon to a large skillet over medium heat. Cook, stirring often, until the bacon is crisp, about 4 minutes. Remove to a paper-towel-lined plate to drain.

Increase heat to medium high, and scatter in the sliced mushrooms. Let sit, without stirring, for a minute to brown the underside, then season with the salt and stir. Continue to cook until the mushrooms are tender, about 3 to 4 minutes. Remove to the plate with the bacon using a slotted spoon, leaving the fat behind in the pan.

Reduce the heat to low, and add the mustard. Whisk in the vinegar, then the remaining 2 tablespoons olive oil. Taste, and add more olive oil if necessary to balance the acidity. Season with salt.

In a large bowl, combine the greens, mushrooms, and bacon. Pour the dressing over all, season with black pepper, and toss. Serve immediately.

CAESAR SALAD WITH BABY KALE
AND FOCACCIA CROUTONS

Insalata alla Cesare con Cavolo Nero e Crostini di Focaccia

Caesar salad was one of the most popular things on the menus at my first two restaurants. It is familiar and much loved, but here I add some kale for diversity and flavor. All of the components of this salad—the romaine, the kale, and the dressing—can be prepared before-hand, and kept in the refrigerator until you are ready to dress the salad, just before serving. You can use all romaine for a more traditional Caesar, if you prefer.

Serves 4 to 6

One 5-to-6-inch square of focaccia, rosemary or plain, cut into ½-inch cubes (about 3 cups cubes)

4 oil-packed anchovy fillets, drained

2 large hard-cooked egg yolks

2 tablespoons white wine vinegar

Juice of 1 lemon

1 tablespoon Dijon mustard

2 small cloves garlic, crushed and peeled

½ teaspoon kosher salt, plus more to taste

6 tablespoons extra-virgin olive oil

5 cups loosely packed chopped romaine hearts (about 1 heart)

5 cups loosely packed baby kale

½ cup grated Grana Padano

Freshly ground black pepper

Preheat oven to 350 degrees. Scatter the focaccia cubes on a baking sheet, and bake until light golden and crispy, about 8 to 10 minutes. Let cool.

In a mini–food processor (or in a bowl, if you're working by hand), combine the anchovies, egg yolks, vinegar, lemon juice, mustard, garlic, and ½ teaspoon salt. Process until smooth. With the machine running, add the olive oil in a steady stream to make a smooth dressing.

When ready to serve, combine the romaine and kale in a large bowl. Drizzle with the dressing, and toss well. Add the focaccia croutons and grated cheese, and toss again. Taste, and season with black pepper and additional salt if necessary. Toss once more, and serve immediately.

CUCUMBER SALAD

Insalata di Cetrioli

This salad can be prepared several hours ahead and refrigerated; serve cold or at room temperature. It's a crunchy and refreshing recipe, but to make a more substantial dish you can add shredded cooked chicken, or salami and ham, cut into julienne slices. The Italians love their salads, and will often turn them into a meal course, especially in the summer, by adding some proteins. It is a clever way to use leftover chicken or fish.

Serves 6

2 English cucumbers, sliced into ¼-inch-thick rounds

1 small red onion, thinly sliced

2 teaspoons kosher salt, plus more to taste

¼ cup white wine vinegar

½ tablespoon honey

¼ cup extra-virgin olive oil

3 stalks celery, sliced ¼ inch thick on the bias, plus ½ cup inner celery leaves

Freshly ground black pepper

In a large colander, toss the cucumbers and red onion with the salt. Let drain in the sink 30 minutes, to purge the excess water.

Rinse and drain the cucumbers and onions well, and pat dry.

In a large serving bowl, whisk together the vinegar and honey. While continuing to whisk, pour in the olive oil in a slow, steady stream to make a smooth dressing. Add the cucumber and onions and celery and leaves. Toss to coat with the dressing. Taste, and season with salt and pepper. Toss again, and serve.

PANZANELLA WITH SHRIMP AND FENNEL

Panzanella con Gamberi e Finocchio

The ingredients for this salad can be prepped ahead of time. Toss the bread and vegetables together 15 to 20 minutes before serving, giving the bread some time to soak up the dressing and soften. Then toss in the shrimp, which can be chilled or warm when you add them, depending on your preference. Perfect for summer entertaining, whether for twenty or a romantic lunch for two.

Serves 4 to 6

1-pound chunk 1- or 2-day-old bread, cut into 1-inch cubes (about 6 cups cubes)

3 beefsteak tomatoes, cut into 1-inch wedges

1 small fennel bulb, trimmed, and thinly sliced by hand or on a mandoline

1 bunch scallions, white and green parts, chopped

½ English cucumber, sliced into half-moons

¼ cup red wine vinegar

1½ teaspoons kosher salt

½ cup plus 2 tablespoons extra-virgin olive oil

1 pound medium shrimp, peeled and deveined

Preheat oven to 350 degrees. Spread the bread cubes on a baking sheet, and toast until crisp throughout but not browned, about 7 minutes. Let cool.

In a large bowl, combine the tomatoes, fennel, scallions, and cucumber. Sprinkle with the vinegar and 1 teaspoon salt. Toss well. Add the bread cubes, and toss to soak in the vinegar. Drizzle with ½ cup of the olive oil, and toss again. Let sit while you cook the shrimp.

Add the remaining 2 tablespoons olive oil to a large skillet over high heat. When the oil is hot, add the shrimp and season with the remaining ½ teaspoon salt. Cook and toss until the shrimp are just cooked through, about 3 minutes. Remove the skillet from the heat, and let cool 5 minutes.

Add the shrimp to the salad, and toss well. I like to serve it warm, but it is wonderful cold as well.

PASTA SALAD WITH TOMATO, MOZZARELLA, AND GREEN BEANS

Insalata di Cavatappi, Mozzarella, Pomodori, e Fagiolini

This dish is great for buffets, picnics, and large family gatherings. My daughter, Tanya, is the expert pasta-salad maker in my family. The recipe is easy to multiply, it keeps well, and it's economical. This pasta can be dressed several hours ahead, but hold about half of the dressing to toss in at the last minute, since the pasta will have absorbed much of the first batch.

Serves 6 to 8

1 teaspoon kosher salt, plus more for boiling and to taste

1 pound green beans, trimmed

1 pound cavatappi or elbows

2 pints cherry tomatoes, halved lengthwise

1 pound small mozzarella balls (bocconcini), halved if on the larger side

1 cup loosely packed fresh basil leaves

1 cup loosely packed fresh Italian parsley leaves

2 ripe plum tomatoes, seeded and cut into chunks

½ cup toasted skinned almonds

2 cloves garlic, crushed and peeled

2 tablespoons red wine vinegar

½ cup extra-virgin olive oil

Bring a large pot of salted water to boil. Add the green beans, and cook until tender, about 6 to 7 minutes. Remove with a spider to a bowl of ice water to stop the cooking. Drain, pat dry, and cut into thirds.

Add the pasta to the same water, and cook until al dente. Drain, rinse, and pat dry. Put in a large bowl, and add the green beans, cherry tomatoes, and mozzarella.

For the dressing, in a mini–food processor (or a bowl, if you're working by hand), combine the basil, parsley, plum tomatoes, almonds, garlic, vinegar, and salt. Process until smooth. With the machine running, add the olive oil in a steady stream to make a creamy dressing. Pour the dressing over the pasta, and toss well. Season with salt if necessary, and serve.

ARUGULA SALAD WITH PORCINI MUSHROOMS AND SHAVINGS OF GRANA PADANO

Insalata di Funghi Porcini e Grana Padano

Porcini are my absolute favorite mushrooms, and I have very fond memories of foraging for them in the hills of Emilia-Romagna with Dante Laurenti, who was a captain at my restaurant Felidia when we first opened, in 1981. This delicious salad is very time-sensitive, since all the ingredients are tender, so toss at the last minute. If you have no porcini, very thinly sliced shiitake or cremini mushrooms may be substituted. Whichever type of mushroom you choose, make sure they are firm and as free of blemishes as possible. Before slicing, trim any tough parts from the stems—cut the shiitake stems off completely—and wipe the caps clean with a damp paper towel.

Serves 4 to 6

One 2-ounce piece Grana Padano
2 tablespoons extra-virgin olive oil
1 tablespoon freshly squeezed lemon juice
¼ teaspoon kosher salt
Freshly ground black pepper, to taste
4 ounces baby arugula
2 ounces fresh porcini mushrooms, wiped clean, trimmed, and finely sliced (about 2 cups)
Truffle oil, to taste

Make 1-inch shards of cheese by shaving it with a vegetable peeler. You should have about 1¼ cups. Set the shards aside.

In a large bowl, whisk the olive oil and lemon juice with the salt and pepper to taste until blended. Add the arugula and mushrooms. Toss until the salad is coated with dressing, then fold in the shaved Grana Padano, and divide salad among serving plates. Drizzle with truffle oil to taste.

LEEK, WALNUT, AND GORGONZOLA SALAD

Insalata di Porri, Noci, e Gorgonzola

Good leeks are always in season, and when you want a salad, especially in the winter months, this is the recipe to go to. You can cook the leeks ahead of time, but don't assemble the salad until the last minute. You can also serve it over a bed of greens, for a more substantial meal.

Serves 4 to 6

3 bunches leeks (6 large or 9 medium)
½ teaspoon kosher salt
2 tablespoons red wine vinegar
¼ cup extra-virgin olive oil
4 ounces Gorgonzola, crumbled
½ cup toasted coarsely chopped walnuts

Trim the dark-green parts, roots, and any tough outer leaves from the leeks. Put the whole leeks in a large saucepan with salted water to cover by an inch or two. Bring to a simmer, and cook until leeks are tender all the way through, about 15 to 18 minutes, depending on the size. Drain, and let cool.

Slice the cooled leeks into 1-inch rounds and separate the rounds with your fingers into a serving bowl. Season with the salt, and toss. Sprinkle the vinegar, then the oil over the leeks, and toss well.

Mound the leeks on a platter, and top with the Gorgonzola, then the walnuts. Serve.

RAW AND COOKED SALAD FOR WINTER

Insalata Cotta e Cruda

While visiting the vegetable stall at Palermo's La Vucciria market, I discovered the unique and flavorful combination of a salad made with both raw and cooked vegetables. Although it was summer when I first tasted it, here I give you a winter version with squash and kale. A perfect combination of different seasonal vegetables, it can also be made with fried eggplant and roasted peppers when summer comes around.

Serves 6

SALAD

1 pound sweet onions, such as Vidalia, sliced into
   ¼-inch-thick rings
4 tablespoons extra-virgin olive oil
1½ teaspoons kosher salt, plus more for the cooking
   water
2 cups peeled, seeded, and cubed butternut squash
½ cup golden raisins
1 pound new red potatoes
8 ounces green beans, trimmed
6 ounces baby kale
¼ cup toasted slivered almonds

DRESSING

⅓ cup toasted slivered almonds
⅓ cup red wine vinegar
½ teaspoon kosher salt
½ cup extra-virgin olive oil

To prepare the cooked vegetables for the salad, preheat oven to 375 degrees. Bring a large saucepan of salted water to a boil to cook the potatoes and string beans. Spread the onion slices on a rimmed sheet pan lined with parchment paper, brush both sides of the onions with 2 tablespoons olive oil, and season with ½ teaspoon salt. Toss the butternut squash with 2 tablespoons olive oil and 1 teaspoon salt. On another rimmed sheet pan lined with parchment paper, spread the squash. Roast squash and onions, turning onions once, until tender and golden, about 20 minutes. Let both cool, then separate the onions into rings.

Put the raisins in a small bowl, and ladle some of the hot water over them. Let the raisins soak 5 minutes, then drain well. Add the potatoes to the boiling water, and simmer until just tender, about 10 to 15 minutes, depending on their size. Drain, cool, and halve.

When the potatoes are out, add the green beans to the boiling water, and cook until just tender, about 4 to 5 minutes. Drain, and cool under cold running water to set the color. Pat dry and, with a paring knife, "French" the green beans by splitting them lengthwise at the seam. Put the onions, squash, potatoes, and green beans in a large salad bowl. Add the raisins, kale, and almonds.

For the dressing, in a mini–food processor (or a bowl, if you're working by hand), combine the almonds, vinegar, and salt. Process to make a paste. With the machine running, add the olive oil in a steady stream to make a smooth, thick dressing. With the machine still running, drizzle in warm water (up to ¼ cup) to thin the dressing.

Drizzle half of the dressing over the salad, and toss. Serve the remaining dressing on the side.

CABBAGE SALAD

Insalata di Cappuccìo

This is a great salad to make on days when you do not have the time or opportunity to go out and shop for ingredients. A good head of cabbage will keep for a week or more, and everyone always has some bacon in the refrigerator. Although you can do all of the prep well in advance, this salad should be served as soon as it is made: What makes it special is the warm bacon dressing. The heat wilts the cabbage somewhat, giving it an interesting texture. And, of course, bacon makes everything better.

Serves 8

3 tablespoons extra-virgin olive oil, plus more if necessary
8 ounces thickly sliced bacon, julienned
1 large white onion, thinly sliced
½ cup white wine vinegar
1 teaspoon kosher salt, plus more to taste
Freshly ground black pepper, to taste
1 medium head green cabbage, cored, and thinly sliced on a mandoline or by hand

Add the olive oil to a large skillet over medium heat. When the oil is hot, add the bacon, and cook until crisp, about 6 minutes. Drain on paper towels, then put it in a large serving bowl.

You should have about ⅓ cup fat left in the pan. If not, add more olive oil; if there's more than ⅓ cup, pour out and discard the excess. Over medium heat, add the onion, and cook until wilted, about 3 minutes. Whisk in the vinegar and season with the salt and lots of black pepper. Let cook for 2 minutes.

Toss the cabbage in the bowl with the pancetta, and pour the hot dressing over all. Toss well, adjust the seasoning, and serve right away.

SUMMER TOMATO SALAD WITH ANCHOVIES AND CAPERS

Insalata Estiva di Pomodori, Acciughe, e Capperi

This salad is easily doubled for a larger crowd. It can be made a few hours ahead, but add the eggs right before serving so they don't cloud up the dressing. It is great for buffets or barbecues, or as an appetizer for summer dinner parties, and makes a fantastic lunch as well.

Serves 6

¼ cup drained capers in brine

6 anchovy fillets, chopped

1 medium shallot, finely chopped

3 tablespoons chopped fresh Italian parsley

½ teaspoon salt, plus more to taste

3 tablespoons red wine vinegar

¼ cup extra-virgin olive oil

2 pounds ripe heirloom tomatoes (varied sizes and colors), cut into 1-to-2-inch chunks, or halved if cherry tomatoes

4 hard-boiled eggs, cut into rough chunks

In a large serving bowl, combine the capers, anchovies, shallot, parsley, and salt. Whisk in the red wine vinegar, then the olive oil.

Add the tomatoes, and toss to coat in the dressing. Let sit at room temperature for 15 minutes to let the tomatoes give up their juices. Just before serving, gently toss with the hard-boiled eggs.

GRILLED APPLE AND RADICCHIO SALAD WITH GORGONZOLA

Insalata di Radicchio e Mele alla Griglia con Gorgonzola

Crisp apples are a nice addition to any salad, adding both texture and flavor. In this salad, I like them grilled, adding an extra dimension to the plate of grilled radicchio. This dish is ideal for vegetarian guests. It should be made with warm vegetables so the cheese softens when crumbled on top.

Serves 4 to 6

2 large heads radicchio, quartered through the root end
½ cup extra-virgin olive oil
1¼ teaspoons kosher salt
4 small Golden Delicious apples, cored and cut into sixths
Juice of 1 lemon
4 ounces Gorgonzola or other blue cheese

Preheat grill to medium heat. In a large bowl, toss the radicchio with 2 tablespoons oil and ½ teaspoon salt. Put radicchio on the grill, and cover. Grill until charred on one side, about 4 minutes. Turn, and cover again until marked, about 3 minutes. Uncover, and grill a few minutes more, moving the radicchio to char any spots that you've missed. Remove to a platter.

In the same bowl, toss the apples with 2 tablespoons oil and ¼ teaspoon salt. Grill, uncovered, turning frequently, until just tender, about 10 to 15 minutes. Remove to the platter with the radicchio.

In a small bowl, whisk together the lemon juice, remaining ½ teaspoon salt, and remaining ¼ cup olive oil. Drizzle over the radicchio and apples. Crumble the Gorgonzola over all, and serve.

GRILLED CALAMARI SALAD WITH TOMATO COULIS

Insalata di Calamari alla Griglia

My grandkids come running when they hear that I am serving calamari. They like them fried, grilled, or stuffed—any way will do. This salad is easily doubled for a larger group. If you have leftover coulis, it can be used to dress other fish, grilled chicken, or a hearty green salad, and it keeps well in the refrigerator for several days. This salad is also a delight when served while the calamari are still warm.

Serves 4

CALAMARI AND SALAD

¼ cup extra-virgin olive oil

2 cloves garlic, thinly sliced

2 tablespoons fresh thyme leaves

¾ teaspoon kosher salt

1 pound calamari tubes and tentacles, cleaned

2 cups thinly sliced celery on the bias (about 4 stalks), plus ½ cup inner celery leaves

3 tablespoons drained capers in brine

1 tablespoon red wine vinegar

COULIS

1½ pounds plum tomatoes

3 tablespoons extra-virgin olive oil

1 medium shallot, chopped (about ¼ cup)

2 tablespoons red wine vinegar, plus more as needed

1 teaspoon kosher salt, plus more as needed

For the calamari, in a large bowl, stir together 2 tablespoons of the oil, the garlic, thyme, and ½ teaspoon salt. Add the calamari, and toss to coat. Let marinate at room temperature for 30 minutes.

For the coulis, halve and core the tomatoes. Seed the tomatoes in a sieve over a bowl to catch the juices, pressing on the seeds to extract the juice. Discard the seeds, but reserve the juice.

In a blender, combine the seeded tomatoes, olive oil, shallot, vinegar, and salt. Blend until smooth. Pass through a sieve to make a silky, smooth sauce. Adjust the seasoning with salt and a little more vinegar if needed.

For the calamari, preheat a grill pan or cast-iron skillet over high heat. When it is very hot, scrape the marinade from the calamari and set calamari on the grill. Weight with another heavy skillet or pot and grill, turning once, until crisp and just cooked through, about a minute or so per side—but do not overcook. Remove to a cutting board, and cut into 1-inch rings.

Put the calamari in a large serving bowl, add the celery and capers, and season with the remaining ¼ teaspoon kosher salt. Drizzle with the remaining 2 tablespoons olive oil and 1 tablespoon vinegar, and toss well.

To serve, spoon about half of the sauce as a base in a shallow serving bowl or platter. Mound the calamari salad on top. Serve the rest of the sauce in a bowl on the side.

SHRIMP AND MIXED BEAN SALAD

Insalata di Gamberi e Fagiolini

I don't think there has ever been a buffet-style meal at my house where this salad has not been on the table, and rarely is there any left over. I enjoy this recipe when made with warm shrimp and beans, but these can both be cooked and chilled in advance if desired. Just dress the salad close to serving time, so the acid in the vinaigrette doesn't discolor the beans. This dish is also great as a main course for a summer meal; just add an additional ½ pound of shrimp to the recipe.

This dish can be made with frozen or canned fava beans. Follow preparation instructions on the package or the can.

Serves 4 to 6

¼ teaspoon kosher salt, plus more for the cooking water
1 pound fresh cranberry beans, shelled from pod
1 pound fresh fava beans, shelled from pod
½ small onion, chopped
2 fresh bay leaves
1 small carrot, chopped
1 stalk celery, chopped
1 pound large shrimp, peeled and deveined
3 tablespoons extra-virgin olive oil
3 tablespoons red wine vinegar
Freshly ground black pepper, to taste

Bring a large pot of salted water to boil. Add the fresh cranberry beans, and simmer 4 minutes. After 4 minutes, add the favas, and simmer until both are tender, about 4 to 5 minutes more. Drain and refresh the beans under cold running water, and remove the outer skins from the favas.

In a medium saucepan, combine the onion, bay leaves, carrot, celery, and 6 cups of water. Simmer 15 minutes, to blend the flavors. Add the shrimp, and cook just until opaque throughout, about 1 to 2 minutes. Remove and drain the shrimp, and allow them to cool.

In a serving bowl, whisk together the olive oil, vinegar, salt, and pepper. Add the beans and shrimp, and toss to coat the solids thoroughly. Serve warm or at room temperature.

LOBSTER SALAD

Insalata d'Aragosta

I had this salad for the first time in Alghero, Sardinia, where it is known as aragosta alla catalana. *The island of Sardinia was under Spanish rule for a few years, and some of that influence remains in this recipe. Depending on the juiciness of your tomatoes, you may have a little extra dressing. Serve it on the side, or it will keep in the refrigerator for a day or two to dress other salads. You can cook the lobsters and prep the other ingredients here ahead of time; just toss the salad at the last minute. This is an impressive dish and looks generous on a buffet table, but it also works well as an appetizer or main course for a sit-down meal.*

Serves 6 as an appetizer or 4 as a main course

1 teaspoon kosher salt, plus more for cooking the lobsters

Two 1½-pound lobsters

2 small ripe plum tomatoes, cored and cut into chunks

3 hard-boiled eggs, whites and yolks separated

Juice of 1 large lemon

⅓ cup extra-virgin olive oil

3 beefsteak or other large tomatoes, cut into wedges

1 large fennel bulb, trimmed, and very thinly sliced on a mandoline or with a very sharp knife

4 inner stalks celery, thinly sliced on the bias, plus ½ cup inner celery leaves

Bring a very large pot of water to boil, and salt it liberally. When the water is at a rolling boil, add the lobsters, and cover the pot. Once the water is boiling again, cook the lobsters 10 to 12 minutes (for this size lobster). Drain, and run the lobsters under cold water. Let cool completely.

When the lobsters are cool, twist off the claws (and cut off any rubber bands). Twist the smaller knuckle segment from each claw. Crack the claws and knuckle segments with the back of your knife to make digging the meat out easier for your guests. Twist the tails from the bodies, split lengthwise, then cut each tail half into two or three pieces. Cut the bodies in half (you can remove the tomalley and roe or leave them in, whichever you prefer). Put all of the lobster pieces in a large serving bowl, and set aside.

For the dressing, in a mini–food processor (or a bowl, if you're working by hand), combine the plum tomatoes, egg yolks, lemon juice, and salt. Process until smooth. With the machine running, add the olive oil in a steady stream, to make a thick and smooth dressing.

Add the tomato wedges, fennel, and celery slices and leaves to the bowl with the lobster. Coarsely chop the egg whites, and add those as well. Drizzle with the dressing (but don't overdress), and toss well. Serve.

Engagement Party—Two Families Meet

Engagement parties are often the first time two families that will eventually be joined are meeting. Keep things simple, but include some recipes that are important to your family (so you have something to talk about, should the conversation lag). Find out from the future bride- or groom-in-law what are some dishes he or she enjoys, and try to include a few of those as well.

For an engagement party, I feel that less formal is the best way to go. Standing and mingling allows for more conversation, and for everyone to get to know each other. If they are not accustomed to formal sit-down dinners, these can make your guests feel uncomfortable, and you run the risk that people who end up sitting next to each other don't have that much in common. I prefer an elegant buffet style. Have plenty of seating available, and if possible set it up in clusters, so small groups can form and have more intimate conversations. Make sure to open the festivities with a sparkling-wine toast as you welcome your guests, soon to be family, into your home and into your lives.

As for the buffet, this is when you take out your best plates, flatware, and linens. Do not hold back. Around the space where people will be eating, put out some roasted olives with orange and rosemary (page 34), with a small plate nearby where they can leave the discarded pits, as well as some carrot and chickpea dip (page 37) with bread sticks and chips. The buffet should be diversified with baked stuffed vegetables (page 30), marinated mushrooms (page 43), herb frittata roll-ups (page 51), bruschetta with kale (page 64) or cannellini and pancetta (page 62), and crispy shrimp (page 90), all favorites. And always keep in mind that some of your guests may be vegetarians.

You'll certainly want some salads, such as panzanella with shrimp and fennel (page 111) or the salad of leeks, walnuts, and Gorgonzola (page 115). Some dishes hot out of the oven, such as baked stuffed shells (page 221), are sure to go down well; with the oven going, perhaps also make a crostata with kale, butternut squash, and ricotta (page 75) and my crostata with mushrooms and onion (page 76); cut both crostate into squares, so the pieces can easily be picked up and put on a plate or popped into the mouth. People love deviled eggs (page 49) and stuffed mushrooms (page 29), so be sure to include those as well. And if you want to be a bit fancier, serve the Prosciutto di Parma "purses" stuffed with Grana Padano (page 36). Rice balls stuffed with sausage ragù (page 78) are always a big hit, and you can make them in advance, keep them warm in the oven, then serve in a pretty ceramic baking dish straight to the buffet table on a trivet. Put a cloth over the side, so your guests will know that the baking dish might still be hot. I would serve all of these items on platters on a large table. You should also include some room-temperature fish dishes served on platters, such as the poached salmon salad (page 129) or the poached seafood salad (page 126), both made in advance and easily placed on the buffet, so you, too, can get to know and enjoy your guests.

For big protein items, I like chicken with tuna sauce (page 275), which is delicious served cold, and *cima genovese* (page 292), a vegetable-stuffed poached breast of veal that's wonderful cold or at room temperature. Complement any large protein dishes with some vegetables, such as grilled corn, figs, and portobellos (page 162), all grilled earlier and then served at room temperature. You should do this when figs are in season, but they should not be too ripe. Balsamic braised onions (page 173) can also be made in advance and served at room temperature; this dish is out of the norm and sure to impress with its vibrant flavor. The layered beef casserole (page 310) is a one-pot main dish that you can keep warm and bring out to the buffet at the last minute.

I like to serve the desserts buffet style as well. Set them up in a separate area, if you have the room, with lots of seasonal fruits as well as three or four cakes, depending on the number of guests. Serving the desserts in a different place will allow you to have some of them preset, so you can move between courses smoothly without having to dismantle the whole savory buffet. An almond torte with chocolate chips (page 335), chocolate sponge cake with sour cherries and chocolate zabaglione filling (page 336), chocolate ricotta cheesecake (page 340), and peach almond cake (page 343) are a grouping I would love to find on any dessert buffet, but any two should suffice. Include a typical Italian spoon dessert (*al cucchiaio*), such as a berry tiramisù (page 349) or coffee panna cotta (page 351). Put out some whipped cream, fresh berries, and chocolate sauce on the side, so everyone can top their desserts as they wish. And, of course, the celebration of this (future) marriage made in heaven is best celebrated with some heavenly cake (page 339).

POACHED SEAFOOD SALAD

Insalata di Frutti di Mare

This dish truly speaks of Italy. Every region of the country that is on the sea has some version of this seafood salad. It's one of those recipes you can take in any direction you like. You can use whatever seafood is available—scungilli, crabmeat, scallops, or any firm fish fillets. You can use lemon juice in place of part or all of the vinegar, and dress the salad up with capers, black olives, roasted peppers, or diced tomatoes, as you see fit. However you make it, it's best prepared about half an hour before serving, to give the flavors a chance to develop. You can refrigerate the salad, but not for too long. And be sure to bring it to room temperature and check the seasonings before you serve it. When I am having family over, I know this will be a favorite, served in a large bowl on the table—everyone digs in.

Serves 6 to 8

COURT BOUILLON

½ cup dry white wine
2 stalks celery, chopped
2 medium carrots, chopped
4 fresh bay leaves
1 teaspoon black peppercorns
2 teaspoons kosher salt

SALAD

1 pound medium shrimp, peeled and deveined
1 pound small calamari (bodies 4 to 6 inches long), cleaned, bodies cut into ½-inch rings, tentacles reserved
1½ pound mussels, scrubbed and debearded if necessary
4 inner stalks celery with leaves, thinly sliced (about 1½ cups)
1 teaspoon chopped garlic
½ cup extra-virgin olive oil, plus more as needed
2 tablespoons white wine vinegar, plus more as needed
1 teaspoon kosher salt, plus more to taste
Pinch crushed red pepper flakes, plus more to taste
2 tablespoons chopped fresh Italian parsley

For the court bouillon, bring 2 quarts cold water, the wine, celery, carrots, bay leaves, peppercorns, and salt to a boil in a medium Dutch oven. Adjust the heat to a simmer, cover, and cook 15 minutes, to blend the flavors.

Add the shrimp to the court bouillon, and cook until just opaque, about 3 to 4 minutes. Fish the shrimp out with a spider, and spread them on a baking sheet. (Don't worry if they aren't completely drained—you'll use some of the liquid to finish the salad.)

Add the calamari to the court bouillon, and poach just until they are firm and tender, about 3 minutes. Fish out the calamari, and add them to the shrimp.

Return the court bouillon to a boil. Stir in the mussels, cover the pot, and cook until the shells open and the mussels are firm but not tough, about 4 minutes. Remove with a spider, discard any that haven't opened, and add to the other poached seafood. When the mussels are cool enough, pluck the meat from the shells directly into a large serving bowl.

To make the salad, transfer the cooled shrimp and

(recipe continues)

calamari to the bowl with the mussels, shaking off peppercorns as you do. Add the celery and garlic; then pour in the olive oil and vinegar. Toss until mixed, drizzling in some of the reserved cooking liquid to taste. Season the salad with the salt and pepper flakes. It should be very moist and glisten with dressing. If not, add a dash of olive oil, vinegar, and a little more of the cooking liquid. Let the salad stand at room temperature for about 30 minutes, tossing once or twice. Check the seasoning, toss in the parsley, and mix well just before serving.

POACHED SALMON SALAD

Insalata di Salmone

Salmon is a popular and much-liked fish in the United States but is not eaten so much in Italy. This recipe—in which salmon is dressed in a light Italian style—combines elements of the cooking of the two countries I call home. All of the components can be made ahead and chilled; just assemble the salad at the last minute. This recipe works well on buffet tables, for family-style dinners, or as individual appetizers or a main course for a sit-down event. I personally think it is also perfect for an intimate dinner: everything can be done ahead, so more time can be spent with the one you love.

Serves 6 as a main course, 8 as an appetizer

SALMON
Kosher salt
1 cup dry white wine
1 lemon, sliced
1 handful sprigs fresh dill
2 fresh bay leaves
½ teaspoon black peppercorns
2 pounds center-cut salmon fillet

SALAD
1½ teaspoons kosher salt, plus more for the cooking
   water
2 bunches medium-thick asparagus, trimmed, lower
   third of stalks peeled (about 2 pounds)
2 hard-boiled eggs, yolks and whites separated
2 tablespoons Dijon mustard
2 tablespoons white wine
Juice of 1 lemon
¼ cup extra-virgin olive oil
2 to 3 tablespoons grated fresh horseradish
1½ cups thinly sliced radishes
2 tablespoons chopped fresh dill

For the salmon, put 6 cups water in a straight-sided skillet large enough to hold the salmon in one layer lying flat. Season the water liberally with salt, and add the wine, lemon slices, dill, bay leaves, and peppercorns. Bring to a simmer, and cook 10 minutes to blend the flavors; then slide the salmon into the simmering water. Simmer gently until the salmon is just cooked through, about 10 minutes, depending on thickness. Remove from the poaching liquid, and cool to room temperature.

For the salad, bring another large pot of salted water to boil. Add the asparagus, and simmer until just tender, about 6 to 8 minutes, depending on thickness. Drain, cool under running water to set the color, and pat very dry. Spread the asparagus on a serving platter.

In a mini–food processor (or a bowl, if you're working by hand), combine the egg yolks, mustard, white wine, lemon juice, and 1 teaspoon of the salt. Process to make a smooth paste, then add the olive oil with the machine running, to make a thick dressing. Add the horseradish, and process to combine.

Drizzle a few tablespoons of the dressing over the asparagus. Flake the salmon in large chunks into a large bowl. Chop the egg whites, and add to the bowl, along with the radishes and dill. Season with the remaining ½ teaspoon salt. Drizzle with the remaining dressing, toss, and serve the dressed salmon mounded on top of the asparagus on the platter.

CHICKEN AND ZUCCHINI SALAD WITH HORSERADISH DRESSING

Insalata di Pollo e Zucchine con Salsa di Rafano

This salad can be served warm or at room temperature and is easily doubled for a larger gathering. It is also perfect for a buffet table, or just set the bowl in the middle of the table for a family-style dinner. Horseradish adds a nice sparkle. Jarred horseradish is good, but if you have an opportunity to get fresh horseradish, grate the root abundantly just before tossing the salad. I have found that most people like chicken and most people like zucchini, so I consider this dish a safe bet for entertaining.

Serves 4 as a main course or 6 as an appetizer

1 teaspoon kosher salt, plus more for the cooking water

2 fresh bay leaves

4 medium zucchini (about 6 to 8 ounces each)

1 large red onion (about 5 ounces), thickly sliced

1¼ pounds boneless, skinless chicken breast

1 tablespoon freshly grated or 2 tablespoons drained jarred horseradish

3 tablespoons red wine vinegar

¼ cup extra-virgin olive oil

2 hard-boiled eggs, cut into wedges

Bring to a boil a pot of water large enough to hold the zucchini, onion, and chicken together. Add the bay leaves, and salt liberally.

When the water is boiling, add the zucchini and red onion, and reduce the heat to a simmer. Simmer until they just begin to become tender, about 8 to 10 minutes, depending on the size of the zucchini.

Add the chicken, and continue to simmer until the zucchini is tender all the way through when pierced with a knife and the chicken is cooked through. Drain, and let sit in the colander until cool enough to handle. Remove bay leaves.

Slice the chicken on the bias into thin strips. Slice the zucchini into ½-inch rounds, and leave the onion as is. Toss all in a large bowl. Season with the 1 teaspoon salt. Sprinkle with the horseradish, vinegar, and oil. Toss well. Add the eggs, and toss gently. Mound onto a platter, and serve.

Gita in Campagna—Picnic Italian Style

Italians love a good picnic, and the most famous day for picnicking is Pasquetta, Easter Monday. Classic dishes for a Pasquetta picnic include Easter pies filled with boiled eggs, cheese, and herbs, as well as baked pastas such as baked stuffed shells (page 221) and sweet cakes such as chocolate ricotta cheesecake (page 340). Asparagus is in season then, and it makes excellent appetizers and salads, such as asparagus and leeks in lemon vinaigrette (page 104), to accompany heartier fare.

To give myself more room for my picnic spread, I like to sit on the grass as I did when I was a child. I take an old sheet and top it with a large tablecloth to sit on; this gives me more space to spread out the picnic foods. Frittata is a picnic staple; it travels well and tastes best at room temperature. Accompanied by some nice focaccia bread, it makes a great centerpiece for my picnic. (Try my rice frittata, page 56.) Leafy salads will wilt, so I usually stick with bean or vegetable salads, such as shrimp and mixed bean salad (page 122), cucumber salad (page 110), poached seafood salad (page 126), or any of the other heartier salads in this chapter. Roasted olives with orange and rosemary (page 34) and spicy giardiniera (page 45) add a welcome crunchiness to the outdoor feast.

Grilled polenta (page 67) and baked stuffed vegetables (page 30) are a nice addition, perhaps with some grissini (page 99) and some sliced prosciutto to wrap around them, and a chunk of Grana Padano to nibble on. I like to have some sliced-up fennel to add a crunchy, cool touch to the savory meal. And before the ants get to it, finish with a slice of almond torte with chocolate chips (page 335) and slices of ripe melon. Cool lemonade, a chilled bottle of rosé wine, and a crusty loaf of semolina bread are givens at any real Pasquetta picnic, so be sure to have some on hand. Now you just need to find the perfect picnic spot!

Soups

Soups are part of any Italian holiday meal. Whether it's a wedding or a christening, on celebratory occasions a soup is almost always served. Simple chicken stock (page 148), grated pasta soup (page 147), and wedding soup (page 138) are the most likely to appear.

Americans love to serve soups with sandwiches or salads, and any of the soups included in this chapter would pair well with some bruschetta from the appetizer chapter at a lunch party. For this type of event, I also include a few salads for my guests to choose from—a perfect meal for a school lunch meeting or an informal office get-together. A lovely chilled tomato soup (page 145) or a hearty chicken stock (page 148) with some pastina, accompanied by a few prosciutto bruschette or ham and cheese on country bread, would also be an ideal choice for a kids' party.

Soups are great because they can be prepared in advance and be refrigerated or even frozen until needed, then brought back to temperature and served. A bowl of soup is a welcome sight at a buffet table in the cold winter months and during the holidays, but soups such as corn and zucchini soup (page 143) and butternut squash soup (page 142) also are good at room temperature, whereas in the summer a chilled tomato soup (page 145) is always a treat.

CANNELLINI BEAN AND LENTIL SOUP

Zuppa di Cannellini e Lenticchie

Soups are always a great choice as a first course when serving a sit-down dinner. You can make them, for the most part, ahead of time, and simply ladle them hot into bowls when you are ready to sit down to eat. This hearty soup can be made a day or two in advance, though you may need to add a little water when reheating if it thickens too much. Serve with crusty bread and a salad of bitter greens for a casual lunch. Round the meal out with a platter of cheese and salumi, or turn the soup into a meal in itself by adding links of sausages in the last 40 minutes of cooking. When ready to serve, either cut the sausages into slices and serve in the soup, or transfer the sausages whole to a platter and serve with some salad as a second course. This soup will warm not only the stomach but the heart for a romantic winter dinner—and it's ready to eat without cooking on the spot, leaving you more time to spend with your loved one.

Serves 10 to 12

4 ounces slab bacon, cut into chunks

4 cloves garlic, crushed and peeled

¼ cup extra-virgin olive oil, plus more for drizzling

1 medium onion, cut into chunks

1 large carrot, cut into chunks

2 stalks celery, cut into chunks

2 tablespoons tomato paste

1 pound dried cannellini beans, soaked overnight and drained

4 fresh bay leaves

¼ teaspoon crushed red pepper flakes

1 medium green cabbage, shredded (about 2 pounds)

1 pound brown lentils, rinsed

3 tablespoons kosher salt

Grated Grana Padano, for serving

In a food processor, combine the bacon and garlic and process to make a smooth paste, or *pestata*. In a large Dutch oven or soup pot, heat the olive oil over medium heat. When the oil is hot, add the *pestata*, and cook until the bacon renders its fat, about 5 minutes.

Meanwhile, in the same food processor, process the onion, carrot, and celery together to make a second *pestata*. Scrape this *pestata* into the pot with the bacon, and cook, stirring occasionally, until it dries out, about 6 minutes.

Clear a space in the pan and add the tomato paste. Cook and stir the tomato paste in that spot until it is toasted and darkens a bit, about 1 minute. Stir the tomato paste into the vegetables, and add 7 quarts cold water. Bring the soup to a simmer, and add the drained cannellini, bay leaves, and crushed red pepper. Simmer, uncovered, until the cannellini are almost tender and the soup has reduced an inch or two in volume, about 1 hour.

Add the cabbage, and simmer until it is tender, about 20 minutes more. Add the lentils, and continue to simmer until the lentils and cannellini are very tender and the soup is thick, about 30 minutes more. Add salt and stir. Serve in soup bowls, with a drizzle of olive oil and a sprinkle of grated cheese.

ESCAROLE AND WHITE BEAN SOUP

Zuppa di Cannellini con Scarola

This easy, very traditional Italian soup is hearty, delicious, and easy to make. You can make substitutions or add to it as you like, using more vegetables, or you can add a rind of Grana Padano for even more flavor. This recipe is easily doubled to serve a larger group. Remember to soak the beans the day before cooking.

Serves 6

1½ cups cannellini or other small dried white beans, soaked overnight and drained
2 fresh bay leaves
½ cup extra-virgin olive oil, plus more for drizzling
Kosher salt, to taste
8 cups loosely packed escarole leaves, preferably the tough outer leaves, coarsely shredded, washed, and drained
8 cloves garlic, crushed and peeled
6 whole dried peperoncini
Grated Grana Padano, for serving
Grilled bread, for serving

Transfer drained beans to a large Dutch oven. Pour in water to cover by 2 inches, add the bay leaves, and bring to a boil. Adjust the heat to simmering, pour in ¼ cup of the olive oil, and cook until beans are tender, about 1 to 1½ hours. By the time the beans are tender, they should be covered by about 1 inch of cooking liquid; add more water if they're not. Season the beans to taste with salt. Stir in the escarole, and cook, stirring occasionally, until it is quite tender, about 20 to 30 minutes. Remove the pot from the heat.

Heat the remaining ¼ cup oil in a small skillet over medium heat. Add the garlic and peperoncini, and cook, shaking the pan, until the peppers change color, about 1 minute or less. Remove from the heat, and carefully (it will spatter quite a bit) pour one ladleful of soup into the skillet. Swirl the pan to blend the two, and then stir the panful of seasoned soup back into the large pot. Remove bay leaves, check the seasoning, add salt if needed, and let the soup rest off the heat, covered, 10 to 15 minutes. Serve with grated cheese and grilled bread.

WEDDING SOUP
Zuppa Maritata

I am still not 100 percent certain how this soup got its name, but I've narrowed the possibilities down to two passed-down explanations. One is that there is a marriage between all the vegetables and the meatballs. The other is that nutritional reinforcements are needed by the bride and groom, hence the addition of meat to a vegetable soup that is served at the meal before the wedding night. The latter might have more credence, since an alternative name for this soup in Italian is zuppa di rinforzamento. *In any case, this festive vegetable soup with little meatblls can be a whole meal by itself. It also works very well as a holiday antipasto course, to be followed by a roast. As with a wedding, it takes a lot of preparation to get this recipe together, but it can be done a day or two in advance and reheated when your guests come. When you reheat the soup, always bring it back to a boil, to give it that just-cooked flavor.*

Serves 10 to 12

SOUP

2 pounds veal bones
2 pounds bone-in beef short ribs
2 pounds chicken wings, backs, or necks, or a
  combination
2 medium leeks, white and light-green parts, cut
  into 2-inch chunks
1 pound carrots, trimmed but left whole
4 stalks celery, halved crosswise
2 medium onions, halved
1 piece rind from a wedge of Grana Padano left
  from grating
½ tablespoon black peppercorns
½ bunch fresh Italian parsley
3 tablespoons tomato paste
1 tablespoon kosher salt, plus more to taste
1 large bunch spinach, stemmed and coarsely
  chopped (about 10 cups loosely packed leaves)
1 cup orzo or other small pasta (optional)

MEATBALLS

1 teaspoon kosher salt, plus more for the cooking
  water
1 pound ground turkey
8 ounces ground pork
1 cup fine dried bread crumbs
½ cup grated Grana Padano
2 tablespoons chopped fresh Italian parsley
1 large egg, beaten

Extra-virgin olive oil, for drizzling
Grated Grana Padano, for serving

For the soup, in a large Dutch oven or soup pot, combine the veal bones, short ribs, chicken parts, leeks, carrots, celery, onions, cheese rind, peppercorns, parsley, tomato paste, salt, and 6 quarts water. Cover, heat, and simmer for 2 hours, occasionally skimming and discarding the scum and foam that rise to the

(recipe continues)

surface. Uncover, and simmer until reduced by about half, about 1 hour more.

Drain the solids, and return the broth to a cleaned pot. Shred any meat from the short ribs and chicken parts, discarding the fat and bone, and reserve. Cut the carrots into ½-inch pieces, and reserve.

For the meatballs, bring a large pot of salted water to boil. In a large bowl, combine the turkey, pork, bread crumbs, grated cheese, parsley, egg, and salt. Mix well with your hands. Roll into 1-inch meatballs, and add to the boiling water. Simmer for 5 minutes, then transfer with a spider or slotted spoon to the stock.

Return the soup to a simmer. Add the reserved shredded meats, the reserved carrots, and the spinach. Simmer until the spinach is tender, about 10 to 15 minutes, adding the orzo in the last 7 or 8 minutes if desired. Serve in soup bowls with a drizzle of olive oil and a sprinkle of grated cheese.

MIXED FISH STEW

Zuppa di Pesce

This soup can be either a hearty first or a main course, if served with thick slices of grilled bread. I use grouper and monkfish here, but any firm white fish can be substituted, such as halibut or swordfish. You can also swap in clams or shrimp for the mussels, adjusting the cooking time according to the fish you have chosen.

Serves 6 to 8

1 pound skinless grouper fillet
1 pound monkfish fillet, gray outer membrane trimmed
All-purpose flour, for dredging
¼ cup extra-virgin olive oil
6 cloves garlic, sliced
¼ teaspoon crushed red pepper flakes
1½ cups dry white wine
6 sprigs fresh thyme
2 fresh bay leaves
1½ teaspoons kosher salt
1½ pounds mussels, scrubbed and debearded if necessary
2 bunches scallions, white and green parts, chopped
1 tablespoon white wine vinegar
3 tablespoons chopped fresh Italian parsley
Grilled bread, for serving (optional)

Bring 2 cups water to a simmer in a small saucepan, and keep it hot. Cut the grouper and monkfish into six or eight pieces (depending on how many people you are serving).

Spread the flour on a plate. Lightly dredge the fish pieces in flour, tapping off the excess. Heat the olive oil in a large, wide Dutch oven over medium-high heat. Scatter in the garlic and red pepper flakes, and cook for a minute or so, until sizzling. Quickly lay the fish pieces in the pan in a single layer, leaving as much space as possible between them. Without mov-

ing the pieces, fry the fish for about 2 minutes, until a light crust forms. Flip, and sear the other side for 2 to 3 minutes, until a crust forms, then remove all the fish to a large plate.

Raise the heat, and pour in the white wine and the hot water. Drop in the thyme sprigs, bay leaves, and the 1½ teaspoons salt, and bring to a boil. Simmer vigorously for 5 minutes or so, until the volume has reduced by about a third.

Lay the fish pieces back in the saucepan, and add the mussels, taking care not to break up the fish. Sprinkle with the scallions, and simmer for another 4 to 5 minutes, until the fish is cooked through and the mussels are cooked; discard any that haven't opened.

Sprinkle on the vinegar and chopped parsley; stir and swirl the pan to blend them with the *zuppa*. Remove the bay leaves and thyme sprigs. Serve immediately, over a piece of grilled bread in the bottom of the bowl if desired.

BUTTERNUT SQUASH SOUP

Zuppa di Zucca

In the winter and fall, this soup really warms me up. For a more refined presentation, you can pass it through a strainer after blending to give it a silky-smooth texture, although it's not absolutely necessary. This is an easy-to-make recipe, and it can be prepared a day or two in advance. If you want to embellish it and make it a fabulous antipasto, you can add croutons or some poached shrimp just before serving.

Serves 8

3 tablespoons extra-virgin olive oil
1 medium onion, chopped
2 stalks celery, chopped
3-pound butternut squash, peeled, seeded, and cut into 2-inch chunks
2 sprigs fresh sage
2 fresh bay leaves
Zest and juice of 1 large orange
2 teaspoons kosher salt, plus more to taste
Pinch crushed red pepper flakes
8 slices bacon, cooked and crumbled
⅓ cup thinly sliced scallion, for garnish

Add the olive oil to a medium Dutch oven over medium heat. When the oil is hot, add the onion and celery, and cook until wilted, about 4 minutes. Add the squash, sage, and bay leaves. Cook and toss until the sage is fragrant, about 2 minutes.

Add 8 cups water, the orange zest and juice, salt, and crushed red pepper. Set the cover ajar, and simmer the soup until the squash is very tender, about 30 minutes. Remove bay leaves.

Carefully purée the soup in batches in a blender. Return it to the cooking pot, and bring to a simmer. Adjust the seasoning with salt. Serve the soup in bowls, garnished with the bacon and scallions.

CORN AND ZUCCHINI SOUP

Minestra di Zucchine e Mais

If you are making this soup ahead, do not add the rice. When you are ready to serve, cook the rice separately in some salted water, drain, and add it to the reheated soup just before serving. You can also omit the rice entirely, for a lighter version.

Serves 10 to 12

¼ cup extra-virgin olive oil, plus more for drizzling

2 pounds Yukon Gold potatoes, peeled and cut into ½-inch chunks

2 large carrots, cut into ¼-inch dice

2 stalks celery, cut into ¼-inch dice

2 large leeks, white and light-green parts, halved and sliced ½ inch thick

4 cloves garlic, finely chopped

3 fresh bay leaves

Pinch crushed red pepper flakes

1 tablespoon kosher salt, plus more to taste

4 ears corn, kernels removed, cobs reserved

1 pound zucchini, sliced into ¼-inch-thick half-moons

1 pound green beans, trimmed and cut into ½-inch pieces

1 cup Arborio rice

¼ cup pesto, homemade (page 51), prepared without mayo, or store-bought

Grated Grana Padano, for serving

Heat a large Dutch oven over medium heat. Add the olive oil. When the oil is hot, add the potatoes, and cook, stirring occasionally, until they begin to stick to the bottom of the pot and form a crust, about 5 to 6 minutes. Add the carrots, celery, and leeks, and cook until the leeks wilt, about 5 minutes.

Add the garlic, and cook, stirring, until fragrant, about 1 minute. Add 5 quarts cold water, the bay leaves, red pepper flakes, salt, and reserved corn cobs. Bring to a rapid simmer, and cook to concentrate and blend the flavors, about 30 minutes.

Add the zucchini and green beans, and cook, simmering rapidly, until the potatoes begin to fall apart and thicken the soup and it is dense and flavorful, about 1 hour.

Add the rice and corn kernels, and simmer until the rice is al dente, about 15 minutes. Remove bay leaves. Stir in the pesto, adjust the seasoning with salt if necessary, and serve in soup bowls with a drizzle of olive oil and some grated cheese.

CHILLED TOMATO SOUP

Zuppa Fredda di Pomodori allo Yogurt

This soup should be made a day ahead of time to allow the flavors to develop. It's a great dish to begin a barbecue or buffet, especially in the summer months.

Serves 8

3 tablespoons extra-virgin olive oil

2 medium leeks, white and light-green parts, thinly sliced

1 large carrot, chopped

1 large stalk celery, finely chopped

Two 28-ounce cans whole San Marzano tomatoes, crushed by hand

4 leafy stalks fresh basil

Zest of 1 orange, removed with a vegetable peeler, and juice of 1 orange

1½ teaspoons kosher salt, plus more to taste

¼ teaspoon celery seeds

Pinch crushed red pepper flakes

1½ cups plain Greek yogurt

1 English cucumber, peeled and chopped

In a medium Dutch oven or soup pot, heat the olive oil over medium heat. When the oil is hot, add the leeks, carrot, and celery, and cook until the leeks have wilted, about 6 minutes.

Add the tomatoes, slosh out the can with 1½ cups of water, and add that to the pot along with the basil, orange zest and juice, salt, celery seeds, and red pepper flakes. Set the lid ajar, and simmer until the soup is flavorful and the vegetables are very soft, about 35 to 40 minutes. Let cool slightly, then remove the basil and orange peel.

Purée the soup in batches in a blender with the yogurt and cucumber. (If a very silky-smooth soup is desired, you can strain the soup through a sieve after blending.) Transfer to a bowl or pitcher, and refrigerate until very cold, at least 3 hours. Taste, and season for salt again once the soup is chilled.

SPICY ITALIAN-STYLE VEGETABLE SOUP

Zuppa di Verdura Calabrese alla Sangiovannese

Every region of Italy has a vegetable soup, yet each one is distinctly different. Each version uses different vegetables or legumes, or, as in this one, different intensities of spice. This recipe is from the region of Calabria, more specifically from an area called the Sangiovannese, which is well known for its cultivation and use of the peperoncino chili.

Serves 8 or more

¼ cup extra-virgin olive oil, plus more for drizzling
1 slab spare ribs, cut into ribs
1 medium onion, chopped
2 medium leeks, white and light-green parts, sliced
4 cloves garlic, chopped
¼ teaspoon crushed red pepper flakes or 2 or 3 small dried Calabrian chiles
1 pound cannellini beans, soaked overnight and drained
2 fresh bay leaves
1 small savoy cabbage, cored and coarsely shredded
1½ pounds russet potatoes, peeled and cut into 1-inch chunks
1 piece of rind from a chunk of Pecorino
Kosher salt
2 cups cubed day-old country bread
¼ cup chopped Italian parsley
Grated Pecorino, for serving

Heat the olive oil in a large Dutch oven over medium heat. When the oil is hot, add the ribs and brown on all sides, about 5 to 6 minutes in all. Remove to a plate. Add the onion, leeks, garlic, and red pepper flakes or chiles. Cook until the onions and leeks begin to wilt, about 5 minutes. Add the beans, bay leaves, and 6 quarts cold water. Bring to a simmer, partially cover and let cook until the beans just begin to become tender, about 20 to 30 minutes.

Add the browned ribs, cabbage, potatoes, and cheese rind, and simmer, uncovered, until the beans and ribs are tender and the soup begins to thicken, about 30 to 40 minutes.

Once the beans are tender, season the soup with salt and add the bread cubes. Bring to a rapid simmer and cook, stirring often, until the bread breaks down and thickens the soup, about 20 minutes more.

To serve, remove the cheese rind and bay leaves, and stir in the parsley. Serve each portion with a rib or two and sprinkle with grated Pecorino and a drizzle of olive oil.

GRATED PASTA SOUP

Pasta Grattata in Brodo

This is a simple concept: you make a batch of dough, let it chill, and then grate it into boiling soup to cook. A good homemade chicken stock is essential for this recipe. Once the dough is made and chilled, this soup comes together in minutes. For bigger crowds, you can easily double the recipe, and the dough freezes well for future use or unexpected guests.

Serves 6

1 cup fine semolina
¼ cup all-purpose flour, plus more for working the dough
¼ cup grated Grana Padano, plus more for serving
2 large eggs
½ teaspoon kosher salt
8 cups chicken stock (recipe follows)
2 tablespoons chopped fresh Italian parsley

In a food processor, combine the semolina, all-purpose flour, and grated cheese. Pulse to combine. In a small bowl, beat the eggs with the salt. With the processor running, pour in the eggs, and process to make a stiff, smooth dough, about 20 to 30 seconds. If it is still crumbly, add a tablespoon or 2 of water until it forms a stiff dough.

Dump the dough onto a floured counter, and knead until it comes together into a ball. Wrap in plastic, and chill until firm, about 2 hours or up to overnight.

When ready to serve, heat the stock in a soup pot. Lay out a kitchen towel, and dust it with flour. Grate the chilled dough, on the large holes of a box grater, directly onto the kitchen towel, spreading the pieces out so they don't stick together; the shreds should be ¼ of an inch.

Add shreds of dough to the simmering stock, and simmer until al dente, about 8 to 10 minutes. Stir in the parsley. Serve with a sprinkling of grated cheese.

CHICKEN STOCK

Brodo di Pollo

This basic stock works for any recipe in this book calling for chicken stock or broth. It can be made ahead and refrigerated for up to 4 days, or frozen for several months. I always have pints of chicken stock in my freezer, just in case unexpected guests drop by.

Makes 4 quarts

4 pounds chicken (and/or turkey) backs, necks, wings, and giblets (except liver)
1 large onion, halved
5 cloves garlic
1 pound carrots, peeled and halved
4 stalks celery, cut in half
1 handful sprigs fresh Italian parsley
3 fresh bay leaves
1 teaspoon whole black peppercorns
Kosher salt

Rinse the chicken pieces well, and remove any excess fat. Put them in a large stockpot with 8 quarts cold water. Bring to a boil, reduce heat so the liquid is simmering, and cook 1 hour, skimming and discarding any scum that rises to the surface.

Meanwhile, using tongs, brown the onion halves over a burner flame (or in a cast-iron pan) until well browned all over.

After simmering the chicken an hour, add the onion, garlic, carrot, celery, parsley, bay leaves, peppercorns, and salt to the pot. Partially cover, and simmer until broth is flavorful and liquid level is reduced by about half, about 2 hours more.

Strain the stock, let it cool to room temperature, then chill until cold. When it's cold, remove the layer of solidified fat on top and discard.

Panini, Panini . . . Panini Everywhere

In American culture, "panini" usually denotes a ciabatta bread or flatbread sandwich heated in a sandwich press. However in Italy, it refers to all kinds of sandwiches. In fact, the Italian word "panini" is simply the plural of "panino," meaning sandwich. The varieties of Italian panini are endless. They can be made with classic cold cuts, such as prosciutto crudo, salami, prosciutto cotto, or mortadella, or any combination thereof, and served on not just ciabatta but crispy bread, or rolls, or made into a hoagie or sub on a long Italian loaf.

Frittate make a wonderful Italian-style sandwich stuffer, as do braised meats such as thin slices of beef, sausages cooked in tomato sauce, or breaded chicken or veal. Italians stuff their sandwiches with braised vegetables, such as broccoli rabe, fried or grilled zucchini, peppers, and eggplants. Sandwiches using sliced white bread that is toasted are called "toast" in Italy, and usually made with a slice of ham and a slice of cheese toasted in a sandwich press, like the typical American grilled cheese. There are also a large variety of vegetarian options; mozzarella-and-tomato sandwiches, or rolls filled with grilled vegetables like eggplant and zucchini and cooked in a sandwich press, are particularly popular.

Rarely are spreads or condiments added to sandwiches in Italy, but some crunchy vinegar-cured vegetables, such as spicy giardiniera (page 45), are a good accompaniment, as is a smear of pesto (page 51). No matter how you prepare them, Italian-style sandwiches are great for a picnic or an informal gathering.

Vegetables and Sides

I love cooking and eating vegetables and always have loads of them on my table, whether I'm hosting a dinner party or just cooking for my family. Italians are particularly fond of vegetables with pronounced flavors. The more diverse and the more intense the better.

The prime rule in cooking vegetables is to use whatever is local and in season; if they are from your garden, even better.

If you are hosting a fully vegetarian event, make it exciting; diversify the vegetables and legumes as well as the manner of cooking them. Include a few salads, maybe some with beans or cheese for extra protein, and perhaps a few different kinds of stuffed vegetables and some vegetable casseroles, such as portobellos stuffed with quinoa and kale (page 170), Swiss chard and mashed potato gratin (page 176), and crispy baked tomatoes (page 179). Vegetables are best served family style, on platters, so that all the guests help themselves. This way, people can take as much of each vegetable as they like, and in an atmosphere of conviviality. At a more formal dinner, you might already have the vegetables plated with the protein, or, if you have help serving, have them butlered around the table. There are two types of butlered service—French service, in which the person serving puts the vegetables directly onto the guests' plates, and Russian service, in which a platter is extended to the guests with serving utensils and people serve themselves. Choose whichever way of serving the vegetables you feel will enhance the mood and style of the event you have created.

ASPARAGUS GRATIN

Asparagi Gratinati

You can assemble this gratin ahead of time and just broil it at the last minute. If it's refrigerated, return it to room temperature before broiling. The recipe can be multiplied easily for a large group. It looks beautiful on a platter served family style, or on a buffet table. I like it hot out of the oven, but it is also delicious at room temperature. You can easily turn it into a lunch or brunch by topping the baked asparagus with a poached or fried egg.

Serves 6

½ teaspoon kosher salt, plus more for the cooking water

2 bunches medium-thick asparagus (about 2 pounds)

½ stick unsalted butter, melted

½ cup grated Grana Padano

¼ cup fine dried bread crumbs

1 teaspoon grated lemon zest

Bring a large pot of salted water to boil. Trim the woody ends from the asparagus, and peel the lower half of the stalks. Add the asparagus to the boiling water, and simmer until crisp-tender, about 5 minutes. Drain, and cool under running water. Pat very dry.

Preheat broiler. Brush a gratin dish just large enough to hold the asparagus in one layer with 1 tablespoon of the melted butter. In a small bowl, toss together the grated cheese, bread crumbs, lemon zest, and salt. Brush asparagus tops with half of the remaining melted butter. Sprinkle with an even layer of the crumbs. Drizzle with the remaining melted butter. Broil until the crumbs are golden brown, about 3 to 4 minutes, watching carefully so the crumbs don't burn.

BEET SALAD WITH YOGURT DRESSING

Insalata di Barbabietole allo Yogurt

The beets, greens, and dressing can all be made ahead of time. Just compose the salad at the last minute. This is a refreshing and delicious dish for picnics, buffet tables, or a family lunch or dinner.

Serves 8

½ teaspoon kosher salt, plus more for the cooking water

3 bunches medium beets with full tops (about 9 or 10 beets)

5 tablespoons extra-virgin olive oil

3 tablespoons white wine vinegar

1 cup plain Greek yogurt

4 ounces goat cheese, at room temperature

¾ cup milk, to thin the dressing (or less)

¼ cup toasted sliced almonds

Preheat oven to 375 degrees. Bring a large pot of salted water to boil. Trim the beets from the tops, leaving about ½ inch stem top attached to each beet. Wash the beets well, and wrap individually in foil. Set them on a rimmed sheet pan, and roast until tender, about 45 minutes to an hour, depending on their size.

Unwrap, let cool, and then peel and cut each beet into six wedges. Meanwhile, wash the beet greens well, and cut the leaves and tender stems into 1-inch pieces. Add the beet greens and stems to the boiling water, and simmer until very tender, about 15 minutes. Drain, rinse under cool water, and pat very dry. In a large bowl, toss the beet greens with 3 tablespoons of the oil, 2 tablespoons of the vinegar, and salt to taste.

For the dressing, in a mini–food processor (or in a bowl, if you're working by hand), combine the yogurt, goat cheese, remaining 3 tablespoons oil, remaining 1 tablespoon vinegar, and remaining ½ teaspoon salt. Process until smooth. With the machine running, pour in enough milk to thin the dressing so it drizzles from a spoon.

Spread the dressed beet greens on a platter. Mound the beets on top. Drizzle with desired amount of dressing, and sprinkle the almonds on top. Pass remaining dressing at the table.

ITALIAN BAKED BEANS

Cannellini al Forno

These baked beans add a delightful Italian touch to an American barbecue. A comforting dish that everyone will love, this recipe can be multiplied easily. It is great for a buffet table, or served family style at big dinner gatherings. The beans can be prepared earlier in the day and reheated on the stovetop, though you will need to add a little water. Just remember to soak them the day before.

Serves 6 or more

1 pound dried cannellini beans, soaked overnight
3 tablespoons extra-virgin olive oil
1 medium onion, chopped
4 ounces thickly sliced pancetta, diced
¼ cup tomato paste
2 sprigs fresh sage
¼ cup balsamic vinegar
2 tablespoons honey
1 teaspoon kosher salt

Preheat oven to 350 degrees. Drain soaked beans, and rinse well. Add the olive oil to a medium Dutch oven over medium heat. When the oil is hot, add the onion and pancetta, and cook, stirring often, until the fat is rendered, about 4 minutes.

Clear a space in the pan, and add the tomato paste. Cook and stir the tomato paste in that spot until it is toasted and has darkened a shade or two, about 1 or 2 minutes. Stir the tomato paste into the onions, and add the sage sprigs and the drained beans. Add water to cover by about an inch (about 5 to 6 cups) and the vinegar and honey. Bring to a simmer, cover, and bake until beans are tender, about 1½ hours.

Uncover the beans, add the salt, and if beans look dry add ½ cup of water. Bake, uncovered, until the sauce has thickened and coats the beans, about 30 minutes more.

LENTILS WITH BUTTERNUT SQUASH

Lenticchie Brasate con Zucca

This recipe makes an ideal side dish for pork or chicken, and is perfect for buffets. You can also add a cooked protein to the cooked lentils (chicken, shrimp, etc.) at the end, to transform it into a rustic one-pot meal. Or you can eliminate the cheese to make it vegan. The recipe can be prepared ahead of time, though you may need to add a little water when reheating. Add the cheese just before serving.

Serves 8

6 tablespoons extra-virgin olive oil, plus more for
   drizzling
3 medium stalks celery, chopped
1 medium onion, chopped
1 pound brown lentils, rinsed and drained
2 fresh bay leaves
½ cup golden raisins
2-pound butternut squash, peeled and cut into
   ½-inch chunks
1½ teaspoons kosher salt
1 bunch scallions, white and green parts, chopped
   (about 1 cup)
1 cup grated Grana Padano

Heat 3 tablespoons of the olive oil in a medium Dutch oven over medium heat. When the oil is hot, add the celery and onion, and cook, stirring occasionally, until the vegetables begin to soften, about 5 minutes. Add the lentils, bay leaves, and 4 cups water. Adjust the heat so the lentils are just simmering, and cover the pot. Cook until they just begin to loose their bite, about 20 minutes.

Add the raisins, butternut squash, and salt. Add 1 more cup water (or enough barely to cover the lentils), and simmer until the squash and lentils are tender, about 10 to 15 minutes more, adding a little more water if the water level falls below the lentils.

Stir in the scallions, and cook until they're just wilted, about 2 minutes. Remove bay leaves and take the lentils off the heat. Drizzle in the remaining 3 tablespoons oil, stir in the grated cheese, and serve.

SKILLET BRUSSELS SPROUTS WITH LEMON SAUCE

Cavolini di Bruxelles in Padella al Limone

You can prep the sprouts ahead of time, but don't cook them until the last minute. The lemon sauce can be made earlier in the day and reheated. This recipe will make more lemon sauce than you need, but it is great on almost all other cooked vegetables and keeps in the refrigerator for several days.

Serves 4 to 6

LEMON SAUCE

Peel of 2 lemons, removed with a vegetable
  peeler
⅓ cup lemon juice
5 cloves garlic, crushed and peeled
2 medium onions, cut into 1-inch chunks
½ teaspoon kosher salt, plus more to taste
¼ teaspoon crushed red pepper flakes
2 tablespoons extra-virgin olive oil

BRUSSELS SPROUTS

1½ pounds firm, unblemished Brussels sprouts
3 tablespoons extra-virgin olive oil
4 cloves garlic, sliced
½ teaspoon kosher salt
¼ teaspoon crushed red pepper flakes

For the lemon sauce, in a medium saucepan, combine the lemon peels and juice, garlic, onions, salt, red pepper flakes, and 1½ cups water. Cover, and cook at a gentle simmer for 20 minutes.

Uncover, and simmer a bit more rapidly until the onions are very tender and barely covered in liquid, about 20 to 30 minutes more. Scrape the contents of the pot into a blender, and carefully blend as you drizzle in the olive oil through the hole in the top, until smooth. Return to the saucepan, season with salt if necessary, and keep warm.

For the Brussels sprouts, trim any tough or yellowed outer leaves. Trim about ¼ inch from the base to free the outer leaves. Pluck off the leaves, trimming more of the base to loosen them as you go. Once you get to the tiny heart of the sprout and the leaves can't be separated, just cut into slivers. Separate the leaves from all of the sprouts this way.

Heat the olive oil in a large skillet over medium heat. When the oil is hot, add the garlic, and let it sizzle until just golden around the edges, about 1 to 2 minutes. Add the sprout leaves, and season with the salt and crushed red pepper flakes. Toss to coat in the oil, cover, and cook, shaking the pan occasionally, until the leaves begin to wilt, about 4 minutes. Toss with tongs and cover the skillet again.

Cook until the leaves are wilted and tender but not falling apart, about 4 to 5 minutes more. Increase the heat to boil away any liquid in the pan. To serve, spread about ½ cup of the lemon sauce on a platter, and mound the Brussels sprouts on top.

SKILLET BROCCOLI WITH CREAMY GARLIC SAUCE

Broccoli al Tegame con Crema d'Aglio

This recipe is delicious with broccoli, but it's just as good with cauliflower, if you prefer. The sauce can be made a day ahead and will keep well in the refrigerator, and any that's left over will pair well with any sort of cooked cruciferous vegetables.

Serves 6

CREAMY GARLIC SAUCE

2 cups milk, plus more if needed for thinning the sauce
2 heads garlic, separated into cloves and peeled
4 fresh bay leaves
¼ teaspoon kosher salt, plus more to taste
1 tablespoon extra-virgin olive oil

BROCCOLI

2 pounds broccoli
¼ cup extra-virgin olive oil
6 cloves garlic, sliced
½ teaspoon kosher salt, plus more to taste
Pinch crushed red pepper flakes

Put the milk, garlic, bay leaves, and salt in a small saucepan. Bring to a simmer, and simmer until the contents have reduced to 1 cup, about 30 minutes.

Pour the contents of the saucepan into a sieve set over a bowl. Remove the bay leaves, and press and scrape the soft garlic through the sieve into the bowl. Whisk the sauce until smooth, then whisk in the tablespoon of olive oil and salt to taste. Reheat the sauce on the stove until warm. Thin with milk, if you wish. Keep warm while you make the broccoli.

For the broccoli, separate the stalks into medium-size florets, 2 to 3 inches wide at the top. Peel the tough skin from the stem pieces, and slice them lengthwise in half, or in quarters if they are thick. You can also peel or slice off the tough fibrous layer of the large branches and central stems and slice up the fresh core into 4-inch sticks. Discard all dry and hard pieces.

Heat the olive oil in a large skillet over medium heat. When the oil is hot, add the garlic, and cook until just golden around the edges, about 1 to 2 minutes.

Add the broccoli, and sprinkle with the salt and crushed red pepper. Toss to coat the broccoli in the oil. Add ½ cup water. Cover, and cook, tossing the broccoli occasionally, until it's bright green and tender, about 10 minutes. Increase the heat to boil away any cooking liquid left in the pan. To serve, spread the warm garlic sauce on a platter, and top with the broccoli.

CARROTS BAKED IN RICOTTA

Carote al Forno con Ricotta

This recipe can easily be multiplied for large crowds, and is great for family-style dinners and buffets. Carrots are my favorite vegetable to use here, but parsnips and squash are also superb prepared this way.

Serves 6 to 8

1 tablespoon unsalted butter, softened
¼ cup bread crumbs, plus more for the baking dish
½ teaspoon kosher salt, plus more for the cooking water
2 pounds medium carrots, cut into sticks about 3 inches long and ½ inch wide
One 8-ounce container mascarpone
½ cup fresh ricotta
½ cup grated Grana Padano
1 tablespoon fresh thyme leaves

Preheat oven to 425 degrees. Butter a 3-quart gratin dish with the butter, and line with bread crumbs, tapping out the excess. Bring a large pot of salted water to boil. Add the carrots, and cook until just tender, about 12 minutes. Drain well.

In a large bowl, stir together the mascarpone, ricotta, ¼ cup of the grated cheese, the thyme, and salt. Add the hot carrots, and mix well.

Spread the carrots in the buttered baking dish. Sprinkle with the ¼ cup bread crumbs and remaining ¼ cup grated cheese. Bake until the sauce is bubbly and the top is golden brown, about 30 minutes. Serve hot.

CARROTS AND MUSHROOMS IN MARSALA

Funghi e Carote al Marsala

Prep all of your ingredients ahead of time, and cook this at the last minute so that the carrots maintain their vibrant orange color. This recipe can easily be doubled for large family gatherings or buffets.

Serves 6 to 8

½ teaspoon kosher salt, plus more for the cooking water

2 pounds large carrots, cut into ¼-inch-thick rounds on the bias

6 tablespoons unsalted butter

2 tablespoons extra-virgin olive oil

4 cloves garlic, crushed and peeled

1 pound mixed mushrooms (white, cremini, shiitake, oyster, etc.), thickly sliced

6 fresh sage leaves

¾ cup dry Marsala

2 tablespoons chopped fresh Italian parsley

Bring a large saucepan of water to boil, and salt it liberally. Add the carrots, and simmer until just tender, about 8 minutes. Drain well.

In a large skillet, melt 4 tablespoons of the butter in the olive oil over medium-high heat. When the butter is melted, add the garlic. Once the garlic is sizzling, add the mushrooms, sage leaves, and ½ teaspoon salt. Cover, and cook until mushrooms are wilted and have given up their liquid, about 5 minutes.

Uncover, and add the carrots and the Marsala. Bring to a boil. Cook and toss until the Marsala reduces and lightly glazes the vegetables, about 2 minutes. Stir in the parsley and remaining 2 tablespoons butter, and serve.

GRILLED CORN, FIGS, AND PORTOBELLOS

Mais, Fichi, e Funghi alla Griglia

This salad can be served warm or at room temperature. To turn it into a vegetarian entrée for four, you can toss the corn and figs together and serve inside the whole portobellos. Use ripe but firm figs for this recipe; very soft ones will fall apart on the grill.

Serves 6 to 8

1 cup balsamic vinegar
2 fresh bay leaves
1 tablespoon honey
4 medium portobello mushrooms, gills scraped and
    stems removed
6 tablespoons extra-virgin olive oil
1¼ teaspoons kosher salt
6 ears corn, shucked
8 black figs, halved crosswise

In a small saucepan, combine the balsamic vinegar, bay leaves, and honey. Bring to a rapid simmer, and cook until reduced to a thin syrup (it will thicken as it cools), about a scant ½ cup. Let cool, and discard the bay leaves.

Preheat a grill to medium-high heat. In a large bowl, toss the portobellos with 2 tablespoons oil and ½ teaspoon salt. Grill, turning occasionally, until tender all the way through, about 12 to 14 minutes.

In the same bowl, toss the corn with 1 tablespoon olive oil and ½ teaspoon salt. Grill until charred lightly all over, about 8 to 10 minutes.

In the same bowl, gently toss the figs with 1 tablespoon oil and remaining ¼ teaspoon salt. Grill, cut side down, just until they are slightly charred, about 2 to 4 minutes, depending on ripeness. Use a metal spatula to slide them gently from the grill so they don't tear or stick.

Cut the corn from the cob into a large bowl. Slice the portobellos into ½-inch-thick strips, and add to the bowl. Add the figs and the remaining 2 tablespoons oil, and toss gently. Mound on a platter, drizzle with some of the balsamic reduction, and serve the rest on the side at the table.

SKILLET ESCAROLE GRATIN

Scarola in Padella al Taleggio

To make the Taleggio easier to slice, stick it in the freezer for 15 minutes to firm it up. The melting Taleggio makes for a rich and creamy dish. It is a wonderful appetizer, side dish, or main course for the vegetarians at your table.

Serves 4 to 6

2 large heads escarole (about 2 pounds), washed but left whole, outer leaves trimmed
¼ cup extra-virgin olive oil
4 cloves garlic, crushed and peeled
2 anchovy fillets, chopped
½ teaspoon kosher salt
¼ teaspoon crushed red pepper flakes
6 ounces Taleggio, sliced thinly
¼ cup grated Grana Padano

Preheat broiler. Quarter each head of escarole lengthwise, through the root end, to make eight wedges.

Add the olive oil to a large skillet over medium heat. When the oil is hot, add the garlic and anchovies, and cook, stirring, until the anchovies dissolve into the oil, about 1 to 2 minutes.

Arrange the escarole in the pan, cut side down, like spokes in a wheel, and cook, turning once, until browned, about 7 to 9 minutes, adjusting the heat so it doesn't burn. Season with the salt and red pepper flakes.

Layer the Taleggio slices on top, then sprinkle with the grated cheese. Cover the skillet, and cook until the escarole is tender and the cheese has melted, about 3 to 4 minutes.

Place the skillet under the broiler, and broil until the top is browned and bubbly, about 2 minutes, depending on the heat of your broiler.

EGGPLANT PARMIGIANA STACKS

Parmigiana di Melanzane

This dish requires a bit of work to prepare the eggplant and the sauce, but once assembled they can be served hot or, as I like to serve them during the summer months, at room temperature. This is not a dish to make every day, but the results will impress your guests.

Makes 16 to 18 small stacks, serving 8 or more

½ cup extra-virgin olive oil, plus more as needed

All-purpose flour, for dredging

2½ pounds small Italian eggplants (about 5), sliced into ½-inch-thick rounds

1 teaspoon kosher salt, plus more to taste

3½ cups marinara sauce (page 234)

¼ cup packed fresh basil leaves, shredded

1½ cups grated Grana Padano

Preheat oven to 400 degrees. Heat the olive oil in a large nonstick skillet over medium-high heat. Spread some flour on a rimmed sheet pan. Season the eggplant with 1 teaspoon salt, and lightly toss in the flour. When the oil is hot, brown the eggplant in batches, until golden and crisp, about 4 to 5 minutes per batch. (It doesn't need to be completely cooked through at this point, just browned.) Drain on paper towels, and season with more salt while still hot.

Warm the marinara in a small saucepan, and stir in the basil. Line a sheet pan with parchment. Arrange a third of the eggplant on the sheet pan, the pieces not touching. Spread the slices with ¾ cup of the sauce. Sprinkle with ½ cup of the grated cheese. Make another layer of eggplant, then ¾ cup sauce, then ½ cup cheese. Finish with a final layer of ¾ cup sauce and the remaining ½ cup grated cheese. Save the remaining sauce for plating.

Loosely cover the stacks with foil (but don't let it touch them). Bake 10 minutes, until heated through, then uncover, and bake until the tops of the stacks are golden, about 10 minutes more. Rewarm the remaining sauce, and spoon onto the bottom of the platter, then set the eggplant stacks on top.

ENDIVE AND PROSCIUTTO GRATIN

Gratin d'Indivia e Prosciutto

This dish can be assembled ahead of time, but don't broil it until the last minute. Make sure it's at room temperature (or warm) before broiling, so the cheese doesn't brown before the insides are hot. For a more rustic presentation, you can also broil straight in the skillet used to cook the endive. It is an ideal dish for a buffet table, and a tasty side dish for a family dinner.

Serves 6 to 8

2 tablespoons unsalted butter, plus more for greasing the baking dish
2 tablespoons extra-virgin olive oil
8 large Belgian endives, halved
1 teaspoon kosher salt
2 cups chicken stock (page 148)
2 cups shredded Italian Fontina (about 4 ounces)
½ cup grated Grana Padano
1 cup marinara sauce (page 234)
2 ounces prosciutto, thinly sliced

Preheat broiler. Butter a 9-by-13-inch baking dish. In a large skillet over medium heat, melt the butter in the olive oil. When the butter is melted, add the endives, and turn to coat them in the butter. Season with the salt. Add the chicken stock, and bring to a simmer. Simmer rapidly until the endives are tender when pierced with a fork, about 15 minutes. When the endives are tender, increase the heat and boil to reduce the chicken stock down to a thin glaze.

Transfer the contents of the skillet to the baking dish, and arrange the endives in rows. In a medium bowl, toss together the Fontina and Grana Padano. Spread the marinara over the endives. Tear half of the prosciutto in shreds over the sauce. Top with half of the cheese mixture. Repeat with the remaining prosciutto, and top with the remaining cheese.

Broil until the sauce is bubbly and the cheese is golden brown, about 3 to 4 minutes. Serve right away.

GREEN BEANS WITH MINT PESTO

Fagiolini con Pesto alla Menta

The pesto can be made ahead, but add the cheese and hot green beans right before serving. This pesto is great on a lot of things—other steamed green vegetables (such as broccoli or asparagus), pasta, grilled chicken, or white fish fillets.

Serves 6 to 8

1½ teaspoons kosher salt, plus more for the cooking water
2 pounds green beans, trimmed
1 cup loosely packed fresh mint leaves
1 cup loosely packed fresh Italian parsley leaves
½ cup toasted pine nuts
6 tablespoons extra-virgin olive oil
½ cup freshly grated Grana Padano

Bring a large pot of salted water to a boil. Add the green beans, and cook until very tender, about 6 to 8 minutes, depending on size.

Meanwhile, in a mini–food processor (or in a bowl, if you're working by hand), combine the mint, parsley, pine nuts, and salt, and pulse to make a coarse paste. With the machine running, add the olive oil to make a smooth pesto.

Scrape the pesto into a serving bowl, and stir in the grated cheese. When the beans are ready, drain well and add to the bowl with the pesto. Toss well, season with salt if necessary, and serve.

LEEK AND PROSCIUTTO GRATIN

Porri con Prosciutto Gratinati

Prosciutto is often used in Italy to add extra flavor to vegetables, but this dish is delicious even without it, or with thin slices of ham substituted. The recipe can be turned into a perfect brunch dish with the addition of one poached egg per serving.

Serves 4 to 6

2 tablespoons unsalted butter

6 medium leeks, white and light-green parts, ends trimmed, halved lengthwise but still attached at root end

¼ teaspoon kosher salt

3 ounces prosciutto, thinly sliced

4 ounces Gruyère, shredded

½ cup coarsely chopped walnuts

Preheat oven to 400 degrees. Spread the butter in the bottom of an 11-by-7-inch gratin dish.

Arrange the halved leeks in the bottom of a large skillet in one layer, and add water to cover. Bring to a simmer, and cook until the leeks are just tender, about 10 minutes.

Fish the leeks out with tongs and a spider, draining off excess water as you go, and arrange in one layer in the baking dish, rolling to coat in the butter. Season with the salt. Tear the prosciutto into rough shreds, and layer these over the leeks. Bake until the prosciutto is crisp, about 20 minutes.

Sprinkle over the leeks the cheese, then the walnuts, and bake until the cheese is melted and bubbly, about 8 to 10 minutes. Serve hot.

MUSHROOMS AND CELERY

Sedano e Funghi Saltati

This side dish is delicious warm, but can also be served at room temperature. Celery and mushrooms are available year-round, making this ideal for entertaining in winter, when fresh seasonal vegetables are scarce; it's great on buffet tables, served family style, or as a vegetable to pair with a grilled protein. If you leave out the cheese, this recipe makes an excellent option for your vegan guests.

Serves 6 to 8

¼ cup extra-virgin olive oil

1 large onion, sliced ½ inch thick

6 large stalks celery, peeled if stringy, sliced into ½-inch-thick half-moons (about 4 cups)

1 teaspoon kosher salt, plus more to taste

1½ pounds small button mushrooms, trimmed but left whole

8 fresh sage leaves

¼ cup grated Grana Padano (optional)

In a large straight-sided skillet or Dutch oven, heat the olive oil over medium heat. When the oil is hot, add the onion and celery, and cook, stirring occasionally, until wilted, about 5 minutes. Season with ½ teaspoon of the salt.

Add the mushrooms and sage, and season with the remaining ½ teaspoon salt. Toss to coat the mushrooms in the oil. Cover, and cook, stirring occasionally, until mushrooms are softened, about 15 minutes. (Add up to ½ cup water during cooking if it starts to burn.)

Uncover, and increase the heat to boil away any excess liquid and brown the vegetables, about 5 minutes. Remove from the heat, adjust seasoning with salt to taste, and sprinkle with the grated cheese if desired.

PORTOBELLOS STUFFED WITH QUINOA AND KALE

Cappelle di Funghi Ripieni di Quinoa e Cavolo Nero

This serves 6 as a vegetarian entrée. You can also cut the portobellos into halves or wedges after baking, to serve as a contorno *or part of an antipasto buffet. Or you can slice the mushrooms and sauté everything together, making it a stunning tossed vegetable dish. The portobellos are so satisfying that they could be served whole as a main dish for vegetarian guests.*

Serves 6

7 tablespoons extra-virgin olive oil, plus more if needed
2 cloves garlic, crushed and peeled
One 5-ounce box baby kale
1 teaspoon kosher salt
Pinch crushed red pepper flakes
1 cup cooked quinoa (or barley or farro)
1 cup fine dried bread crumbs
½ cup grated Grana Padano
¼ cup toasted coarsely chopped pine nuts
6 portobello mushrooms, gills scraped and stems removed
½ cup dry white wine
½ cup chicken stock (page 148)
One 4-ounce log goat cheese, cut into 8 slices

Preheat oven to 400 degrees. Add 2 tablespoons of the olive oil and the garlic to a large skillet over medium-high heat. Once the garlic is sizzling, add the kale and season with ¼ teaspoon salt and the crushed red pepper flakes. Cook, stirring occasionally, until kale is wilted and all of the liquid from the pan has evaporated, about 5 minutes. Let cool, then squeeze out any additional liquid and coarsely chop the kale.

In a large bowl, combine the kale, quinoa, bread crumbs, grated cheese, and pine nuts. Season with ¼ teaspoon salt, and toss well to combine. The stuffing should be moist and clump together when pressed in your fist. If not, drizzle in a little more oil, a tablespoon at a time.

In another large bowl, toss the portobellos with 2 tablespoons oil and the remaining ½ teaspoon salt. Divide the stuffing among the mushrooms, and place on a rimmed sheet pan. Pour in the wine and stock. Drizzle the remaining 3 tablespoons oil over the mushrooms and into the pan. Tent with foil, and bake until the mushrooms give up their juices and soften, about 15 to 20 minutes. Uncover, and top each portobello with two slices of goat cheese. Bake until the mushrooms and cheese are nicely browned and the pan juices are reduced and bubbly, about 20 minutes more. Serve hot, with the pan juices spooned over, or at room temperature on a buffet.

RED ONIONS STUFFED WITH RICE

Cipolle Rosse Farcite con Riso

You can make these with any type of onion—red, yellow, or sweet. Just choose ones that are about the size of tennis balls. They are good served hot or at room temperature, and make a welcome addition to a buffet table. They also look fabulous served as a side dish at a formal dinner if you are going to plate the main course with proteins and side dishes on individual dinner plates.

Serves 6, or more as part of a buffet

1 cup Arborio rice
1½ teaspoons kosher salt
6 medium red onions
6 tablespoons extra-virgin olive oil
4 ounces ham, diced
1 cup diced roasted red bell peppers
½ cup grated Grana Padano
¼ cup chopped fresh Italian parsley
1 large egg, beaten
1 cup chicken stock (page 148)
½ cup dry white wine
4 tablespoons unsalted butter, cut into bits

Preheat oven to 400 degrees. In a small saucepan, combine the rice, ½ teaspoon salt, and 2 cups water. Bring to a simmer, cover, and cook until rice is al dente, about 14 to 15 minutes. Spread on a baking sheet to cool.

Peel the onions and halve crosswise. Cut a small piece from each end so the onions will sit up straight, making a cup shape. Cut and scoop out the interior of the onion halves to leave shells that are about 2 or 3 layers thick. Chop the onion flesh that you scooped out, and set aside. In a large bowl, toss the onion shells with 2 tablespoons olive oil and ½ teaspoon salt.

Heat the remaining 4 tablespoons olive oil in a large skillet over medium heat. Add the chopped onion pieces, and cook, stirring often, until soft, about 10 minutes. Add the diced ham, and cook until the ham is just golden on the edges, about 3 minutes. Scrape into a large bowl, and let cool slightly, about 10 minutes.

To the large bowl, add the cooked rice, the roasted peppers, grated cheese, parsley, egg, and remaining ½ teaspoon salt. Toss well to combine and make a cohesive stuffing. Mound the filling into the onion shells, and set them in a baking dish large enough to hold the onions without crowding them.

Pour the stock and wine into the dish, and scatter 2 tablespoons of the butter in the liquid. Dot the tops of the onions with the remaining 2 tablespoons butter. Cover the pan with foil (without letting it touch the onions), and bake until the onions are tender, about 35 minutes. Uncover, and bake until the tops are brown and crusty, about 20 to 25 minutes more. Serve hot, with the pan juices, or at room temperature.

FRIED ONION RINGS

Anelli di Cipolla Fritti

Italian onion rings use a light pastella *batter to coat the onions, to which Grana Padano cheese is added for flavor and crunch. The key to frying is to keep the oil at the right temperature. Invest in a deep-fry/candy thermometer, and make sure your oil stays between 355 and 365 degrees as you cook these onion rings, which are a wonderful addition to a grilling party or barbecue.*

Serves 4 to 6

2 large Spanish onions (about 1¾ pounds total)
2 cups milk
Vegetable oil, for deep-frying
1¼ cups all-purpose flour, plus more for dredging
½ teaspoon baking powder
1 teaspoon kosher salt, plus more to taste
1 cup grated Grana Padano

Peel and slice the onions into ½-inch rings, and separate them (don't use the tiny ones from the middle; save them for something else). Place in a large bowl, and pour the milk over them. Let soak 30 minutes, tossing occasionally.

Heat 2 inches of vegetable oil to 365 degrees in a medium Dutch oven. Drain the onions, and reserve the milk. In a large bowl, whisk together the flour, baking powder, and salt. Whisk in the reserved milk to make a smooth batter. A couple of lumps are okay—don't overmix. Whisk in the grated cheese.

Spread some flour on a plate. Dredge the onions lightly in flour. Dip the onions in the batter to coat, and fry, in batches, turning once, until golden brown and crisp, about 2 minutes per side. Drain, and season lightly with salt. Serve immediately.

BALSAMIC BRAISED ONIONS

Cipolline al Balsamico

This is one of those very versatile dishes that are perfect for entertaining. It can be made ahead and served warm or at room temperature, and works really well as part of an antipasto buffet or served with cheeses and salumi. It's also a good side dish for roasted chicken, pork, or beef. Make sure you purchase cipolline onions that are all about the same size, so they cook at the same rate. These onions also make a good side dish for vegans and vegetarians.

Serves 6 to 8

½ cup golden raisins
½ cup balsamic vinegar
¼ cup extra-virgin olive oil
2½ pounds cipolline onions, peeled, roots trimmed but left whole
1 teaspoon kosher salt
2 fresh bay leaves
1 leafy sprig rosemary
¼ cup toasted pine nuts

Put the raisins in a small bowl, and pour the vinegar over them. Let soak while you brown the onions.

Add the olive oil to a large skillet (large enough to hold the onions in one snug layer) over medium heat. When the oil is hot, add the onions and season with the salt. Toss to coat in the oil. Reduce heat to medium low, cover the skillet, and cook, tossing occasionally, until onions are browned all over and almost tender, about 15 to 20 minutes, depending on size.

Add the raisins and balsamic vinegar, bay leaves, rosemary, and ½ cup water. Cover, and cook until onions are tender all the way through, about 10 to 15 minutes. Uncover, increase the heat to medium high, and cook, tossing frequently so the onions don't burn, until they are glazed all over, about 2 to 3 minutes. Remove bay leaves and rosemary sprig, sprinkle with pine nuts, and serve.

MASHED PARSNIPS AND SCALLIONS

Purea di Pastinaca con Scalogno Verde

A tasty substitute for mashed potatoes, easy to prepare, and very flavorful, the parsnips in this recipe can be cooked and mashed a few hours in advance, but the chopped scallions should be added just before reheating and serving, so their color and flavor remain vibrant.

Serves 6 to 8

1½ pound parsnips, peeled and cut into 2-inch lengths
2 medium russet potatoes (about 16 ounces), peeled and quartered
1 teaspoon kosher salt, plus more for salting the water
1 bunch scallions, white and green parts, coarsely chopped (about 1 cup)
½ cup milk, plus more as needed
4 tablespoons unsalted butter
1½ teaspoons grated lemon zest
Freshly ground black pepper, to taste

Pour enough cold water over the parsnips and potatoes in a large saucepan to cover them by three fingers. Season generously with salt, and bring to a boil over high heat. Cook until tender, about 15 minutes. Add the scallions, and cook until bright green, about 3 minutes.

Meanwhile, heat the milk and butter in a small saucepan over low heat until the butter is melted. Drain the vegetables thoroughly, and return them to the empty cooking pot. Mash them with a potato masher, gradually adding the milk and butter, to get a smooth texture. (Add a little more milk if it seems dry.) Stir in the lemon zest, and season with salt and pepper. Serve immediately.

EGGPLANT AND BARLEY STUFFED PEPPERS

Peperoni Farciti di Melanzane ed Orzo

Italians stuff peppers in many ways, but this recipe, which uses barley, is one of my favorites.
A delicious appetizer or side dish hot out of the oven, it is equally good at room temperature.
You could also stuff smaller peppers to make this part of an antipasto buffet table.

Serves 8 as an entrée

PEPPERS

1 teaspoon kosher salt, plus more for the cooking pot
¾ cup pearled barley
¼ cup extra-virgin olive oil
1 small onion, chopped
3 small Italian eggplants (about 1½ pounds total), peeled and chopped into ½-inch pieces
1 bunch scallions, white and green parts, chopped (about 1 cup)
2 hard-boiled eggs, chopped
1 cup diced low-moisture mozzarella
½ cup grated Grana Padano
¼ to ½ cup fine dried bread crumbs
8 medium bell peppers (a mix of red, yellow, and orange is nice)

SAUCE

¼ cup extra-virgin olive oil
6 cloves garlic, chopped
Two 28-ounce cans whole San Marzano tomatoes, crushed by hand
1 teaspoon kosher salt

Preheat oven to 400 degrees. For the peppers, bring a large saucepan of salted water to boil, and add the barley. Cook until still quite al dente, about 20 minutes. Drain, rinse, and pat dry.

Add the olive oil to a large skillet over medium-high heat. When the oil is hot, add chopped onion and the eggplant and season with ½ teaspoon of the salt. Drizzle in ¼ cup water, and cook, tossing occasionally, until the eggplant is cooked, about 10 minutes. Add the scallions, and cook until wilted, about 3 minutes. Scrape into a large bowl, and let cool slightly.

To the cooled eggplant, add the barley, eggs, mozzarella, grated cheese, remaining ½ teaspoon salt, and enough bread crumbs to make the mixture hold together as a stuffing. Toss well to combine.

Cut out the stems of the peppers and trim away enough of the tops to open them for stuffing. Scoop out the seeds and discard. Divide the stuffing among the peppers.

For the sauce, in a large Dutch oven (wide enough to hold the peppers standing up), heat the olive oil over medium heat. When the oil is hot, add the garlic, and cook until fragrant, about 1 minute. Add the tomatoes, slosh out the tomato cans with 2 cups water, and add this to the Dutch oven. Season with the salt. Bring to a simmer, and cook until slightly thickened, about 15 minutes.

Nestle the peppers into the sauce, cover, and simmer until the peppers are tender, uncovering halfway through the cooking process, about 45 minutes in total.

SWISS CHARD AND MASHED POTATO GRATIN

Bietole e Patate Gratinate

This dish brings me right back to my grandmother's garden, where both of these vegetables were almost always available. The gratin can be assembled ahead; just bring it to room temperature before placing in the oven, cover it with foil, and bake for 15 minutes before uncovering and proceeding with the recipe. This is one of those casserole-like vegetable dishes that are easy to double if you're feeding a crowd. It is great on a buffet table as well, and any leftovers can easily be reheated the next day, in a pan on top of the stove.

Serves 6 to 8

4 tablespoons unsalted butter, cut into pieces, plus 1 tablespoon softened butter for lining the baking dish

½ cup fine dried bread crumbs, for lining the baking dish

2 medium bunches (about 2 pounds) white-stemmed Swiss chard, washed well

1½ teaspoons kosher salt, plus more for the cooking pot

2 pounds russet potatoes (about 6 potatoes), peeled, left whole

2 tablespoons extra-virgin olive oil

1 large onion, thinly sliced

¾ cup grated Grana Padano

1 cup grated white cheddar

Preheat oven to 400 degrees. Grease a 9-by-13-inch baking dish with the 1 tablespoon softened butter. Sprinkle with bread crumbs to coat the dish lightly, tapping out the excess. Strip the leaves from the chard stems, and cut the stems crosswise into ½-inch pieces. Coarsely chop the leaves.

Bring a large pot (large enough to hold the potatoes and chard together) of salted water to a boil, and add the potatoes and chard stems. Simmer the potatoes, about 10 minutes.

When the potatoes and stems have cooked about 10 to 12 minutes, add the chard leaves. Simmer until all are tender, about 10 minutes more. Dump all into a colander, and drain very well.

Add the olive oil to a large skillet over medium heat. When the oil is hot, add the onion, and cook until softened, about 7 minutes. Add the chard and potatoes and 1½ teaspoons salt. Cook for a few minutes, pressing the potatoes and chard with a potato masher, then continue mixing with a wooden spoon until mixture is homogeneous. Remove from the heat, and stir in the 4 tablespoons butter pieces and ½ cup of the grated Grana Padano.

Spread the mixture evenly in the prepared baking dish. In a small bowl, toss together the remaining ¼ cup grated Grana Padano and the cheddar. Sprinkle this over the potatoes and chard evenly. Bake until the top is brown and bubbly, about 30 to 35 minutes. Serve hot.

POTATOES STUFFED WITH SAUSAGE AND MUSHROOMS

Patate Farcite con Funghi e Salsicce

These potatoes can be stuffed and roasted ahead of time, then covered with foil and reheated in a 350-degree oven before serving. They're also good at room temperature. To turn this recipe into finger food, use small Red Bliss potatoes (about 20 to 24) and mind the baking time: it should take half as long, depending on the size of the potatoes used. When my family comes over in the colder months, this is a rich, filling favorite.

Serves 8

4 large russet potatoes (about 12 ounces each)
½ cup extra-virgin olive oil
2 teaspoons kosher salt
1 small onion, finely chopped
3 links sweet Italian sausage without fennel seeds, removed from casings (about 10 ounces total)
12 ounces mixed mushrooms (white, cremini, shiitake, oyster, etc.), thinly sliced (about 4 cups)
1 cup grated Grana Padano
3 tablespoons chopped fresh Italian parsley

Preheat oven to 425 degrees. Halve the potatoes lengthwise, and scoop out the flesh to make a boat or shell. Finely chop the flesh you've scooped out. In a large roasting pan, toss the scooped-out potatoes with ¼ cup of the olive oil, and season with 1 teaspoon salt.

Add the remaining ¼ cup olive oil to a large skillet over medium heat. When the oil is hot, add the onion, and cook until just softened, about 3 to 4 minutes. Add the chopped potato, and crumble in the sausage. Cook, stirring to break up the sausage, until the sausage is no longer pink, about 5 to 6 minutes.

Add the mushrooms, and season all with the remaining teaspoon of salt. Cook and stir until the mushrooms and chopped potato are just tender, about 10 to 12 minutes. Remove from heat, and scrape into a large bowl to cool slightly, about 5 minutes.

To the sausage mixture, stir in ½ cup of the grated cheese and the parsley. Fill the potato shells with the mixture, and arrange, filled side up, in the roasting pan. Sprinkle the tops with the remaining grated cheese. Pour ½ cup water into the bottom of the roasting pan, and cover the pan with foil, making sure not to touch the filling. Bake until potato shells are just tender, about 40 minutes. Uncover, and bake until tops are golden brown, about 25 minutes more.

CRISPY BAKED TOMATOES
Pomodori Croccanti al Forno

These can be served warm or at room temperature, either as a side dish or as part of an anti-pasto buffet. When cold, they are marvelous cut and tossed in green salads, because baking brings out the true summer-tomato taste. Roughly chopped, they make a great topping for a bruschetta.

Serves 6

6 large plum tomatoes
2 tablespoons extra-virgin olive oil, plus more for drizzling
1½ teaspoons kosher salt
1 cup panko bread crumbs
½ cup grated Grana Padano
½ cup finely chopped scallions
2 tablespoons chopped fresh Italian parsley
¼ teaspoon crushed red pepper flakes

Preheat oven to 425 degrees. Halve the tomatoes crosswise, and cut out the cores. Squeeze out the seeds. In a large bowl, toss the tomatoes with the olive oil and 1 teaspoon of the salt.

In a medium bowl, toss together the panko, grated cheese, scallions, parsley, red pepper flakes, and remaining ½ teaspoon salt. Press the stuffing into the tomatoes, opening the tomatoes up with your fingers as you go to get some stuffing into the smaller cavities.

Set the tomatoes, cut side up, on a parchment-lined rimmed sheet pan. Drizzle the tops with olive oil. Bake on the top rack of the oven until the tomatoes are tender but still hold their shape and the stuffing is browned, about 20 to 25 minutes.

Move the tomatoes to the bottom rack, and bake to dry them out a bit, about 10 to 15 minutes more.

SKILLET PEPPERS AND POTATOES

Peperoni e Patate

This is one of those simple recipes that inevitably becomes a family favorite. The recipe suggests bell peppers, but when summer comes around and there are mounds of different peppers available, you can replace the bell peppers with sweet banana peppers, gypsy peppers, jalapeño, cayenne, or Calabrian chile peppers. Keep in mind the heat or spiciness of the different varieties as you use them in this recipe.

Serves 4 to 6

5 tablespoons extra-virgin olive oil

2 large russet potatoes, peeled and cut into thin wedges

1 teaspoon kosher salt

1 medium red onion, sliced

1 red bell pepper, cut into ½-inch strips

1 yellow bell pepper, cut into ½-inch strips

2 teaspoons chopped fresh rosemary

¼ teaspoon crushed red pepper flakes

2 tablespoons chopped Italian parsley

Heat a large skillet over medium-high heat. Add 3 tablespoons of the olive oil. When the oil is hot, add the potatoes, tossing and shaking the skillet to coat them in the oil. Season with ½ teaspoon of the salt. Cook the potatoes, tossing occasionally, until browned on the edges, about 5 to 6 minutes.

Reduce the heat to medium-low and add the remaining 2 tablespoons olive oil. Add the red onion, bell peppers, rosemary, and red pepper flakes. Season with the remaining ½ teaspoon salt. Toss to combine the vegetables and cover the skillet. Cook, stirring occasionally, until the peppers and potatoes are tender, about 10 to 15 minutes more.

Uncover the skillet and increase the heat to reduce any liquid left in the pan and caramelize the vegetables slightly, about 2 minutes. Sprinkle with the parsley, toss, and serve.

ROASTED BUTTERNUT SQUASH WITH OLIVES AND WALNUTS

Zucca Arrostita Condita con Olive e Noci

This can also be served as a salad, atop baby arugula, with some shavings of ricotta salata on top. It is a great vegetable dish for holiday gatherings, especially when served with a festive roast, such as turkey or rack of lamb.

Serves 6 to 8

1 large butternut squash (about 4 pounds), peeled and cut into 1½-inch chunks
¼ cup extra-virgin olive oil
1 teaspoon kosher salt
½ cup chopped pitted oil-cured black olives
Grated zest and juice of 1 large orange
2 tablespoons chopped fresh Italian parsley
½ cup coarsely chopped toasted walnuts

Preheat oven to 425 degrees. In a large bowl, toss the squash with the olive oil and salt. Spread on a sheet pan and roast, tossing once or twice, starting on the bottom rack and moving to the top halfway through, until very golden, about 25 to 30 minutes.

While it's still warm, scrape the squash into a serving bowl, and sprinkle with the olives, orange juice, zest, and parsley. Toss well. Sprinkle the chopped walnuts on top, and serve.

SPICY POTATO SALAD WITH BACON

Insalata di Patate e Pancetta Piccante

This salad is best served warm, but is also good at room temperature. Just don't serve it chilled: the bacon fat will congeal, and the potatoes will become waxy. It is ideal for barbecues, buffet tables, or family dinners.

Serves 6 to 8

3 pounds new red potatoes
1 teaspoon salt, plus more to taste
3 tablespoons extra-virgin olive oil
6 ounces slab bacon, diced
1 medium red bell pepper, cored, seeded, and chopped
1 medium red onion, chopped
¼ cup drained chopped pickled peperoncini
6 tablespoons red wine vinegar, plus more to taste
2 tablespoons chopped fresh Italian parsley

In a large saucepan, cover the potatoes with cold water by 1 inch. Bring to a simmer, and cook until tender all the way through when pierced with a knife. Drain. Once the potatoes are cool enough to handle (but still warm), quarter them, and put them in a large serving bowl. Season with the salt, and toss.

In a large skillet, heat the olive oil over medium heat, and add the bacon. Cook until the edges of the bacon are crispy but the fat is not totally rendered, about 3 minutes. Add the bell pepper and onion, and cook until crisp-tender, about 3 minutes.

Increase the heat to high, and add the chopped peperoncini and vinegar. Bring everything to a boil, and pour over the still-warm potatoes. Sprinkle with the parsley, and toss well. Season with salt and more vinegar if necessary, and serve warm.

LEMON AND OREGANO POTATOES

Patate al Limone e Origano

This is a unique rendition of a traditional potato salad, best when served warm, but good at room temperature. It is wonderful as a side dish at a barbecue, for picnics, and at the dinner table. So simple.

Serves 6 to 8

3 pounds russet potatoes, peeled and cut into 2-inch chunks

1½ teaspoons kosher salt, plus more for the cooking water

Juice of 4 lemons, plus grated zest of ½ lemon

6 tablespoons extra-virgin olive oil

3 tablespoons chopped fresh Italian parsley

1 teaspoon dried oregano, preferably Sicilian on the branch

½ teaspoon spicy paprika

Put the potatoes in a large saucepan, and add water to cover. Salt the water liberally, and add the lemon juice. Bring to a simmer, and cook until potatoes are tender, about 13 to 15 minutes, depending on size.

Meanwhile, in a large serving bowl, whisk together the grated lemon zest, olive oil, parsley, salt, dried oregano, and paprika.

When the potatoes are tender, drain well, shaking off any excess water, and add to the bowl. Toss well to coat the potatoes in the oil, and serve.

BRAISED KALE AND CHICKPEAS

Cavolo Nero Brasato con Ceci

You can substitute another leafy, slightly bitter green, such as escarole or Swiss chard, for the kale, or use a combination of several different greens. You can also use other beans, such as cannellini, in place of the chickpeas. Make sure to put them to soak the day before. This vegetable dish is easily reheated once ready. Just make sure not to overcook it, because the chickpeas can turn to mush.

Serves 6 to 8

1 pound dried chickpeas, soaked overnight
1 teaspoon kosher salt, plus more to taste and for the cooking pot
2 bunches kale, stemmed, leaves coarsely chopped (about 2 pounds)
¼ cup extra-virgin olive oil, plus more for drizzling
4 ounces slab bacon, diced
4 cloves garlic, thinly sliced
2 tablespoons tomato paste
1 cup canned whole San Marzano tomatoes, crushed by hand
Pinch crushed red pepper flakes
2 fresh bay leaves

Drain and rinse the beans. Put them in a large pot with cold water to cover by 2 inches. Bring to a simmer, and cook, with the lid ajar, until the chickpeas are tender throughout, about 1 hour (cooking time varies depending on the age of the beans, so check them often). Remove from the heat, stir in ½ tea-spoon of the salt, and let cool in the cooking liquid. When cooled, drain, reserving 2 cups of the soaking liquid.

Meanwhile, bring a large pot of salted water to boil. When it is boiling, add the kale, and cook until the leaves are tender, about 15 minutes. Drain well.

Add the olive oil to a large Dutch oven over medium heat. When the oil is hot, add the bacon, and cook until the fat is rendered, about 4 minutes. Add the sliced garlic, and let sizzle a minute; then clear a space in the pan, and add the tomato paste to it. Cook and stir the tomato paste in that spot until it is toasted and darkens a shade or two, about 1 minute. Add the tomatoes and 1 cup bean-cooking liquid. Season with the remaining ½ teaspoon salt, the crushed red pepper flakes, and the bay leaves. Add the drained beans and chard and enough of the remaining bean-cooking liquid to make a sauce. Cook to blend and concentrate the flavors, about 10 minutes. Season with salt, drizzle with a little olive oil, and serve.

SQUASH AND SAUSAGE IN TOMATO SAUCE

Ragù di Zucca e Salsicce

Served over polenta or toasted bread, this dish can become a main course, a snack, or a lunch. Any leftovers can be used to make a risotto. It is delicious as is as part of a buffet or at family gatherings.

Serves 6 to 8 as a side dish

¼ cup extra-virgin olive oil

1 small onion, chopped

12 ounces sweet Italian sausage, removed from casings

6 fresh sage leaves

¼ teaspoon crushed red pepper flakes

One 28-ounce can whole San Marzano tomatoes, crushed by hand

1 large butternut squash, peeled, seeded, and cut into 1-inch chunks

1 teaspoon kosher salt

½ cup grated Grana Padano

Add the olive oil to a large skillet over medium heat. When the oil is hot, add the onion. Toss the onion to coat in the oil, then add ½ cup water. Bring to a simmer, and cook until the water has reduced away and the onion softens, about 7 minutes.

Crumble in the sausage, and increase the heat so the sausage and onion brown, crumbling the sausage with a wooden spoon, about 5 minutes. Add the sage and red pepper flakes, and let sizzle a minute. Add the tomatoes, slosh out the can with 1 cup water, and add that to the pan along with the salt. Bring to a simmer, stir in the squash, and cover the skillet. Cook until the squash is tender, about 15 minutes.

Uncover, and increase the heat to reduce and thicken the sauce. Once the sauce is reduced to your liking, remove the skillet from the heat, stir in the grated cheese, and serve.

ROASTED SUNCHOKES

Topinambour Arrosto

Sunchokes have become quite popular in the last few years. They are easy to prepare and taste like a mixture of potato and artichoke. Be sure to select fresh sunchokes for this recipe. Their skins should be taut, not wrinkled, and they should feel heavy for their size. If they are fresh, they don't need to be peeled, just washed well. Depending on how big your sunchokes are, you can roast them whole or halve them.

This dish is a good substitute for roasted potatoes. It is delicious hot, but also good at room temperature for a buffet table.

Serves 8

2½ pounds sunchokes, scrubbed well, halved if large
¼ cup extra-virgin olive oil
½ tablespoon kosher salt
4 sprigs fresh rosemary

Preheat oven to 425 degrees. In a large bowl, toss the sunchokes with the oil, salt, and rosemary sprigs. Spread on a sheet pan.

Roast until tender, tossing occasionally so they brown evenly, about 30 minutes. Remove the whole rosemary stems, and serve.

WINTER RATATOUILLE
Caponata Invernale

This recipe takes some time to put together but feeds a crowd once you've got it done. It can be served warm or at room temperature. The shaved ricotta salata on top is optional, but a nice savory touch to complement the sweetness of the roasted vegetables. The ratatouille can be made 3 or 4 days in advance, and keeps well. It can be served on its own as an appetizer, or makes a great side dish or a tasty topping for bruschetta.

Serves 10 or more as a side dish

¾ cup extra-virgin olive oil

3 medium parsnips, peeled and cut into 1-inch chunks (about 1 pound)

1 small celery root, peeled and cut into 1-inch chunks (about 1¼ pounds)

3 stalks celery, cut into 1-inch chunks

3 medium carrots, cut into 1-inch chunks (about 1 pound)

1 pound sunchokes, peeled if the skin is thick or wrinkly, and halved

1 small butternut squash, peeled and cut into 1-inch chunks (about 1½ pounds)

3 small onions, cut into 6 wedges each through the root end

2 teaspoons kosher salt, plus more to taste

Freshly ground black pepper

4 anchovy fillets, chopped

4 cloves garlic, crushed and peeled

8 fresh sage leaves

3 tablespoons tomato paste

1½ cups dry white wine

1 cup chicken stock (page 148)

⅓ cup drained capers in brine

Preheat oven to 425 degrees. Heat 1 tablespoon of the oil in a large skillet over medium heat. Add the parsnips, and cook and toss until the edges begin to soften and caramelize, about 5 minutes. Add them to a large roasting pan. Repeat this procedure with each vegetable (cooking each type separately, about 5 minutes per batch) and a tablespoon of oil at a time, until all of the vegetables are in the roasting pan. Season with the 2 teaspoons kosher salt and some black pepper. Drizzle with 2 tablespoons more oil. Toss well to combine.

Return the skillet to the heat, and increase to medium high. Add the remaining 3 tablespoons olive oil. When the oil is hot, add the anchovies, garlic, and sage. Once they begin to sizzle, clear a space in the pan and add the tomato paste. Cook and stir the tomato paste in that spot until it is toasted and darkens a shade or two, about 1 minute. Add the wine, and stir to combine. Bring to a boil, and add the stock and capers. Boil until reduced by half, about 5 minutes. Pour this over the vegetables in the roasting pan, and roast on the bottom rack of the oven, tossing occasionally, until the vegetables are tender and glazed, about 20 minutes.

Polenta, Risotto, and Pasta

Pasta, rice, and polenta make fabulous additions to any party, dinner, or gathering, and they're equally good as the stars of the show. People of all ages love pasta, and it's a highly economical and fun way to fuel a night of friends coming to visit. You should prepare a mix of different pasta dishes, from skillet-finished to baked recipes. Most of my pasta recipes are served with lots of vegetables and proteins, and you can easily add more of each to any pasta recipe I have included here.

Also consider substituting different shapes of pasta in these recipes. The shapes carry the different sauces in different ways. For a chunky sauce, a pasta with nooks and crannies—such as fusilli, rigatoni, candele, or rotelle—is good. Shapes are also fun when you are cooking pasta for kids, particularly farfalle, ditalini, mezza manica, and the like. Some shapes are more resilient and remain al dente longer than others, which is especially helpful when you have a big crowd. Penne, ziti, and gemelli hold particularly well.

If you're not having a pasta party but instead serving pasta as the main course, a big bowl of salad, such as kale Caesar with focaccia croutons (page 109) or raw and cooked salad for winter (page 116), is always welcome as an appetizer and a balancing element. If you want a small, intimate pasta party for a few chosen friends, have a go at making fresh pasta (page 226). Make the pasta together, cook it together, and then all sit down together to eat it.

A risotto party is also a lot of fun. I start with a diversified antipasto buffet, including lots of vegetables, and then like to make risotto in front of everybody while they are all sipping their drinks and gathered around the stove watching me cook. If you feel up to it, you can give them a risotto lesson, so they can try it themselves at home. Once the risotto is finished, it needs to be served immediately in hot bowls, but if you have some left over the next day, you can make patties (*riso al salta*) and fry them until crispy. You can also freeze any extra risotto and turn it into arancini for your next cocktail party. Once the risotto has defrosted, add a beaten egg and some grated Grana Padano cheese, shape the mixture into small balls, and then roll them in flour, then in beaten eggs and bread crumbs. Fry the patties in vegetable oil and serve them hot.

Depending on the pasta or risotto that you choose to cook, you may want to select an appetizer that can be plated ahead of time, such as a salad, and possibly a main course that comes hot out of the oven, affording yourself the time to pay close attention to the pasta or risotto you are cooking. You could also consider a baked pasta, such as baked shells (page 221) or lasagna (page 224), which is prepared in advance and then baked when needed. Timing, especially with pasta and risotto, is very important in the kitchen.

Polenta is a very good alternative *primo,* because it can be cooked when needed and served hot, topped with some shrimp alla buzara (page 245), with chicken liver spiedini (page 281), with a Bolognese sauce (page 220), or baked into a torta with Gorgonzola and savoy cabbage (page 194). When I serve it as a main course, I like to let it cool in a baking pan until solid and then cut it into slices, which I serve grilled or fried and topped with winter ratatouille (page 187), or squash and sausage in tomato sauce (page 185). When tightly wrapped, polenta keeps in the refrigerator for a few days and freezes well for a few weeks.

BASIC POLENTA

Polenta

Polenta is similar to grits. In northern Italy, where it is most common, it can be prepared and served in many different ways. In its most basic preparation, polenta is a smooth and dense porridge. It can be served alongside many different foods, such as cheese, vegetables, fish, meat, and game, the proteins most often cooked in a sauce or guazzetto. *When chilled, polenta can be fried, grilled, or baked.*

Serves 6

5 cups water (or half water and half milk, for a richer taste)
1 tablespoon extra-virgin olive oil
1 fresh bay leaf
1 tablespoon kosher salt
1½ cups coarse yellow cornmeal

Cooked polenta is delicious served as is, but if you would like to add additional flavor, all or just one or two of the following additions, whipped into the hot polenta, are great options:

4 tablespoons unsalted butter, at room temperature, cut into pieces
1 cup grated Grana Padano
½ cup mascarpone
½ cup crumbled Gorgonzola

In a large saucepan, combine the water (or water and milk), olive oil, bay leaf, and salt, and bring to a simmer over medium heat. Very slowly, sift the cornmeal by handfuls into the pot, through the fingers of one hand, stirring constantly with a wooden spoon or whisk to remove any lumps.

Once all of the cornmeal is added, adjust the heat so just a few lazy bubbles pop to the surface. Continue to cook and stir until the polenta is smooth and thick and pulls away from the sides of the pan as it is stirred, about 30 to 35 minutes.

To serve, beat in the finishing items of your choice. Discard the bay leaf, pour the polenta into a serving bowl or onto a wooden board, and allow it to rest a few minutes. To serve from the bowl, dip a large spoon into hot water and scoop the polenta onto individual dishes, dipping the spoon into the water between scoops. To serve from the board, cut polenta into segments with a thin, taut string or knife, and transfer to plates with a spatula or cake server.

POLENTA TORTA WITH GORGONZOLA AND SAVOY CABBAGE

Torta di Polenta, Gorgonzola, e Verze

This is an ideal preparation for a crowd. You can assemble the tart the day before and then bake it the day of your gathering, and it also reheats well. It's delicious with Gorgonzola and cabbage, but you can vary the filling in this torta however you wish. I love vegetables with polenta but you can treat this cake like a pizza and stuff it with sliced grilled sausages, mozzarella, and some tomato sauce to moisten the filling. I also like using a leftover ragù or a combination of other sautéed vegetables with the potato-and-cheese base. Save the extra sauce and serve it on the side when slicing the torta di polenta.

Serves 6 to 8

2 tablespoons unsalted butter, at room temperature, plus more for greasing the pans

1 recipe basic polenta (preceding recipe), hot

Fine dried bread crumbs, for the pan

2 medium Idaho potatoes, peeled and quartered (about 1½ pounds)

2 teaspoons kosher salt, plus more for the cooking water

1 small head savoy cabbage

2 tablespoons extra-virgin olive oil

2 teaspoons chopped fresh thyme

4 cloves garlic, lightly crushed and peeled

Pinch crushed red pepper flakes

1½ cups crumbled Gorgonzola or grated Taleggio or Montasio cheese

½ cup grated Grana Padano

Butter a 9-inch round cake pan. Pour the just-cooked polenta into the greased cake pan. Let stand until cool, then refrigerate until completely chilled, about 4 to 5 hours.

When the polenta is firm, preheat oven to 400 degrees. Butter a 10-inch, 4-inch-tall springform pan, coat with bread crumbs, and shake any excess out of the pan. Put the potatoes in a large saucepan with ample salted water. Bring to a simmer, and cook 5 minutes.

Meanwhile, remove any wilted or yellow leaves from the cabbage and cut out the core. Cut the cabbage into 1-inch chunks. Add these to the pot with the potatoes, and cook until both vegetables are tender, about 15 minutes more.

Drain the vegetables thoroughly. In a large skillet, heat the oil over medium heat. Add the thyme and garlic, and cook until garlic is just golden, about 2 to 3 minutes. Add the cabbage-potato mixture, the salt, and the pepper flakes. Cook, turning the vegetables occasionally, until the liquid is evaporated and the vegetables begin to sizzle. Mash the vegetables coarsely with the spoon as you turn them, leaving plenty of lumps. Be careful not to scorch the mixture—just cook it until the liquid has evaporated. Remove the garlic cloves (if they haven't mashed into the mixture) and discard.

Invert the cooled polenta cake onto a cutting board. With a long, thin knife, slice the cake into

(recipe continues)

three even horizontal layers. Place the top layer upside down in the bottom of the buttered 10-by-4-inch springform pan. Top with half of the potato-cabbage mixture and half of the Gorgonzola. Top the cheese with the center layer of polenta, and top that with the remaining potato-cabbage mixture and Gorgonzola. Place the bottom layer of the polenta cake upside down over the torta and press gently. Brush the top of the torta with the 2 tablespoons butter, and sprinkle with the grated Grana Padano. Bake the torta until the top layer of cheese is lightly browned and the torta is heated through, about 40 minutes.

Remove, and let cool 10 to 15 minutes. Remove the sides of the springform pan, and cut the torta into slices to serve.

RICE WITH CHICKEN AND VEGETABLES

Riso alla Pitocca

This is a very satisfying one-pot dish, perfect for casual entertaining. The vegetable pestata *adds great flavor, but you can also leave the vegetables chunky—or add additional vegetables, such as leeks or fennel, for a different taste. The recipe is easily doubled for larger parties.*

Serves 6 to 8

5 cups chicken stock (page 148) or water
1 small onion, cut into chunks
1 large carrot, cut into chunks
2 stalks celery, cut into chunks
3 cloves garlic, crushed and peeled
¼ cup extra-virgin olive oil
1½ pounds boneless, skinless chicken thighs, trimmed of all fat and cut into 1-inch chunks
1 fresh bay leaf
1 teaspoon kosher salt, plus more to taste
1 cup dry white wine
2 cups Arborio or Carnaroli short-grain rice
2 tablespoons unsalted butter, cut into pieces
3 tablespoons chopped fresh Italian parsley
½ cup grated Grana Padano, plus more for passing

In a small saucepan, warm the stock over low heat, and keep it hot. In a food processor, combine the onion, carrot, celery, and garlic, and process to a smooth-textured paste, or *pestata*.

Heat the olive oil in a medium Dutch oven over medium-high heat. When the oil is hot, add the *pestata*. Cook, stirring frequently, until the *pestata* has dried out and begins to stick to the bottom of the pan, about 5 minutes.

Add the chicken pieces and the bay leaf, and season with the salt. Cook and stir the chicken in the pan until browned and caramelized all over, about 4 minutes. Raise the heat, pour in the white wine, and cook, stirring and scraping up the browned bits in the pan, until the wine has almost completely evaporated.

Pour in the hot stock, stirring, then all the rice. Bring to a boil over high heat, cover the pan, and reduce the heat to keep the rice bubbling gently. Simmer until both the rice and the chicken chunks are fully cooked and the consistency is creamy, about 14 minutes.

Turn off the heat, remove the bay leaf, drop in the pieces of butter, and stir vigorously until they are melted and thoroughly combined; then stir in the parsley and ½ cup of grated cheese. Spoon the rice into warm bowls, and serve immediately, passing additional grated cheese at the table.

RISOTTO WITH MUSHROOMS
Risotto ai Funghi

Risotto with mushrooms is one of the best-loved Italian classics at my house, and in the restaurants as well. It is a recipe than can be easily doubled, and it's fun to cook in front of your guests as they mingle in your kitchen. If you have time, you can add more flavor to your chicken stock by simmering the trimmings from the mushrooms and leeks in it. This is always a perfect first course for an elegant meal.

Serves 6

7 cups chicken stock (page 148)

¼ cup extra-virgin olive oil

1½ cups thinly sliced shallots (about 4 large shallots)

1½ cups thinly sliced leeks, white and light-green parts (about 2 medium leeks)

2 cups Arborio or other short-grain rice

1 cup dry white wine

1 teaspoon kosher salt, plus more to taste

2 pounds mixed mushrooms (white, cremini, shiitake, oyster, chanterelle, etc.), thickly sliced

¼ cup chopped fresh Italian parsley

½ cup grated Grana Padano

4 tablespoons butter, cut into bits

In a medium saucepan, heat the stock to a simmer; keep it hot. Add the olive oil to a large straight-sided skillet over medium heat. When the oil is hot, add the shallots and leeks. Cook and stir, adjusting the heat so they don't color, until the leeks have wilted, about 5 minutes. Add the rice, and stir to coat it in the oil. Toast the rice in the oil, stirring, until the edges of the kernels become translucent, about 2 minutes.

Add the wine, bring to a simmer, and cook until the wine is absorbed, about 3 minutes. Season with the salt, and add enough hot stock just to cover the rice, about 1½ cups. Simmer gently, stirring, until almost all of the liquid is absorbed.

After the first addition of stock is absorbed, add the mushrooms and stir to incorporate. Continue adding ladlefuls of stock periodically until the rice is creamy but al dente, about 18 minutes from the time you added the wine. (You may not use all of the stock.) Stir in the parsley. Remove the skillet from the heat, and whisk in the grated cheese. Drop in the butter, and mix well until the rice is creamy and smooth. Season with salt if necessary. Serve immediately.

MILAN-STYLE RISOTTO

Risotto alla Milanese

In Milan or in the Lombardy region, risotto alla milanese is on just about every menu, so why not bring some Milanese style to your table? What makes this risotto unique is the inclusion of saffron and bone marrow. You can purchase marrow bones from your butcher; marrow from the shank bones is best. Keep in mind you may have to order the bones ahead of time. Ask the butcher to split the bones so you can scoop out the marrow for this recipe. When serving risotto as an appetizer at a dinner party, you should consider keeping the main course light, or serving a smaller-sized portion, because risotto can be very filling.

Serves 6

7 cups homemade beef stock or canned low-sodium beef broth
½ teaspoon saffron threads
3 tablespoons extra-virgin olive oil
1 medium onion, finely chopped (about 1 cup)
1 large shallot, finely chopped (about ¼ cup)
2 cups Arborio or other short-grain rice
½ cup dry white wine
½ teaspoon kosher salt, plus more to taste
2 ounces beef marrow, chopped
2 tablespoons unsalted butter, cut into bits
½ cup grated Grana Padano
Freshly ground black pepper, to taste

Warm the stock in a small saucepan over low heat; keep it hot. Pour ½ cup of the hot stock over the saffron in a small heatproof bowl.

In a large straight-sided skillet or Dutch oven, heat the olive oil over medium heat. When the oil is hot, add the onion and shallot, and cook until just golden, stirring often, about 8 minutes. Add the rice, and stir to coat it with the oil. Toast the rice until the edges become translucent, 1 to 2 minutes. Pour in the wine, and stir until evaporated. Add ½ cup of the remaining hot stock, and the salt. Cook, stirring constantly, until all the stock has been absorbed. Stir in the beef marrow.

Continue to add hot stock in small batches, just enough to moisten the rice completely, and cook until each successive batch has been absorbed. About 10 minutes after the first addition of stock, stir in the saffron mixture. Stir constantly, and adjust the level of heat so the rice is simmering very gently, until the rice mixture is creamy but al dente, about 18 minutes from the time the wine was added.

Remove the casserole from the heat. Beat in the butter until it's completely melted, and then beat in the cheese. Adjust the seasoning with salt if necessary, and add pepper. Serve immediately, ladled into warm shallow bowls.

BARLEY, KALE, AND BUTTERNUT SQUASH RISOTTO

Risotto d'Orzo, Cavolo Nero, e Zucca

The barley brings a nutty, earthy element to this risotto, adding another complex layer of flavor. A hearty dish, it can serve as a vegetarian main course (if you use water instead of chicken stock) or as a first course or side dish to accompany braised or roasted pork or poultry.

Serves 6 to 8

1 teaspoon kosher salt, plus more for the cooking water and to taste

2 fresh bay leaves

2 cups pearled barley

8 cups chicken stock (page 148)

¼ cup extra-virgin olive oil

1 medium onion, finely chopped

1 large carrot, finely chopped

2 stalks celery, finely chopped

1 cup dry white wine

1 medium bunch kale (about 1 pound), stemmed, leaves coarsely chopped

4 cups ½-inch cubes butternut squash

3 tablespoons butter, cut into bits

¾ cup grated Grana Padano

Bring a large saucepan of salted water to a boil. Add the bay leaves and barley, and simmer until the barley is about halfway cooked (just beginning to become tender on the outside, hard in the center), about 30 minutes. Drain well.

Bring the stock to a bare simmer in a medium saucepan over low heat; keep it hot. Add the olive oil to a large Dutch oven over medium heat. When the oil is hot, add the onion and about ⅓ cup of the hot stock. Simmer until the stock reduces away, about 3 minutes. Add the carrot and celery, and cook until slightly softened, about 4 minutes.

Add the drained barley, and toss to combine. Let the barley dry in the pot for a minute, then add the wine. Simmer until the wine is absorbed, then add enough of the stock just to cover the barley. Add the kale and butternut squash, and stir to combine. Simmer until the first batch of stock is absorbed, about 7 minutes. Season with the salt, and keep adding stock to cover, until the barley is creamy and the vegetables are cooked, about 15 minutes more.

Off heat, add the butter and grated cheese, mix well to combine, season with salt if necessary, and serve.

RISOTTO WITH ARTICHOKES, SUNCHOKES, AND MINT

Risotto con Carciofi, Topinambour, e Menta

Purchase artichoke hearts from the deli that are marinated in oil, as opposed to canned in brine. If making this for vegetarian guests, you can substitute a vegetable stock for the chicken stock, or just use plain water instead.

Serves 6

1 pound sunchokes
7 cups chicken stock (page 148)
3 tablespoons extra-virgin olive oil
1 medium onion, finely chopped
2 cups Arborio or other short-grain rice
1 cup dry white wine
1 teaspoon kosher salt, plus more to taste
2 cups drained marinated artichoke hearts, coarsely chopped
¼ cup chopped fresh mint leaves
¼ cup chopped fresh Italian parsley leaves
1 cup grated Grana Padano
3 tablespoons butter, cut into bits

Wash and scrub the sunchokes well, using a vegetable brush. Halve them, and slice ¼ inch thick.

In a medium saucepan, heat the stock to a simmer; keep it hot. Add the olive oil to a large straight-sided skillet over medium heat. When the oil is hot, add the onion. Cook and stir, adjusting the heat so the onion pieces don't color, until they are softened, about 8 minutes. Add the rice, and stir to coat it in the oil. Toast the rice in the oil, stirring, until the edges of the grain become translucent, about 2 minutes.

Add the sunchokes and wine, bring to a simmer, and cook until the wine is absorbed, about 3 minutes. Season with the salt, and add enough hot stock just to cover the rice, about 1½ cups. Simmer gently, stirring, until almost all of the liquid is absorbed.

After the first addition of stock is absorbed, add the artichokes, and continue adding ladlefuls of stock periodically until the rice is creamy but al dente, about 18 minutes from the time you added the wine. (You may not use all of the stock.) Stir in the mint and parsley.

Remove the skillet from the heat, and sprinkle with the grated cheese. Drop in the butter, and mix well until the rice is creamy and smooth. Season with salt if necessary. Serve immediately.

CAMPANELLE WITH FENNEL AND SHRIMP

Campanelle con Finocchio e Gamberetti

I like to use a variety of different shapes of pasta to make my dishes more interesting. Here I suggest using campanelle, which translates as "little bells." Campanelle carry the sauce well and have an interesting texture. Blanching the fennel in the pasta water adds extra flavor to the pasta. You could also make this with scallops or shelled lobster meat instead.

Serves 6

1 teaspoon kosher salt, plus more for the pasta water
1 medium fennel bulb, trimmed, quartered, plus ½ cup chopped reserved tender trimmings and fronds
¼ cup extra-virgin olive oil, plus more for drizzling
4 cloves garlic, crushed and peeled
1 pound medium shrimp (about 40 to 50), shelled, deveined, tails removed, and cut in half crosswise
2 tablespoons unsalted butter
1 medium leek, white and light-green parts, halved crosswise and thinly sliced
1 pound campanelle
¼ teaspoon crushed red pepper flakes
½ cup dry white wine

Bring a large pot of salted water to a boil. Add the fennel quarters, and simmer until they just begin to become tender, about 5 to 7 minutes. Drain the fennel, and rinse under cold running water until cool enough to handle. Cut out the core section from each piece of fennel, then cut the fennel crosswise into ¼-inch strips. Chop and reserve ¼ cup tender fennel fronds. Return the water to a boil for the pasta.

Add the olive oil to a large skillet over medium heat. When the oil is hot, add the garlic to the pan, and cook until golden brown, shaking the pan, about 3 minutes.

Increase the heat to medium high, scatter the shrimp in the pan, and season with the salt. Cook, tossing constantly, just until the shrimp turn pink, about 2 minutes. Remove the shrimp with a slotted spoon to a small bowl.

Over medium heat, add the butter to the skillet. When the butter is melted, add the leek. Cook until it just begins to wilt, about 5 minutes.

Meanwhile, add the pasta to the boiling water. Once the leek has wilted, add the fennel and red pepper flakes. Stir to coat the fennel in the butter, then add the white wine. Simmer until the wine is reduced away, then ladle in 1 cup of the pasta cooking water. Simmer until the sauce is reduced by half and the fennel and leeks are very tender, about 8 minutes. Stir in the fennel fronds and the reserved shrimp.

When the sauce is ready and the pasta is al dente, remove the pasta with a spider directly to the sauce. Toss to coat the pasta with the sauce. Remove the skillet from the heat, drizzle with a little olive oil, toss again, and serve.

SPAGHETTI WITH CHICKEN AND ZUCCHINI

Spaghetti con Pollo e Zucchine

There's very little prep for this recipe, and the sauce comes together in the time it takes to cook the pasta, so it's perfect for a quick first course when you've got other dishes to attend to, or as a simple entrée for casual weeknight entertaining.

Serves 6

1 teaspoon kosher salt, plus more for the pasta water

¼ cup extra-virgin olive oil, plus more for drizzling

1 pound boneless, skinless chicken breast, sliced into ½-inch strips

2 medium leeks, white and light-green parts, halved and sliced ½ inch thick

1 pound spaghetti

1 pound medium zucchini, cut into 1½-by-¼-inch-thick matchsticks

Pinch crushed red pepper flakes

¼ cup chopped fresh basil

¼ cup chopped fresh Italian parsley

½ cup grated Grana Padano

Bring a large pot of salted water to boil for the pasta. Add 2 tablespoons of the olive oil to a large skillet over medium-high heat. Season the chicken all over with ½ teaspoon of the salt. Add the chicken to the skillet, and toss to brown all over, about 2 to 3 minutes. Remove to a plate.

Reduce the heat in the skillet to medium, and add the remaining 2 tablespoons olive oil and the leeks. As the leeks soften, add the spaghetti to the pasta water. Cook the leeks until just wilted, about 3 minutes.

Add the zucchini to the leeks, season with the remaining ½ teaspoon salt and the red pepper flakes, and toss. Cover, and cook until the zucchini wilts, about 2 to 3 minutes. Uncover, increase the heat to medium high, and cook until the vegetables are caramelized on the edges, about 2 minutes. Add back the chicken and ½ cup pasta water. Simmer while the spaghetti finishes cooking, about 3 minutes.

When the spaghetti is al dente, remove with tongs directly to the sauce. Drizzle with some olive oil, sprinkle with the basil and parsley, and toss. Add a little pasta water if it seems dry. Remove the skillet from the heat, sprinkle with the grated cheese, toss, and serve.

LAGANE PASTA WITH CHICKPEAS

Lagane e Ceci

This is one of those so-called poor recipes from Calabria that use just a few ingredients to make a tasty nutritious meal. It is a recipe that can be stretched from a pasta dish to a soup by adding some water and a bit more of the condiments, especially when your dining crowd increases. Either way, it is delicious.

Serves 4 to 6

CHICKPEAS

2 tablespoons extra-virgin olive oil, plus more for drizzling

4 ounces pancetta, diced

4 cloves garlic, crushed and peeled

½ teaspoon crushed red pepper flakes or 2 or 3 whole dried Calabrian chiles

8 ounces dried chickpeas, soaked overnight, drained

2 fresh bay leaves

2 sprigs fresh rosemary

Kosher salt

LAGANE

2 cups all-purpose flour, plus more for working the dough

2 large whole eggs

2 tablespoons extra-virgin olive oil

¼ cup chopped fresh Italian parsley

½ cup freshly grated Grana Padano

To make the chickpeas, heat the olive oil in a large Dutch oven over medium heat. When the oil is hot, add the pancetta and cook until the fat has rendered and the pancetta is crispy on the edges, about 3 to 4 minutes. Add the garlic and crushed red pepper flakes or chiles, and cook, stirring, until the garlic is golden on the edges, about 2 minutes. Add the drained chickpeas and enough cold water to cover the chickpeas by about 2 inches. Then add the bay leaves and rosemary sprigs, and bring to a simmer. Partially cover the pot and cook until the chickpeas are tender, about 1 hour. Discard the bay leaves.

To make the lagane, put the flour in the work bowl of a food processor and pulse several times to aerate. In a spouted measuring cup, combine the eggs, olive oil, and ⅓ cup cold water. Beat with a fork to combine.

With the processor running, pour the egg mixture through the feed tube and process until the dough forms a ball around the blade. If the dough doesn't begin to form a ball after about 15 seconds, add a little more flour (if it is too wet) or water (if it is too crumbly) and process until you get a ball. Once the ball forms, process about 30 seconds to get a smooth and homogeneous dough.

Dump the dough onto the counter, and knead a few times to make a completely smooth ball of dough that springs back when pressed. Wrap the dough in plastic, and let rest at room temperature for 30 minutes. (The dough can also be made a day ahead, wrapped, and refrigerated. Return to room temperature before proceeding.)

To roll the pasta, cut the ball of dough into 6 pieces. Keep the pieces covered as you work, and line several baking sheets with floured kitchen towels.

Flatten each piece, then roll it through the widest

setting of a pasta machine several times, folding like a letter (rectangle) each time to smooth and strengthen the dough. Once you have a smooth rectangle, continue to roll the pieces through each setting, stopping at the next-to-last setting. Lay the pieces, without touching, on the floured towels.

Cut the pieces into thirds. Roll lengthwise and cut into strands about ¾-to-1-inch thick (slightly thicker than pappardelle). Dust the strands of pasta with flour and form into loose nests on the floured baking sheets.

Bring a large pot of salted water to boil for pasta. Transfer the chickpeas and enough cooking liquid just to cover them to a large skillet and bring to a simmer. Add the pasta to the boiling water and cook until al dente, just about 2 minutes after the water returns to a boil. Transfer the pasta to the sauce with a spider and tongs. Drizzle with olive oil and add the parsley. Toss to coat the pasta with the sauce, adding a little more chickpea cooking liquid if it seems dry. Remove the skillet from the heat, add the grated cheese, toss, and serve.

ORECCHIETTE WITH ASPARAGUS AND PEAS

Orecchiette con Asparagi e Piselli

If fresh peas are in season, you can substitute them for the frozen, but cook them 3 or 4 minutes more. To make this a heartier (but still light and elegant) pasta entrée, add some sautéed shrimp or lobster meat. As is, it is vegetarian, and if you do not add the cheese, it makes a great dish for vegan guests.

Serves 6

1 teaspoon kosher salt, plus more for the pasta water
¼ cup extra-virgin olive oil, plus more for drizzling
4 cloves garlic, thinly sliced
1 large bunch medium-thick asparagus (about 1 pound), peeled and cut into 1-inch pieces
1 pound orecchiette
One 10-ounce box frozen peas, thawed
1 bunch scallions, white and green parts, chopped (about 1 cup)
¼ cup chopped fresh Italian parsley
1 cup grated Grana Padano

Bring a large pot of salted water to boil for the pasta. Add the olive oil to a large skillet over medium heat. When the oil is hot, add the garlic, and let it sizzle a minute. Add the asparagus, and toss to coat it in the oil. Cook and toss until the asparagus just begins to soften, about 5 minutes. (Add a splash of pasta water if the garlic is in danger of burning.) Cover with a lid.

Uncover the asparagus, and at the same time add the orecchiette to the pasta water. Add the peas to the asparagus, and season with the salt. Toss to combine, and cook about 2 to 3 minutes. Add the scallions, stir, and add 1½ cups pasta water. Bring to a boil, and cook until reduced by about half, about 3 to 4 minutes.

When the pasta is al dente, remove with a spider directly to the sauce. Add the parsley, drizzle with some olive oil, and toss to coat the pasta in the sauce, adding a little pasta water if it seems dry. Remove the skillet from the heat, sprinkle with the grated cheese, toss, and serve.

FUSILLI WITH ROASTED TOMATO PESTO

Fusilli con Pesto di Pomodoro Arrosto

This tomato pesto also makes a flavorful topping for bruschetta and works well as a sandwich spread with some cold cuts and cheese, or on some grilled chicken or fish.

Serves 6

2 small onions, sliced into ½-inch rings

6 ripe plum tomatoes, halved

6 tablespoons extra-virgin olive oil, plus more for drizzling

2 tablespoons tomato paste

1 teaspoon kosher salt, plus more for the pasta water

¼ teaspoon crushed red pepper flakes

1 pound fusilli

1 cup loosely packed fresh basil leaves

½ cup grated Grana Padano

2-ounce piece ricotta salata

Preheat oven to 400 degrees. In a large bowl, toss the onions and tomatoes with 3 tablespoons of the olive oil. Line a sheet pan with parchment. Pick out the onions and spread them on the parchment. Spread the tomato paste on the cut sides of the tomatoes, and place them, cut side up, on the sheet pan, in and around the onions. Sprinkle all with the salt and crushed red pepper. Roast until softened and golden brown, about 30 to 40 minutes.

While the tomatoes roast, bring a large pot of salted water to boil for the pasta. Once the tomatoes and onions are out of the oven, add the fusilli to the pasta water. Scrape the tomatoes and onions onto a cutting board, and sprinkle the basil leaves on top. Coarsely chop the mixture together, and put it in a large serving bowl.

When the spaghetti is al dente, remove it with tongs to the bowl with the pesto. Drizzle with the remaining 3 tablespoons olive oil and ½ cup pasta-cooking water. Sprinkle the grated Grana Padano over all, and toss well. Drizzle with a little more olive oil and pasta water if it seems dry, season with salt if needed, and toss again. Shave the ricotta salata in shreds over the top of the plated pasta, using a vegetable peeler, and serve immediately.

SPAGHETTI WITH ROASTED GARLIC PESTO

Spaghetti con Pesto d'Aglio

The pesto for this dish can be made earlier in the day, but toss it with the hot pasta and cheese just before serving. It is super-flavorful, and economical for a large crowd.

Serves 6

2 whole heads garlic
½ cup extra-virgin olive oil, plus more for drizzling
Kosher salt, for the pasta water and to taste
8 anchovy fillets
½ cup toasted slivered almonds
2 cups loosely packed fresh Italian parsley leaves
Pinch crushed red pepper flakes
1 pound spaghetti
½ cup grated Grana Padano

Preheat oven to 375 degrees. Cut the tops from the two heads of garlic. Place each bulb on a square of foil large enough to wrap it, drizzle each head with 1 tablespoon olive oil, and season with salt. Wrap the heads in foil, and roast the garlic until the cloves are completely softened, about 40 minutes. Let cool.

Bring a large pot of salted water to boil for the pasta. Squeeze the pulp from the garlic cloves into the work bowl of a mini–food processor (or in a bowl, if you're working by hand). Add the anchovies, almonds, parsley, and red pepper flakes. Process to make a paste; then, with the machine running, add the remaining 6 tablespoons olive oil to make a smooth pesto. Scrape the pesto into a serving bowl, and stir in ½ cup of the pasta-cooking water to loosen it up.

Cook the spaghetti until al dente. When the spaghetti is ready, remove it with tongs directly to the bowl with the pesto. Sprinkle with the grated cheese and toss. Season to taste with salt (the anchovies and cheese are salty, so take care), add a little pasta water if it still seems dry, toss, and serve.

MEZZI RIGATONI WITH SAUSAGE AND ESCAROLE

Mezzi Rigatoni con Salsicce e Scarola

If you can't find mezzi rigatoni, use another tube-shaped pasta, such as ziti, penne, gomiti, or rigatoni, to catch the bits of sausage and escarole. This recipe uses only the coarser outer leaves of escarole, so save the inner parts of the head for salad or for a recipe such as skillet escarole gratin (page 164). This is a crowd pleaser.

Serves 6

1 teaspoon salt, plus more for the pasta water
3 tablespoons extra-virgin olive oil
1¼ pounds sweet Italian sausage without fennel seeds (about 6 links), removed from casings
3 cloves garlic, thinly sliced
¼ teaspoon crushed red pepper flakes
Outer leaves from 2 heads escarole, coarsely chopped (about 10 cups)
1 pound mezzi rigatoni
1½ cups chicken stock (page 148)
1 cup grated Grana Padano

Bring a large pot of salted water to boil for the pasta. Add the olive oil to a large skillet over medium heat. When the oil is hot, add the sausage. Break the meat up with a wooden spoon, and cook until it's no longer pink, about 5 to 6 minutes.

Add the garlic and red pepper flakes, and let sizzle a minute. Add the chopped escarole, in batches if necessary, and season with the salt. Cover the escarole, and let it wilt, about 3 to 4 minutes.

Meanwhile, add the pasta to the water. Once the escarole has wilted, uncover and add the chicken stock. Bring to a simmer, and cook until the escarole is tender and the sauce has reduced by half, about 5 minutes.

When the pasta is al dente, remove it with a spider and transfer directly to the sauce. Toss to coat the pasta with the sauce, adding a little pasta water if it seems dry. Turn off the heat, and sprinkle with the grated cheese. Toss and serve.

ZITI WITH KALE PESTO AND CRISPY BACON

Ziti con Pesto di Cavolo Nero e Pancetta Croccante

Recycling leftovers and turning them into new dishes is one of the most noble forms of cooking, in which food is respected and not wasted. This quick dish can be made with the remaining kale pesto from page 274, to serve either as a first course, or for a family dinner the next day.

Serves 6

Kosher salt
1 pound ziti
3 tablespoons extra-virgin olive oil
4 cloves garlic, crushed and peeled
8 ounces slab bacon, cut into lardoons
2 cups kale pesto (page 274)
1 cup grated Grana Padano

Bring a large pot of salted water to boil for the pasta. Add the ziti and stir.

Meanwhile, add the olive oil to a large skillet over medium heat. When the oil is hot, add the garlic and let it sizzle a minute, then add the bacon. Cook and stir until the bacon renders its fat and crisps, about 6 minutes.

Add 1 cup pasta-cooking water to the skillet, and simmer until reduced by half, about 2 minutes.

When the pasta is al dente, remove it with a spider directly to the simmering sauce. Toss to coat the pasta with the sauce, adding a little more pasta water if it is dry.

Scrape the pesto into a large pasta-serving bowl. Pour the pasta over the top, mix well, add the grated cheese, and toss, adding up to ½ cup more pasta water if it seems dry.

BUCATINI WITH EGGPLANT AND TOMATO SAUCE

Bucatini con Melanzane e Pomodoro

Bucatini—large, hollow spaghetti—is a pasta much loved in Rome and southern Italy, as is the combination of tomatoes and eggplant. When you add fresh ricotta to the mix, you are cooking all'italiana, *and your guests will love it. This would be my pasta choice for a summer meal out on the patio or in the backyard.*

Serves 6

1 tablespoon kosher salt, plus more for the pasta
  water and to taste
2 medium eggplants (about 1½ pounds)
5 tablespoons extra-virgin olive oil
4 ounces pancetta, julienned
1 large onion, sliced
One 28-ounce can whole San Marzano tomatoes,
  crushed by hand
1 pound bucatini
½ cup loosely packed fresh basil leaves, chopped
1 cup fresh ricotta
½ cup grated Grana Padano

Bring a large pot of water to boil for the pasta. Cut the stems from the eggplants. With a vegetable peeler, remove strips of peel so the eggplant appears striped. Cut the eggplants into 1-inch cubes. Toss in a colander with 1 tablespoon kosher salt, and let sit in the sink and drain for 30 minutes. Rinse well, and pat very dry.

In a large skillet, heat 3 tablespoons of the olive oil over medium-high heat. When the oil is hot, add the eggplant cubes and brown all over, removing the cubes to a plate with a slotted spoon as they brown, about 6 to 7 minutes in all.

When all of the eggplant is out of the skillet, add the remaining 2 tablespoons olive oil and the pancetta. Cook until the pancetta begins to render its fat, about 3 to 4 minutes. Add the onion, and cook until just wilted, about 4 minutes. Add the tomatoes, slosh out the can with 1 cup pasta-cooking water, and add this to the skillet. Bring the sauce to a simmer, and cook until the eggplant is tender and melting but still holds its shape, and the sauce is thickened, about 20 minutes.

When the sauce is almost ready, cook the pasta. When the pasta is al dente, remove it with tongs directly to the simmering sauce. Sprinkle with the basil, and toss to coat the pasta with the sauce. Remove the skillet from the heat. Stir in the ricotta to combine. Sprinkle with the grated cheese, toss, and serve.

SEDANI WITH SEAFOOD SAUCE

Sedani con Salsa di Crostacei

Sedani pasta is a rather recent arrival in the United States. It has a shape that resembles rigatoni but is longer with ridges. It is the perfect pasta to catch all the seafood and tomato in this sauce, but linguine, though very different, is a good substitute. When you're cooking for guests, most pasta should be cooked and sauced immediately prior to serving, and sedani especially so. Be sure to use enough sauce, or the pasta pieces will begin to stick together.

Serves 6

1 teaspoon kosher salt, plus more for the pasta water

¼ cup extra-virgin olive oil, plus more for drizzling

4 cloves garlic, crushed and peeled

One 28-ounce can whole San Marzano tomatoes, crushed by hand

¼ teaspoon crushed red pepper flakes

18 littleneck clams, scrubbed

2 pounds mussels, scrubbed and debearded if necessary

1 pound sedani

8 ounces sea scallops, side muscle or "foot" removed, scallops halved crosswise

8 ounces jumbo shrimp, peeled and deveined

1 bunch scallions, white and green parts, chopped (about 1 cup)

¼ cup chopped fresh Italian parsley

In a large Dutch oven, bring salted water to boil for the pasta. In a large straight-sided skillet, heat the olive oil over medium heat. When the oil is hot, add the garlic and let it sizzle a minute; then add the tomatoes, slosh out the can with ½ cup water, and add this to the skillet. Add the salt and crushed red pepper flakes. Bring to a simmer, and cook to thicken and blend the flavors, about 10 minutes.

After 10 minutes, add the clams and cover the skillet. Cook until they just begin to open, about 3 minutes.

Uncover the skillet, add the mussels, and cover again. Add the pasta to the boiling water. Cook the mussels until they begin to open, about 3 to 4 minutes.

Uncover, and add the scallops and shrimp. Cook over high heat, uncovered, until the shrimp and scallops are cooked through, about 3 to 4 minutes; discard any clams and mussels that have not opened by then.

When the pasta is al dente, drain, reserving about 1 cup of pasta water. Put the pasta back in the pot, and pour in most of the seafood sauce, reserving some of the fish to add as a garnish. Add the scallions, parsley, and a drizzle of olive oil. Toss to coat the pasta with the sauce and wilt the scallions. Serve right away, topped with the remaining shellfish and sauce.

ZITI WITH PORK RIB GUAZZETTO

Ziti con Guazzetto di Costolette di Maiale

Some sauces are very versatile, and there are many ways to make a meal with them once cooked. This is one of those sauces. Not only is it delicious as a pasta sauce, but it is also good served over polenta or stirred in at the last minute to finish plain risotto. This recipe makes enough to sauce 2 pounds of pasta, with the ribs on the side, and can easily feed twelve people or more. You can serve half, with 1 pound of pasta, shred the remaining meat into the remaining sauce, and freeze for another meal.

Serves 10 to 12

4 pounds pork spareribs, cut into individual ribs
1 tablespoon kosher salt, plus more for the pasta water
¼ cup extra-virgin olive oil, plus more for drizzling
2 medium onions, chopped
3 stalks celery, chopped
4 cloves garlic, crushed and peeled
3 fresh bay leaves
1 cup dry white wine
½ teaspoon crushed red pepper flakes
Two 28-ounce cans whole San Marzano tomatoes, crushed by hand
3 leafy stalks fresh basil
2 pounds ziti
1 cup grated Grana Padano

Season the ribs all over with 1½ teaspoons of the salt. Heat a large Dutch oven over medium-high heat, and add the olive oil. When the oil is hot, add the ribs, in batches if necessary, and brown all over, removing them to a plate as they brown, about 10 minutes.

When all of the ribs are out, add the onions, cel-ery, and garlic, and reduce heat to medium. Cook until the vegetables begin to wilt, about 6 minutes. Add the bay leaves and white wine, and simmer to reduce the wine by half, about 2 minutes. Season with the remaining 1½ teaspoons salt and the red pepper flakes. Add the tomatoes, slosh out the can with 2 cups water, and add that to the pot. Nestle the ribs and basil sprigs in the sauce, and bring to a simmer. Cover, and cook until ribs are very tender, about 1¼ to 1½ hours.

When the ribs are done, bring a large pot of salted water to boil for the pasta. Add the ziti. Remove the ribs to a platter, ladle a little sauce over them, and discard the bay leaves and basil sprigs. Return the sauce to a boil, and reduce to your liking while the pasta cooks.

When the ziti is al dente, remove it with a spider directly to the sauce. Toss to coat the pasta, adding a drizzle of olive oil and a little pasta water if it seems dry. Remove the pot from the heat, sprinkle with the grated cheese, toss, and serve with the ribs on the side.

RIGATONI WITH ITALIAN AMERICAN MEAT SAUCE

Rigatoni con Salsa Italo Americana

This recipe is a traditional Italian American favorite for Sunday lunch. It makes enough sauce for 4 pounds of pasta. If you have a big crowd, you can use the whole batch, but if you only want to cook 1 pound of pasta, don't worry—the rest of the sauce will freeze well for several months. On a Sunday, this brings everyone in my family to the table.

Serves 15 to 20

¼ cup extra-virgin olive oil, plus more for drizzling
2 pounds sweet Italian sausage without fennel seeds (about 12 links)
4 pounds country-style pork ribs
4 teaspoons kosher salt, plus more for the pasta water
10 cloves garlic, chopped
2 cups dry red wine
4 fresh bay leaves
Four 28-ounce cans whole San Marzano tomatoes, crushed by hand
¼ teaspoon crushed red pepper flakes
4 pounds rigatoni
2 cups grated Grana Padano

Heat a very large Dutch oven over medium heat, and add the olive oil. When the oil is hot, add the sausages and brown all over, about 6 minutes. Remove them to a plate. Season the ribs with 1 teaspoon of the salt, and brown all over, about 8 minutes. Remove to the plate with the sausages.

When all of the meat is out of the pot, add the garlic, and let it sizzle a minute, taking care that it doesn't burn. Add the wine and bay leaves, bring to a boil, and boil to reduce the wine by half, about 3 minutes. Add the tomatoes, slosh out the can with 4 cups of water, and add that to the pot. Stir in the remaining tablespoon of salt and the red pepper flakes. Once the sauce is simmering, add the meat back in, cover, and simmer until the ribs are tender, about 1¼ to 1½ hours. Remove the bay leaves.

Bring a very large pot of salted water to boil for the pasta. Add the rigatoni. When the ribs are done, remove them and the sausages to a platter, and ladle a little sauce over the top to keep everything warm. Bring the sauce back to a simmer in the Dutch oven, and simmer while the pasta cooks, to reduce to your liking. When the pasta is al dente, remove it with a spider directly to the pot. Toss to coat the pasta with the sauce, adding a little pasta water if it seems dry. Drizzle with olive oil, and toss again. Remove from the heat, add the grated cheese, and toss. Serve the pasta from the pot, with the platter of meat alongside.

SPAGHETTI WITH BOLOGNESE SAUCE

Spaghetti alla Bolognese

This sauce is most often paired with spaghetti, but it is very versatile and is also great when used to dress fresh pastas, such as fettuccine or gnocchi, or in making a rich lasagna. This recipe makes about 6 cups of sauce, enough for 2 pounds of dry pasta. If you're feeding a smaller crowd, the sauce will keep for several days in the fridge and also freezes well.

Serves 12

1 medium yellow onion, cut into chunks
1 medium carrot, cut into chunks
2 stalks celery, cut into chunks
3 tablespoons extra-virgin olive oil
2 teaspoons kosher salt, plus more for the pasta water
¼ teaspoon crushed red pepper flakes
1 pound ground beef
1 pound ground pork
½ cup dry red wine
1 tablespoon tomato paste
3 cups canned whole San Marzano tomatoes, with their liquid, passed through a vegetable mill or crushed by hand
3 fresh bay leaves
2 pounds spaghetti
1 cup grated Grana Padano

In a saucepan, bring 4 cups water to a bare simmer. In a food processor, pulse the onion, carrot, and celery to make a fine-textured paste or *pestata*.

Heat the olive oil in a large, wide Dutch oven over medium heat. Stir in the *pestata,* and season with 1 teaspoon salt and the red pepper flakes. Cook, stirring, until the *pestata* dries out and begins to stick to the bottom of the pot, about 8 minutes.

Crumble in the ground beef and pork, and continue cooking, stirring to break up the meat, until all the liquid the meat has given off is evaporated and the meat is lightly browned, about 10 minutes.

Pour in the wine, and cook, scraping the bottom of the pan, until the wine is evaporated, 3 to 4 minutes. Stir in the tomato paste, and cook a few minutes. Pour in the tomatoes, toss in the bay leaves, and season with the remaining teaspoon of salt. Bring to a boil, then lower the heat so the sauce is at a lively simmer. Cook, stirring occasionally, until the sauce is dense but juicy and a rich, dark-red color. (Most likely, a noticeable layer of oil will float to the top toward the end of cooking. This oil can be removed with a spoon or, as is traditional, reincorporated into the sauce.) This will take about 2 to 3 hours, and the longer you cook it, the better it will become. While the sauce is cooking, add hot water from the saucepan you heated, as necessary to keep the meats covered. When done, remove the bay leaves.

Bring a very large pot of salted water to boil for the pasta. Add the spaghetti, and cook until al dente. When the pasta is done, remove it with tongs straight to the simmering sauce. Toss to coat the pasta with the sauce, adding a splash of pasta water if it seems dry. Off heat, sprinkle with the grated cheese, and toss well.

BAKED STUFFED SHELLS

Conchiglie Ripiene al Forno

This recipe multiplies well, so it's good for when you're entertaining large groups. The shells can be stuffed and assembled ahead of time. Return them to room temperature, and add the final topping of sauce and cheese just before baking.

Serves 8

1 teaspoon kosher salt, plus more for the pasta water

¼ cup extra-virgin olive oil

6 cloves garlic, crushed and peeled

¼ teaspoon crushed red pepper flakes

Two 28-ounce cans whole San Marzano tomatoes, crushed by hand

1 pound large pasta shells

1 pound fresh ricotta, drained overnight

16 ounces low-moisture mozzarella cut into small cubes, plus 4 ounces shredded

2 cups grated Grana Padano

1 bunch scallions, chopped

8 ounces frozen peas, thawed

3 tablespoons chopped fresh Italian parsley

1 large egg, beaten

½ cup loosely packed fresh basil

Preheat oven to 400 degrees. Bring a large pot of salted water to a boil for the pasta. In a Dutch oven, heat the olive oil over medium heat. Add the garlic and cook until the edges are just golden, about 2 minutes. Sprinkle in the crushed red pepper. Add the tomatoes, slosh out the can with 1 cup of cooking water, and add that to the pot. Stir in the salt, and bring to a rapid simmer. Cook, uncovered, until thickened, about 20 minutes.

While the sauce cooks, add the shells to the boiling pasta water and cook until just al dente. Drain, and separate shells on baking sheets to avoid sticking.

For the filling, stir together in a bowl the ricotta, cubed mozzarella, 1 cup grated Grana Padano, the scallions, peas, parsley, and egg. Mix the shredded mozzarella and remaining grated Grana Padano in another bowl, and set aside. Stir the basil into the finished sauce.

To assemble, in a 10-by-15-inch or other large baking dish, spread 2 cups of the sauce. Divide the filling evenly among the shells, and arrange them in one layer in the baking dish. Top evenly with 2 cups more sauce. Sprinkle with the reserved cheese mixture. Dollop the remaining sauce evenly over the top. Tent with foil, and bake until bubbly all over, about 25 to 30 minutes. Remove foil, and bake until cheese is golden and crusty, 5 to 10 minutes more. Let sit 5 minutes before serving.

PAPPARDELLE WITH BEEF GUAZZETTO

Pappardelle con Guazzetto di Manzo

This sauce is very hearty, so 1 pound of pasta will feed up to eight people. It is also delicious served with tajarin (page 228).

Serves 6 to 8

6 cups chicken stock (page 148)

½ cup dried porcini mushrooms

2 pounds boneless beef chuck, cut into 2-inch cubes

1½ teaspoons kosher salt, plus more for the pasta water

All-purpose flour, for dredging

5 tablespoons extra-virgin olive oil

1 large onion, chopped

2 cups coarsely grated carrots

¼ cup tomato paste

1 cup dry white wine

3 fresh bay leaves

Pinch ground cloves

1 pound pappardelle

½ cup grated Grana Padano

Bring the stock to a simmer in a small saucepan. Put the porcini in a spouted measuring cup, and add 1 cup of the hot stock. Season the beef all over with ½ teaspoon of the salt. Spread some flour on a plate, and lightly dredge the beef in the flour, tapping off the excess. Heat 3 tablespoons of the olive oil in a large Dutch oven over medium heat. When the oil is hot, add the beef and brown all over, about 8 minutes. Remove the beef chunks to a plate as they brown.

Once all of the beef is out, add the remaining 2 tablespoons olive oil to the Dutch oven. When the oil is hot, add the onion and carrot, and cook until the onion softens, about 6 minutes. Clear a space in the pan, and add the tomato paste. Cook and stir the tomato paste in that spot until it toasts and darkens a shade or two, about 2 minutes. Stir the tomato paste into the vegetables, and add the wine. Bring to a simmer, and cook until reduced by half, about 2 minutes. Add the bay leaves, cloves, and remaining teaspoon of salt. Remove the porcini from the soaking liquid and chop; add them to the pot. Pour the soaking liquid into the pot, leaving the grit behind in the bottom of the cup. Add the beef back to the pot, and ladle in enough of the hot stock just to cover the beef. Cover, and simmer until the beef is very tender and falling apart, about 1½ to 2 hours, adding more stock as you go to maintain the level of liquid (if you run out of stock, add a little water). Remove the bay leaves.

When the beef is almost ready, bring a large pot of salted water to boil for the pasta. Add the pasta. Bring the beef and sauce to a boil, and cook a minute or two to thicken the sauce to your liking. When the pasta is al dente, remove with a spider directly to the sauce. Toss to coat the pasta with the sauce, adding a little pasta water if it seems dry. Remove the pot from the heat. Sprinkle with the grated cheese, toss, and serve.

LASAGNA WITH RICOTTA AND MOZZARELLA

Lasagna con Ricotta e Mozzarella

This recipe will give you twelve long sheets of pasta. Don't worry if there are a few tears, or some sheets are longer than others. The most important layer is the four sheets at the bottom, so reserve the four best for that. After that, use the sheets you have left as instructed below, cutting and patching if necessary.

Buying fresh sheets of pasta is a good option if you are short of time.

The mozzarella will be easier to slice if you pop it in the freezer for 15 to 20 minutes first. You can assemble the lasagna ahead of time, but return it to room temperature before baking.

Serves 8 to 12

PASTA

2 recipes poor man's two-egg pasta dough (recipe follows)

SAUCE

¼ cup extra-virgin olive oil
5 cloves garlic, thinly sliced
Two 28-ounce cans whole San Marzano tomatoes, crushed by hand
¼ teaspoon crushed red pepper flakes
1½ teaspoons kosher salt
½ cup loosely packed fresh basil leaves, chopped

FILLING

3 pounds fresh ricotta, drained overnight
1 cup grated Grana Padano
2 large eggs, beaten
½ cup chopped fresh Italian parsley
½ teaspoon kosher salt

ASSEMBLY

Unsalted butter, softened, for the baking dish
1½ pounds fresh mozzarella, thinly sliced
1½ cups grated Grana Padano

Make the pasta dough, and let it rest 30 minutes at room temperature while you make the sauce. (Don't try to make a double batch at once in a standard food processor—it's too much. Make two single batches.)

Preheat oven to 375 degrees. For the sauce, heat the olive oil in a large Dutch oven over medium heat. When the oil is hot, add the garlic, and cook until it's just golden on the edges, about 1 to 2 minutes. Add the tomatoes, slosh out the can with 1½ cups of water, and add that to the pan. Season the sauce with the red pepper flakes and salt. Simmer until slightly thickened, about 20 minutes. Stir in the chopped basil. You should have about 6 to 6½ cups sauce.

To roll the pasta, cut each dough ball into six pieces. Keep the pieces covered as you work, and line several baking sheets with floured kitchen towels.

Flatten each piece, then roll it through the pasta machine on the widest setting several times, folding it like a letter (rectangle) each time to smooth the dough. Once you have a smooth rectangle, continue to roll the piece through the settings, skipping one setting each time you roll, stopping at the next-to-last setting. A hand pasta machine usually has nine settings and in rolling the sheets of pasta, each new setting will make the pasta thinner. Layer the thin sheets of pasta without touching, on the floured towels. You should have twelve long sheets of dough.

Set up a large roasting pan filled with ice water next to the boiling pasta water. Cook the sheets of pasta, a few at a time, until still quite al dente, about 2 to 3 minutes per batch once the water returns to a boil. As they're cooked, cool the sheets in the ice water, then store them on baking sheets lined with damp kitchen towels.

For the filling, stir together the ricotta, grated cheese, eggs, parsley, and salt in a large bowl. Mix well to combine.

When you are ready to assemble the lasagna, butter a 4-quart lasagna pan. Spread 1 cup sauce in the bottom of the baking dish. Pick out the two longest sheets of pasta and lay them in the baking dish so they overlap in the center of the dish and the ends of the pasta sheets flop over the short sides of the baking dish. Spread another ½ cup sauce over the pasta. Fit two more pasta sheets in the dish, perpendicular to the first layer and flopping over the long sides of the dish. (After these two layers, the pasta should no longer go over the sides—cut the cooked pasta as you are layering the lasagna and fold to fit the pasta to the dimensions of the dish.)

Spread another ½ cup of sauce over the pasta and spread with half of the filling. Layer with half of the sliced mozzarella, and sprinkle with ½ cup grated Grana Padano. Make another layer of pasta, cutting and folding to fit the dish. Spread with another ½ cup sauce, the remaining filling, the remaining sliced mozzarella, and ½ cup grated Grana Padano. Top with another pasta layer, and press lightly.

Add another layer of pasta sheets to cover the lasagna, then 1 cup sauce. Then cut and fold a final layer of pasta on top of the sauce to seal the lasagna. Fold the flopping edges over the top, and spread with the remaining sauce. Sprinkle with the remaining grated Grana Padano. Tent the lasagna with foil (making sure it doesn't touch the top), place on a sheet pan to catch drips, and bake until the edges of the lasagna are bubbly, about 45 minutes. Uncover, and bake until the top is golden and crusty, about 30 minutes more. Let the lasagna rest about 20 minutes before cutting into squares and serving. The lasagna cuts best when it has rested and cooled.

POOR MAN'S TWO-EGG PASTA DOUGH

Pasta Fresca con Due Uova

This is a great basic recipe for rolled pasta for lasagna, manicotti, or fettucine as well as for ravioli, strong yet still tender. For rolling and cutting instructions, see the individual recipes. You can also make this dough by hand, without a food processor, though the kneading time will be longer (about 5 minutes total).

Makes about 1 pound

2 cups all-purpose flour, sifted, plus more as needed
2 large eggs
¼ cup extra-virgin olive oil

Put the flour in the work bowl of a food processor, and pulse several times to aerate. In a spouted measuring cup, combine the eggs, olive oil, and 3 tablespoons cold water. Beat with a fork to combine.

With the processor running, pour the egg mixture through the feed tube and process until the dough forms a ball around the blade. If the dough doesn't begin to form a ball after about 15 seconds, add a little more flour (if it is too wet) or water (if it is too crumbly), and process until you get a ball. Once the ball forms, process about 30 seconds to make a smooth and homogeneous dough.

Dump the dough onto the counter, and knead a few times to make a completely smooth ball of dough that springs back when pressed. Wrap the dough in plastic, and let it rest at room temperature for 30 minutes. (The dough can also be made a day ahead, wrapped, and refrigerated. Return it to room temperature before proceeding.)

TAGLIATELLE WITH PORCINI MUSHROOM SAUCE

Tagliatelle al Funghi Porcini

If you don't have a tagliatelle attachment for your pasta machine, just roll the sheets of pasta like a jelly roll and cut them lengthwise at ½-inch intervals with a sharp knife or pizza cutter, making sure you dust liberally with flour so the pasta does not stick. Or, if pressed for time, you can use store-bought dry tagliatelle nests. This simple yet elegant dish would be a quick and easy first course for a special fall dinner party. It is best with porcini mushrooms, but any good fresh mushroom, or a mixture of different varieties, will make a good sauce as well.

Serves 4 to 6

1 recipe poor man's two-egg pasta dough (preceding recipe)

1 teaspoon kosher salt, plus more for the cooking pot and to taste

¼ cup extra-virgin olive oil

1 pound fresh porcini mushrooms, trimmed and sliced

4 cloves garlic, crushed and peeled

Freshly ground black pepper, to taste

2 tablespoons unsalted butter

3 tablespoons chopped fresh Italian parsley

¾ cup chicken stock (page 148)

½ cup grated Grana Padano

To roll the pasta, cut the dough ball into six pieces. Keep the pieces covered as you work, and line several baking sheets with floured kitchen towels.

Flatten each piece, then roll it through the pasta machine on the widest setting several times, folding it like a letter (rectangle) each time to smooth and strengthen the dough. Once you have a smooth rectangle, continue to roll the piece through each setting, stopping at the next-to-last setting. Layer the pieces, without touching, on the floured towels.

Fasten the pasta-cutting attachment to the machine, and run the sheets through the wider setting for tagliatelle, or cut by hand (see headnote). Dust the strands of pasta, and form them into loose nests on the floured baking sheets. (The pasta can be made earlier in the day and allowed to sit at room temperature, uncovered, until you're ready to cook.)

When you're ready to cook, bring a large pot of salted water to boil for the pasta. Add 2 tablespoons of the olive oil to a large skillet over medium-high heat. When the oil is hot, add half of the mushrooms and garlic, and season with ½ teaspoon salt and some pepper. Cook until the mushrooms are lightly browned on both sides, about 4 minutes. Do not stir the porcini, or they will break; rather, turn them gently with a spatula. Transfer the porcini to a plate, and proceed as before with the remaining oil, garlic, porcini, salt, and pepper.

Discard the excess oil from the skillet, and, over medium heat, return all of the porcini to the pan; add the butter and parsley. Adjust the seasoning, add the stock, and simmer until the mushrooms are tender, about 5 minutes. Meanwhile, add the pasta to the boiling water. As soon as the pasta is done, about 1 to 1½ minutes after it returns to a boil, gently remove with tongs and a spider to the sauce. Add a little pasta water if the sauce seems dry. Sprinkle with the grated cheese, toss, and serve.

TAJARIN PASTA WITH TRUFFLES

Tajarin al Tartufo

This rich dish is the one to make when you want an easy showstopper. The pasta can be made ahead of time, but don't cook it or make the sauce until the very last minute—and shave the truffles tableside if you can, so your guests get the full aroma. The pasta dough here is richer and more delicate than the poor man's two-egg recipe on page 226, but you can also use that one.

Serves 6 to 8

PASTA

2 cups all-purpose flour, plus more for working the dough

9 large egg yolks (about ⅔ cup)

2 tablespoons extra-virgin olive oil

COOKING AND DRESSING THE PASTA

Kosher salt

2 sticks unsalted butter

1 cup grated Grana Padano

1 ounce fresh white truffle (or more!!), brushed clean

For the pasta, put the flour in the work bowl of a food processor, and pulse several times to aerate. In a spouted measuring cup, combine the egg yolks, olive oil, and 3 tablespoons cold water. Beat with a fork to combine.

With the processor running, pour the egg mixture through the feed tube and process until the dough forms a ball around the blade. If the dough doesn't begin to form a ball after about 15 seconds, add a little more flour (if it is too wet) or water (if it is too crumbly), and process until you get a ball. Once the ball forms, process about 30 seconds to make a smooth and homogeneous dough.

Dump the dough onto the counter, and knead

a few times to make a completely smooth ball that springs back when pressed. Wrap the dough in plastic, and let it rest at room temperature for 30 minutes. (The dough can be made a day ahead, wrapped, and refrigerated. Return it to room temperature before proceeding.)

Cut the dough into four equal pieces. Keeping it lightly floured, roll each piece through a pasta machine at progressively narrower settings into sheets that are 5 inches wide (or as wide as your machine allows) and 20 inches or more long. Cut each strip crosswise into three shorter rectangles, each about 7 inches long.

Flour each of these rectangles, and roll it up the long way, into a loose cylinder, like a fat cigar. With a sharp knife, cut cleanly through the rolled dough crosswise at ¼-inch intervals. Shake and unroll the cut pieces, opening them into tajarin ribbons, each about 7 inches long and about ¼ inch wide. Dust them liberally with flour, and fold the tajarin into loose pasta nests and set on floured towels on sheet trays.

When you're ready to cook the pasta, bring a large pot of salted water to a boil. In a large skillet over medium heat, melt the butter. When the butter is melted, add about ½ cup of the hot pasta-cooking water, and bring it to a boil while you cook the pasta.

Shake off excess flour from the tajarin in a colander, and add them to the boiling water. Cook for only a minute, or until the pasta is just al dente, then lift it from the water with a spider and tongs, drain briefly, and drop it into the skillet.

Over low heat, toss the tajarin until well coated with butter. Turn off the heat, and toss in the grated cheese. Shave coin-sized flakes of truffle, using half the piece, over the pasta, and toss in.

Heap individual portions of pasta into warm bowls. Quickly shave the remaining truffle, in equal shares, on top of each mound of tajarin, and serve immediately.

ROMAN-STYLE SEMOLINA GNOCCHI

Gnocchi alla Romana

At our restaurant Lidia's Kansas City, some of the favorite offerings on the menu are the three daily pasta specials served tableside, and these Roman-style semolina gnocchi are always popular with customers. This is a more convenient version of gnocchi that, instead of a kneaded dough, uses semolina flour cooked like polenta, allowed to chill, then cut into pieces. This is a perfect dish for entertaining, because it can be assembled and refrigerated up to a day before you bake it, and you can easily multiply the recipe to make large quantities for a big group.

Serves 6 to 8

GNOCCHI

5 cups milk
4 tablespoons unsalted butter
1 teaspoon kosher salt
1½ cups coarse semolina flour

ASSEMBLY

6 tablespoons unsalted butter, melted, plus softened butter for the baking dish
2 cups shredded Taleggio
1 cup grated Grana Padano

Put the milk, butter, and salt in a saucepan. Set over medium heat, stirring occasionally until the milk is hot and the butter melted, then gradually pour in the semolina, whisking steadily. Cook the semolina slowly, over medium-low heat, for 30 minutes or more, until it's thickened, switching to a wooden spoon when it becomes too thick to whisk. When the semolina is very thick, scrape and flatten it into an even layer, about ½ inch thick, on a rimmed baking sheet. Let it cool to room temperature, or until solid.

Preheat oven to 400 degrees. Generously butter a very large dish (14-inch oval, or two smaller dishes). Flip the semolina out onto the counter, and cut into 2-inch squares with a sharp knife. Lay the squares point side up (so they look like diamonds) in the baking dish, with the gnocchi squares slightly overlapping like shingles.

Drizzle with the melted butter. In a medium bowl, toss together the Taleggio and grated Grana Padano. Sprinkle cheese over gnocchi.

Bake the gnocchi for 30 minutes, or until the butter is bubbling in the pan and the top is a beautiful golden brown. Let the dish sit for about 5 minutes; cut into squares, and serve hot.

PEAR AND PECORINO RAVIOLI WITH CACIO E PEPE SAUCE

Ravioli di Pere e Pecorino con Salsa Cacio e Pepe

These ravioli are a favorite at Felidia Restaurant, so popular that we cannot take them off the menu. They are easy to make, vegetarian, and a flavorful mouthful. They can be frozen—just be certain to freeze them flat on a tray. Once they're frozen, you can collect and seal them in a plastic container. Do not use a plastic bag, because they chip easily when frozen, and if they're broken the filling will seep out during cooking.

Serves 6

FILLING
2 medium Bartlett pears, ripe but firm
8 ounces Pecorino Romano, freshly shredded
4 ounces grated Grana Padano
2 to 3 tablespoons mascarpone

PASTA
1 recipe poor man's two-egg pasta dough (page 226)
1 large egg, beaten, for egg wash
Kosher salt, for the pasta water

SAUCE
1½ sticks unsalted butter
4 ounces Pecorino Romano (aged 12 months), grated
2 ounces grated Grana Padano
Freshly ground black pepper, to taste

For the filling, peel and core the pears, and shred them against the large holes of a box grater. Stir the shreds with the Pecorino Romano and Grana Padano in a bowl, and blend in the mascarpone. Mix the filling well.

Cut the ball of dough into four pieces. Work with one piece at a time, and keep the others moist in a closed plastic bag. Roll the first piece of dough, using a pasta machine, and make sure your strip is 5 inches wide on the first setting. When you have stretched the dough to approximately 20 inches long, having narrowed the setting twice, cut it crosswise into two 10-inch strips. Roll each of these to 20 inches, long enough for five ravioli. Measurements need not be exact. If your dough stretches to 24 inches, make six ravioli; if your strips are a bit shorter, that's all right, too.

Lay the two strips out on a very lightly floured surface. The strips should be the same length and width; stretch them gently by hand to widen or lengthen as needed. If one strip is clearly wider than the other, use that as the top strip, to drape over the filling. Repeat with remaining pieces of dough, keeping the other strips covered with a moist cloth to prevent drying out.

With a spoon (or your fingers), place a dollop of filling in a mound on the left or right end of your designated bottom strip. The center of the mound should be 2 inches away from the edge. Place the next portions of filling at 4-inch intervals from the first filling. You should have room for five or six mounds on the strip. Press the top of the mounds lightly, to flatten and spread them just a bit.

Brush a thin strip of beaten egg along the top, bottom, and side edges of the dough strip and in between all the mounds of filling. Pick up the top strip, and drape it over the filling mounds, lining up the edges with the bottom dough strip on all sides, and stretching it gently so it covers the bottom completely. Press the dough layers together lightly, but only along the stripes of egg glue, leaving a bit of air space around the filling.

With a pastry-cutting wheel, cut along the top, bottom, and side edges of the ravioli strips in straight lines, trimming away as little of the dough as possible. Then cut in between the mounds, separating the ravioli.

Arrange the finished ravioli on a lightly floured towel-lined tray. Cover with a cloth, and make more ravioli from the remaining pieces of dough. The ravioli can stay like this 2 to 3 hours before being cooked.

When you're ready to cook, bring a large pot of salted water to boil for the pasta. Meanwhile, in a large skillet, melt the butter over medium heat. Once it's melted, add 1 cup pasta-cooking water, and bring to a boil while you cook the ravioli.

Gently slide the ravioli into the boiling water. Cook, stirring gently to separate, until they're al dente, about 2 minutes after the water returns to a boil.

Remove ravioli with a spider, lay the cooked ravioli in the skillet, and coat with the hot butter. Mix together the grated Pecorino Romano and Grana Padano. Remove the pan from the heat, and sprinkle with the grated cheeses, mixing gently so the cheese begins to melt into a sauce. Season liberally with black pepper, and serve.

SAUSAGE AND RICOTTA–FILLED RAVIOLI

Ravioli Ripieni di Salsicce e Ricotta

Ricotta is a common filling for ravioli in Italy, usually mixed with other ingredients, such as spinach, Swiss chard, or leftover braised or roasted meats. This recipe, which calls for sausage, is flavorful and easy to prepare.

Serves 6

MARINARA SAUCE

¼ cup extra-virgin olive oil
4 cloves garlic, thinly sliced
Pinch crushed red pepper flakes
One 28-ounce can whole San Marzano tomatoes, crushed by hand
1 teaspoon kosher salt
3 leafy stalks fresh basil, plus ¼ cup leaves, chopped

RAVIOLI

1 small onion, quartered
1 small stalk celery, cut into chunks
1 small carrot, cut into chunks
3 tablespoons extra-virgin olive oil
12 ounces sweet Italian sausage, without fennel seeds, removed from casings
¼ cup dry white wine
1 cup fresh ricotta, drained overnight
¼ cup grated Grana Padano, plus more for sprinkling
¼ cup chopped fresh Italian parsley
1 batch poor man's two-egg pasta dough (page 226)

For the marinara sauce, in a large skillet, heat the olive oil over medium heat. When the oil is hot, add the garlic, and cook until the edges just turn golden, about 1 minute. Season with the red pepper flakes, then add the tomatoes, slosh out the can with 1 cup of hot water, and add that to the pan. Bring to a simmer, add the salt and sprigs of basil, and cook until slightly thickened, about 15 minutes. Remove and discard basil sprigs.

For the filling, in a food processor, pulse the onion, celery, and carrot until finely chopped. Add the olive oil to a large skillet over medium heat. When the oil is hot, add the vegetables, and cook until they release their liquid and begin to soften, about 4 minutes.

In a bowl, crumble the sausage into small pieces, and pour the wine over it. Work the wine into the sausage with your fingers. Add the sausage to the skillet. Cook, crumbling, until the sausage is cooked through and in very small pieces, about 4 to 5 minutes. Scrape filling into a bowl to cool, then stir in the ricotta, grated cheese, and parsley.

To roll the dough, cut it into four equal pieces, and flatten into squares. Roll through the widest setting on a pasta machine, fold like a letter, and roll through again. Fold and roll once more to smooth and straighten the dough, then repeat with the remaining three pieces of dough.

Roll each strip through the progressive settings of the machine, stopping at the next-to-last setting, aiming for strips that are about 6 inches wide.

Lay one strip on a floured counter, and place heaping teaspoons of filling at about 4-inch intervals down the lower half of the strip (to get about 6 to 7 mounds per strip). Brush around the filling with water. Fold the top edge over to meet the bottom and press to seal, leaving a little airspace. Using a pastry-cutting wheel, cut into squares, evenly between the mounds of filling. Repeat with the remaining dough and filling. Store the ravioli on baking sheets lined with floured kitchen towels.

When you're ready to cook, bring a large pot of salted water to boil for the pasta. Heat the marinara to a simmer in a large skillet. Drop the ravioli into the boiling water, stir gently to separate them, and simmer until al dente, about 2 minutes from the time the water boils again.

When the ravioli are cooked, gently remove with a spider to the simmering sauce. Add the chopped basil, and toss gently to coat the pasta with the sauce, adding a little pasta water if it seems dry. Sprinkle with grated cheese, toss gently, and serve.

SPAGHETTI WITH ANCHOVIES AND BREAD CRUMBS

Spaghetti con Acciughe e Mollica

Bread crumbs on pasta are known as poor man's cheese; they are often used as a great sub-stitute for cheese for lactose-sensitive individuals. They bring a nice crunch to the pasta and are quite popular in the southern regions of Italy, such as Sicily, Calabria, and Basilicata.

Serves 6

Kosher salt
One 3-to-4-inch chunk day-old country bread
6 tablespoons extra-virgin olive oil, plus more for
    drizzling
1 pound spaghetti
12 good-quality anchovy fillets, drained
4 cloves garlic, sliced
¼ to ½ teaspoon crushed red pepper flakes (or 1 or
    2 dried Calabrian chiles, crumbled)
¼ cup chopped fresh Italian parsley

Bring a large pot of salted water to boil for the pasta. Grate the bread on the large holes of a box grater (or pulse in a processor) to make ¾ cup coarse crumbs.

Heat 2 tablespoons of the olive oil in a small skillet over medium-low heat. Add the bread crumbs, and cook, tossing frequently, until light golden and crisp, about 5 minutes. Set aside.

Add the spaghetti to the boiling water. Heat the remaining 4 tablespoons olive oil in a large skillet over medium heat. Add the anchovies and garlic, and cook until the anchovies dissolve into the oil and the garlic is golden, about 2 to 3 minutes. Ladle in 2 cups of pasta cooking water and let simmer rapidly. Reduce to about 1 cup while the pasta cooks.

Once the pasta is al dente, remove with tongs and add to the sauce. Add the parsley, and toss to coat the pasta with the sauce, adding a little more pasta water if it seems dry. Add the bread crumbs, and toss to mix.

BAKED RIGATONI WITH TOMATO
SAUCE, MEATBALLS, AND EGGS

Pasta "Chinja"

Although the name here is very Calabrian, the dish is quite universal. Who doesn't love pasta with juicy meatballs and cheese? This recipe makes almost double the sauce and meatballs you'll need, so freeze the rest for dinner another night.

Serves 6 to 8

1 small onion, roughly chopped

1 small carrot, roughly chopped

1 stalk celery, roughly chopped

1 cup loosely packed fresh Italian parsley leaves

4 cloves garlic, crushed and peeled

2 tablespoons extra-virgin olive oil, plus more for drizzling

Two 28-ounce cans whole San Marzano tomatoes, crushed by hand

¼ to ½ teaspoon crushed red pepper flakes

½ teaspoon kosher salt

1 pound sweet Italian sausage, removed from casings

1 large egg

¾ cup fine dried bread crumbs

½ cup freshly grated Pecorino Romano

½ cup freshly grated Grana Padano

1 pound rigatoni

3 hard-boiled eggs, peeled and sliced

3 cups freshly grated Caciocavallo

2 ounces sliced spicy sopressata, cut into strips

Preheat oven to 425 degrees. Bring a large pot of salted water to boil for the pasta. Add the onion, carrot, celery, parsley, and garlic to the bowl of a food processor, and process to make a smooth paste, or *pestata*.

Heat a large Dutch oven over medium-high heat. Add the olive oil. When the oil is hot, add about two-thirds of the *pestata*, and cook, stirring occasionally, until the *pestata* dries out and sticks to the bottom of the pot, about 4 to 5 minutes. Add the tomatoes, red pepper flakes, salt, and 1½ cups pasta water. Bring to a simmer.

Meanwhile, in a large bowl, combine the sausage, raw egg, bread crumbs, and ¼ cup each Pecorino Romano and Grana Padano. Mix well with your hands, and form into about 30 (1-inch) meatballs. Add the meatballs to the sauce, and simmer until the sauce is thick and flavorful and the meatballs are cooked through, about 20 minutes.

When the sauce is almost ready, add the pasta to the pasta water. Remove half of the sauce and meatballs to another container, and reserve for another time. When the pasta is al dente, transfer it to the simmering sauce, drizzle with olive oil, and toss to coat with the sauce.

Spread half of the pasta and meatballs into a 9-by-13-inch baking dish. Cover with the hard-boiled egg slices in an even layer. Sprinkle with half of the remaining Pecorino Romano and Grana Padano, half of the Caciocavallo, and all of the sopressata. Spread the remaining pasta and meatballs over top. Sprinkle with the remaining grated Caciocavallo, Pecorino Romano, and Grana Padano. Bake, uncovered, until browned and bubbly, about 20 to 25 minutes.

Fish and Seafood

I love planning a dinner party based on seafood. It is easier to stay on top of things when cooking just one type of protein, and it makes choosing wine for the evening nice and easy. I try to diversify my seafood choices, perhaps beginning with mussels with fennel and saffron (page 252) or octopus and potato salad (page 254) as an appetizer, and then serving crustaceans, such as lemony shrimp over zucchini (page 244), or a fish, such as swordfish Bagnara style (page 258), for the main course.

Fish is a staple on my table all year long. In the winter months, there's nothing I like more than halibut baked with tomato and onions (page 256) or cabbage rolls stuffed with salmon (page 261). Not everyone likes fish, so I always make sure to have plenty of vegetables on hand, including some that are hearty enough to serve as main courses.

For a summer party based around fish, I prefer to use the grill and make some shrimp spiedini with zucchini and tomato salsa (page 246), perhaps served with a green salad, some asparagus and leeks in lemon vinaigrette (page 104), and maybe some seared tuna or salmon. I really enjoy baked stuffed calamari (page 242), clam soup (page 247), and roasted lobster with fennel (page 253), with stuffed vegetables and baked potatoes as side dishes. The latter is something the whole family can enjoy; depending on how you dress the table and room, you can make it as elegant (with lobster forks) or homey (put out bibs and let your guests get their fingers dirty) as you like. . . . I prefer the latter.

STUFFED CALAMARI

Calamari Ripieni

You can stuff the calamari ahead of time, then just bake at the last minute. Take care not to overfill them, or they may burst as they contract during cooking. Also, make sure not to overcook: the calamari can become tough. This dish is great served family style on platters and is delicious hot out of the oven, but also good served at room temperature. If you are planning an elegant dinner, these calamari become a marvelous appetizer, one per person, when served over grilled polenta (page 67).

Serves 8

CALAMARI

2 cups fine dried bread crumbs
1 cup grated Grana Padano
2 hard-boiled eggs, finely chopped
¼ cup chopped fresh Italian parsley
¼ cup extra-virgin olive oil
¼ teaspoon kosher salt
½ cup white wine, or as needed
2 pounds medium calamari (about 6 inches long), tubes only

SAUCE

1 cup dry white wine
¼ cup extra-virgin olive oil
½ cup drained capers in brine
3 cloves garlic, sliced
Juice of 1 lemon
1 lemon, thinly sliced into half-moons
3 anchovy fillets, chopped
2 tablespoons chopped fresh Italian parsley
½ teaspoon kosher salt
¼ teaspoon crushed red pepper flakes

Preheat oven to 450 degrees. For the calamari, in a large bowl, combine the bread crumbs, grated cheese, chopped eggs, parsley, olive oil, and salt, and toss to combine. Drizzle in about half of the wine, and toss. Continue to add wine until you've got a moist stuffing that clumps together a little when pressed in the palm of your hand.

Loosely fill the calamari with the stuffing. You can seal the larger opening with a toothpick if you want, but it's not essential.

For the sauce, in a 15-by-10-inch or other large baking dish (you want the calamari to sit in one layer), combine the wine, olive oil, capers, garlic, lemon juice, lemon slices, anchovies, parsley, salt, and red pepper flakes. Arrange the calamari in one layer on top, and spoon some of the juices over. Bake on the bottom rack of the oven for 15 minutes.

Baste the calamari with the pan juices, then continue baking until the calamari are tender, about 15 to 20 minutes more. (Add a little water if the pan juices are in danger of reducing away.) Serve hot, with the juices spooned over the calamari.

CALAMARI STEWED WITH POTATOES, FAVAS, AND OLIVES

Calamari Brasati con Fave, Olive, e Patate

This stew should be made right before serving, but most of the work is in the prep (peeling favas, slicing leeks, etc.), and that can be done ahead. You'll need to buy about 4 pounds unshelled favas (or, out of season, use frozen peeled favas) to yield 2 cups. This dish is perfect served family style in the center of the table, or as part of a buffet.

Serves 6

2 cups fava beans
3 tablespoons extra-virgin olive oil
1¼ pounds new red potatoes, cut into 1-inch chunks
1 teaspoon kosher salt, plus more to taste
3 medium leeks, white and light-green parts, halved lengthwise and sliced 1 inch thick
½ cup pitted oil-cured black olives
3 cloves garlic, crushed and peeled
One 28-ounce can whole San Marzano tomatoes, crushed by hand
1 teaspoon crushed celery seeds
Pinch crushed red pepper flakes
1½ pounds medium (4-to-6-inch) calamari, tubes cut into 1-inch rings, tentacles halved
2 tablespoons chopped fresh Italian parsley

Shell fresh favas from the pod. Bring a pot of water to boil, add the fava beans, and simmer for 4 minutes. Drain and refresh fava beans under cold running water, and remove the outer skin from the favas.

Add the oil to a large Dutch oven over medium heat. When the oil is hot, add the potatoes. Season with ½ teaspoon salt, and cook, stirring occasionally, until potatoes are brown and crispy all over, about 8 to 10 minutes.

Add the leeks, olives, and garlic, and cook until the leeks begin to wilt, about 5 minutes. Add the tomatoes, slosh out the can with 1 cup water, and add that to the pan. Bring to a simmer, and stir in the celery seeds, red pepper flakes, and remaining ½ teaspoon salt. Set the lid ajar, and simmer 20 minutes to blend the flavors.

Stir in the favas, and simmer until tender, about 10 minutes. Stir in the calamari and parsley, and cook until calamari just turns opaque and begins to curl, about 2 to 5 minutes. Serve immediately.

LEMONY SHRIMP OVER ZUCCHINI

Gamberoni con Zucchine

These quick and easy shrimp make a delicious appetizer or a main course on their own, and with the zucchini included they become a complete meal. This is an elegant dish when served plated at a sit-down event, and it also looks fabulous on a buffet table.

Serves 6 to 8

ZUCCHINI

3 tablespoons extra-virgin olive oil

4 medium zucchini (about 20 ounces), cut into 1½-inch-by-¼-inch-thick matchsticks

½ teaspoon kosher salt

⅛ teaspoon crushed red pepper flakes

¼ teaspoon dried oregano, preferably Sicilian on the branch

SHRIMP

3 tablespoons extra-virgin olive oil

2 pounds extra-large shrimp, peeled and deveined

1 teaspoon kosher salt

6 cloves garlic, finely chopped

3 tablespoons unsalted butter, cut into bits

1 cup dry white wine

Grated zest and juice of 1 lemon

3 tablespoons chopped fresh Italian parsley

2 to 3 tablespoons bread crumbs

For the zucchini, add the olive oil to a large skillet over medium-high heat. When the oil is hot, scatter in the zucchini. Season with the salt and red pepper flakes. Cook until the zucchini begins to wilt but still has a little bite, about 4 minutes. Sprinkle with the dried oregano, remove from the heat, and keep warm.

For the shrimp, add the olive oil to another large skillet over medium-high heat. When the oil is hot, add half of the shrimp and season with half of the salt. Sear quickly on both sides, about 1 minute, and remove to a plate. Repeat with the remaining shrimp and salt.

When all of the shrimp is out of the skillet, add the garlic and butter to the oil remaining in the pan, and cook until sizzling, 2 minutes. Add the white wine, lemon zest, and lemon juice, and bring to a boil. Add the shrimp back to the sauce, sprinkle with the parsley, and toss. Sprinkle with the bread crumbs and return to a boil to thicken the sauce. Serve the shrimp over the zucchini.

SHRIMP ALLA BUZARA

Gamberoni alla Buzara

I like this dish with meaty U15 shrimp, meaning there are fifteen or fewer shrimp per pound. I leave the shells on because shrimp cooked in the shell will be more flavorful and are a bit more forgiving with respect to cooking time. This dish is always welcome on a buffet table, but also in the center of the table with family and friends. Put out some grilled bread to mop up the sauce, as well as bowls for the shells and wet towels for cleaning hands. My family really enjoys digging in, licking their fingers, and mopping the sauce with Italian bread.

Serves 6 to 8

2 pounds jumbo shrimp, unshelled
6 tablespoons extra-virgin olive oil
1 small onion, finely chopped
4 cloves garlic, finely chopped
1½ teaspoons kosher salt
3 tablespoons tomato paste
1 tablespoon fresh thyme leaves, chopped
1½ cups dry white wine
Pinch crushed red pepper flakes
3 tablespoons unsalted butter, cut into pieces
1 bunch scallions, white and green parts, chopped
   (about 1 cup)
2 to 3 tablespoons bread crumbs
Grilled bread, for serving

Prepare the shrimp by splitting the shells along the back from tip to tail with a sharp serrated paring knife. Remove the dark intestinal tract, and slice the shrimp halfway to butterfly them, always leaving the shells on. Rinse the shrimp, and pat them very dry.

In a large skillet, heat 4 tablespoons of the olive oil over medium heat. When the oil is hot, add the onion and garlic, and season with 1 teaspoon of the salt. Cook just until the garlic begins to turn golden (don't let it burn), about 2 to 3 minutes. Add ½ cup water, and simmer until reduced, about 5 minutes.

When the water is reduced and the onion is ten-der, make a hot spot in the pan and add the tomato paste. Cook and stir the tomato paste in that spot until it is toasted and darkens a shade or two, about 2 minutes. Add the thyme, and pour in the wine with ½ cup more water. Add the red pepper flakes, and bring the sauce to a simmer. Simmer until reduced by half, about 4 to 5 minutes.

Meanwhile, add the remaining 2 tablespoons oil to a second large skillet and heat over medium-high heat. When the oil is hot, season the shrimp with the remaining ½ teaspoon salt. Sear the shrimp (in batches if necessary—don't crowd the skillet) on both sides, about 2 minutes in all, and transfer to the simmering sauce.

Once all of the shrimp are in the sauce, drop in the butter pieces, and toss until the butter is melted and the sauce is creamy. Add the scallions, and sprinkle with the bread crumbs. Simmer a minute to thicken the sauce. Serve immediately with grilled bread.

SHRIMP SPIEDINI WITH ZUCCHINI AND TOMATO SALSA

Spiedini di Gamberoni con Zucchine al Pomodoro

The salsa can be made and the shrimp can be skewered earlier in the day, so all you have to do at the last minute is grill them. This dish can be served many different ways. As a main course, set the shrimp skewers on a plate, and spoon some of the colorful and delicious salsa over them. For a buffet, pile all the shrimp skewers on a plate, and set the salsa next to it for people to serve themselves. And when served family style in the center of the table, the shrimp will disappear in no time.

Serves 4

SALSA

1 large plum tomato, seeded and finely diced
1 small zucchini, finely diced
1 small shallot, finely diced
2 small inner stalks celery with leaves, finely diced
2 tablespoons drained capers in brine, roughly chopped
2 tablespoons chopped fresh Italian parsley
3 tablespoons extra-virgin olive oil
2 tablespoons lemon juice
½ teaspoon kosher salt

SHRIMP

1½ pounds extra-large shrimp (26 to 30 per pound), peeled and deveined, tails left on
3 cloves garlic, sliced
Leaves from 1 sprig fresh rosemary
2 tablespoons extra-virgin olive oil
1 teaspoon sweet paprika
½ teaspoon kosher salt

Soak eight wooden skewers in water for 20 minutes (or use metal skewers). For the salsa, in a medium bowl, combine the tomato, zucchini, shallot, celery, capers, parsley, oil, lemon juice, and salt. Toss well. Let sit at room temperature 30 minutes to allow the flavors to blend, stirring occasionally.

Preheat a grill or grill pan to medium-high heat. For the shrimp, in a large bowl, toss the shrimp, garlic, rosemary, olive oil, smoked paprika, and salt. Rub with your fingers to get the spices all over the shrimp. Let marinate at room temperature for 15 to 20 minutes.

Thread the shrimp onto the skewers, poking the skewers through the bottom and top of the shrimp to secure them firmly.

Grill the shrimp until charred in places and just cooked through, about 2 minutes per side. Mound the skewers on a platter, and spoon a little of the salsa over them, passing the rest at the table.

CLAM SOUP

Zuppa di Vongole

This dish makes a delectable appetizer, and serving it family style is the way to go. Bring it to the table in the cooking pot with the lid on, so it stays warm. Be sure to have plenty of grilled bread on hand, to dunk into the sauce, as well as bowls for the shells.

Serves 6 as an appetizer, 4 as a light main course

¼ cup extra-virgin olive oil, plus more for drizzling

4 cloves garlic, crushed and peeled

2 large leeks, white and light-green parts, halved crosswise and sliced ¼ inch thick

½ teaspoon kosher salt

Pinch crushed red pepper flakes

½ cup dry white wine

One 28-ounce can whole San Marzano tomatoes, run through a food mill or crushed by hand

2 medium zucchini (10 ounces), cut into 1½-by-¼-inch sticks

48 littleneck clams, scrubbed

2 tablespoons chopped fresh Italian parsley

4 or 6 slices lightly toasted or grilled country bread (one for each bowl)

Add the olive oil to a large Dutch oven over medium heat. When the oil is hot, add the garlic. Once the garlic is sizzling, add the leeks, cover, and cook until wilted, about 5 minutes.

Season with the salt and red pepper flakes. Add the wine, and cook until reduced by half, about 2 minutes. Add the tomatoes, slosh out the can with ½ cup water, and add that to the pan. Bring to a simmer, and cook to thicken slightly, about 5 minutes.

Add the zucchini, and simmer just until they begin to droop, about 5 minutes. Add the clams, stir, and cover. Cook about 5 to 6 minutes, until the clams are done; discard any that haven't opened. Stir in the parsley, drizzle with oil, and serve over the bread slices in shallow bowls.

Evviva gli Sposi! Getting Married—Italian Style

Traditional weddings in Italy are usually elegant affairs held in the country, by the sea, or in elaborate palazzos. Some even mutate into a *festa del paese,* in which the whole town participates in a reception held in the main square, with music—often an accordion and a backup local folk band—flowing through the streets. There are certain rituals to be followed besides the white dress, including luxurious gifts for the witnesses or best man and woman—and also for the wedding guests, in the form of *bomboniere,* small favors, usually crystal, silver, or porcelain with candied almonds, always an odd number, gathered in tulle or lace.

Wedding celebrations are more elaborate the farther south you go in Italy. Since a large number of early Italian immigrants to the United States were from southern Italy, the tradition of big weddings was brought along and evolved into the big Italian American wedding. Here in the States, Italian American weddings are usually held in a hotel or a catering hall. There is often a 1- or 2-hour cocktail gathering to start, at which buffet tables are laden with lots of seafood dishes, such as baked clams, oysters, and a shrimp-cocktail bar. This spread is accompanied by salads, grilled vegetables, and stuffed mushrooms, with hors d'oeuvres passed as well. The cocktail hour alone is a veritable feast and would be more than enough food for the event, but this is only the prelude to a full sit-down meal. Usually, there is a first course of salad, pasta, or soup, and then a choice of poultry, fish, or meat, a dessert, or maybe a "Viennese hour" (a large pastry buffet with many varieties of small bite-sized desserts and cookies), and of course the wedding cake.

When my children, Joseph, and four years later, Tanya, married, I made some of the food for both weddings, creating a menu that reflected the elegance of the events and at the same time included some of our family traditions. There was a sumptuous 2-hour cocktail reception with a raw seafood bar, caviar, and shrimp cocktail. A whole roasted suckling pig was also served, as well as passed hors d'oeuvres. The food really could have stopped then, but we continued and, once inside the ballroom, we served the traditional wedding soup (page 138), pear and pecorino ravioli (page 232), and a choice of main-course dishes, followed by the wedding cake and a Viennese hour as well. The brides were gorgeous, the ceremonies touching, and people left talking about the food! So, when planning a wedding, how can you incorporate some Italian family traditions? Let me give you some suggestions.

Wedding Menus

Keep in mind that for large weddings, items cooked in the oven that can be kept warm are easier to serve than items that need to be cooked right before serving.

Our Family Favorite: Formal Sit-Down Wedding Dinner

Start with a cocktail hour with abundant shellfish, whipped cod, octopus salad, caviar, lots of prosciutto, mounds of chunks of Grana Padano, smoked salmon, and plenty of grilled vegetables and cold salads.

APPETIZER: raw and cooked salad (page 116) topped with mozzarella di bufala and a thin slice or two of Prosciutto di Parma

SOUP: wedding soup in a mixed-meat broth (page 138)

PASTA: pear and pecorino ravioli (page 232)

MAIN COURSE: beef tenderloin, roasted vegetables, and porcini sauce (page 318)

DESSERT: heavenly cake (page 339) with baked pineapple (page 330) and vanilla ice cream

In the center of the table, bowls of tangerines and cookies, crostoli (page 356), and chocolate orange truffles (page 355)—all served after dessert

Italian American Wedding

A traditional wedding cocktail hour might include roasted olives with orange (page 34), bruschette with caponata (page 39), marinated mushrooms (page 43), meatless meatballs (page 48), cannellini and pancetta bruschetta (page 62), crostata with mushrooms and onion (page 76), pizzette with various toppings (page 70), arancini with sausage ragù (page 78), mussels with salsa verde (page 84), crispy shrimp (page 90), fried bread (page 98), and spicy stuffed clams (page 93). It could also feature a spread of Italian cured meats, such as prosciutto, mortadella, salami, and various cheeses, including mozzarella (see page 94 for advice on putting together a good selection).

ANTIPASTO: lobster salad (page 123)

SOUP: escarole and white bean soup (page 137)

PASTA: lasagna with ricotta and mozzarella (page 224)

MAIN COURSE: ossobuco (page 288) or roasted guinea hen with balsamic glaze (page 276)

CAKE: wedding cake, bride's choice of filling, which could be fruit (strawberry and pineapple is a good combination) or chocolate pudding, or a rum cake. Additional desserts are always served, and I would include chocolate ricotta cheesecake (page 340), coffee panna cotta (page 351), and *semifreddo al torrone* (page 352).

COOKIES: A big platter can be placed in the center of each table, including pinoli cookies, shortcake cookies with jam, and rainbow cookies, plus chocolate crostoli (page 356) and fig and hazelnut butter cookies (page 359). And perhaps some chocolate orange truffles (page 355) as well.

Wedding Story

Felix, my husband, was born in Istria and immigrated to the United States about the same time my family did. We did not know each other in Istria, but we met in Astoria, Queens, in 1963. Astoria included a large community of Italians and Istrians, and I had two very special girlfriends, Wanda Radetti and Graziella Vlacic; we are still close, up to this very day. Felix was a family friend of Graziella's, and when my sixteenth birthday party was planned, Graziella said she would invite Felix. "Who?" I said. "The one that plays the accordion—you'll like him," she responded. I did. We married in 1966. Felix was a good accordion player and had often been asked to play at weddings when he was still living in Istria. He had a favorite wedding story he always liked to tell.

This particular wedding took place in a private house in Istria. The kitchen and storage were on the first floor, and the festivities took place on the second floor, where Felix was seated in a corner, playing away. With the momentum of the dance escalating, he could feel the wooden floor pulsating beneath his feet. It slowly began to cave in at the center. Fortunately, no one was hurt. They picked Felix up in his chair as he kept playing and carried him outside, where the merrymaking continued on the terrace. Nothing was going to stop that wedding celebration.

MUSSELS WITH FENNEL AND SAFFRON

Cozze con Finocchio e Zafferano

You can serve this fun yet elegant dish in individual portions, piling the mussels high on each plate with a ladle. Make sure you distribute the sauce evenly and have plenty of grilled bread on the table, as well as some bowls to collect the shells. Even without the saffron, this is a delicious dish, but the saffron adds a luxuriousness that I love.

This recipe is easily scaled up; plan on a pound of mussels per person for a first course, 1½ to 2 pounds for an entrée.

Serves 4 as an appetizer

1 cup chicken stock (page 148)

1 teaspoon saffron threads

¼ cup extra-virgin olive oil, plus more for drizzling

1 small onion, thinly sliced

1 medium fennel bulb, trimmed, halved, cored, and thinly sliced lengthwise, ¼ cup chopped tender fronds reserved

1 cup dry white wine

½ teaspoon kosher salt

Pinch crushed red pepper flakes

4 pounds mussels, scrubbed and debearded if necessary

¼ cup chopped fresh Italian parsley

Crusty country bread, for serving

In a small saucepan, heat the chicken stock to a bare simmer. Add the saffron, and let steep 5 minutes. Keep hot.

In a large Dutch oven, heat the olive oil over medium heat. When the oil is hot, add the onion and fennel. Cook and stir until wilted, about 3 to 4 minutes.

Add the white wine, salt, and red pepper flakes. Simmer until reduced by half, about 3 minutes. Add the mussels and hot stock. Bring to a simmer, cover, and cook about 3 to 4 minutes, until the mussels are done; discard any that haven't opened. Stir in the parsley and reserved chopped fennel fronds, stir, and serve with bread.

ROASTED LOBSTER WITH FENNEL

Aragosta al Forno con Finocchio

This is a very impressive dish when brought to the table. The difficult part is prepping the lobsters, but once you've mastered that, the rest is easy. (And you can always ask your fishmonger to prep the lobster for you.) When trimming the fennel, reserve the nicer fronds and tender parts trimmed from the bulb to chop for the stuffing, but discard the tough or woody parts.

Serves 6

Three 1½-pound lobsters

1¼ teaspoons kosher salt, plus more for the cooking pot

3 medium fennel bulbs, trimmed, cored, and cut into 6 wedges each, plus 1 cup chopped tender fronds reserved

½ cup extra-virgin olive oil, plus more for the sheet pans

1 medium onion, finely chopped

2 cups panko bread crumbs

½ cup grated Grana Padano

¼ cup chopped fresh Italian parsley

Grated zest of 1 lemon

Put the lobsters in the freezer about 30 minutes before you want to start cooking. Preheat oven to 400 degrees. Bring a large pot of salted water to boil.

Add the fennel bulbs to the boiling water, and simmer until almost tender, about 7 to 8 minutes. Drain, cool, and put in a large bowl. Toss with 2 tablespoons of the olive oil and 1 teaspoon salt. Set aside.

Add 2 tablespoons of the olive oil to a medium skillet over medium heat. When the oil is hot, add the onion, reserved chopped fennel, and remaining ¼ teaspoon salt. Cook until the fronds wilt, about 2 minutes. Then add ½ cup water, and simmer until the vegetables are tender and the water has reduced away, about 6 minutes. Scrape into a large bowl to cool.

When the fennel and onion are cool, stir in the panko, grated cheese, parsley, lemon zest, and 2 tablespoons olive oil.

To split the lobsters, hold one down on your cutting board, hard shell side up. Split lengthwise through the head first, then down through the tail, separating the lobster into two halves. Remove the nerve tissue and sac from the head cavities, and the thin intestinal tract that goes down the length of the tail. Cut the rubber bands from the claws.

Lightly stuff the head and the tail cavities of the lobsters with the panko stuffing (you will have some extra; that's okay). Set three lobster pieces each on two oiled rimmed sheet pans, with the bodies facing crosswise (parallel to the short side of the pans).

Divide the boiled and seasoned fennel wedges, laying them flat in the pans, and sprinkle the remaining stuffing over the fennel. Drizzle all with the remaining 2 tablespoons olive oil. Tent the pans with foil, making sure it doesn't touch the stuffing. Bake until the fennel is tender and the lobsters have given up their juices, about 20 minutes. Uncover, increase oven heat to 425 degrees, and bake until crumbs are brown and crispy, about 10 to 15 minutes more. Serve hot.

OCTOPUS AND POTATO SALAD

Insalata di Polipo e Patate

This dish can be served warm—toss the salad while the potatoes are still warm or at room temperature—but not cold. It is great as part of a buffet, as a first course, or as a rustic entrée if you have a tableful of octopus lovers. It is a perfect dish to bring to a potluck dinner, but be sure not to dress with the oil and lemon juice too far in advance of serving.

Serves 6, or more as part of an antipasto buffet

2½-pound cleaned octopus
4 cloves garlic, crushed and peeled
2 teaspoons dried oregano, preferably Sicilian on the branch
¼ teaspoon crushed red pepper flakes
¼ cup red wine vinegar
1 medium red onion, sliced ¼ inch thick
1½ pounds russet potatoes
1 cup coarsely chopped marinated artichoke hearts
Juice of 1 large lemon
3 tablespoons extra-virgin olive oil
Kosher salt
¼ cup chopped fresh Italian parsley

Put the octopus in a pot where it will fit snugly. Scatter in the garlic, oregano, and red pepper flakes. Add a cup of water, and bring to a bare simmer. Cover tightly, and cook until octopus is very tender when pierced with a fork, about 2 hours. (Add more water, as necessary, throughout the cooking time, to keep an inch of liquid or more in the bottom of the pan, up to 2 cups more water in all.)

While the octopus cooks, bring 2 cups water and the vinegar to a boil in a medium saucepan. Add the red onion, and simmer until it droops but still has some bite to it, about 5 minutes. Drain. In the meantime, in another saucepan, simmer the potatoes whole until tender, about 25 minutes or so, depending on size. Drain. When they're cool enough to handle, peel and cut into 1-inch chunks.

When the octopus is done, cool slightly and cut into 1-to-2-inch pieces. In a large serving bowl, combine the octopus, red onion, potatoes, and artichoke hearts. Drizzle with the lemon juice and olive oil, and toss. Season with salt, and sprinkle with the parsley. Toss and serve.

MONKFISH IN TOMATO SAUCE WITH GREEN OLIVES AND CAPERS

Coda di Rospo Brasato con Capperi e Olive

Monkfish is a good choice for entertaining because of its mild flavor and because it's also harder to overcook than a lot of fish, so you can relax and focus on spending time with your guests. Just make sure you trim away all of the silver skin and gray bits. This dish is best made with ripe summer tomatoes in season—but it is also excellent with canned tomatoes. You will need about 2 cups. Crush them by hand, or pass them through a vegetable mill. This dish is great served family style, or kept warm on a buffet table.

Serves 6

4 ripe medium tomatoes, or 2 cups canned whole San Marzano tomatoes

2 pounds monkfish fillets, cleaned and cut into 2-inch chunks

1½ teaspoons kosher salt

All-purpose flour, for dredging

¼ cup extra-virgin olive oil

4 cloves garlic, crushed and peeled

Juice and flesh of 1 large lemon, peel removed in strips with a vegetable peeler

½ cup slivered green olives

¼ cup drained capers in brine

1 bunch scallions, white and green parts, chopped (about 1 cup)

Halve the tomatoes. Set a strainer over a bowl, and scoop the seeds from the tomatoes into the strainer. Press on the scooped seeds to extract the juices. Save the juices and discard the seeds. Chop the tomatoes into 1-inch chunks.

Season the monkfish with 1 teaspoon salt. Spread the flour on a plate, and lightly dredge the monkfish in the flour, tapping off the excess.

Add the olive oil to a nonstick skillet over medium-high heat. When the oil is hot, add the garlic and let sizzle a minute. Add the monkfish, and brown all over, about 3 to 4 minutes.

Add the tomatoes, lemon peel, and juice, and bring to a simmer. Stir in the olives and remaining ½ teaspoon salt. Cover, and cook about 10 minutes.

Add enough water so the liquid films the bottom of the pan (about ½ cup water). Stir in the capers, cover, and simmer until monkfish is cooked through, about 10 minutes more. Uncover, stir in the scallions, return to a boil, and serve.

HALIBUT BAKED WITH TOMATOES AND ONIONS

Rombo al Forno con Pomodori e Cipolle

You can easily double this recipe (in two baking pans) to feed a larger crowd. The components can be assembled ahead of time, but bake the fish right before serving. It is good served individually or family style, and will keep well on a buffet.

Serves 4

½ cup extra-virgin olive oil

2 medium onions, cut into thin rings

1½ teaspoons kosher salt

3 medium tomatoes, sliced ½ inch thick

Four 6-ounce skinless halibut fillets, about
    1½ inches thick

6 leafy sprigs fresh thyme

Preheat oven to 425 degrees. In a large skillet, heat ¼ cup of the olive oil over medium heat. When the oil is hot, add the onions, and season with 1 teaspoon of the salt. Cover, and cook, stirring occasionally, until onions are wilted, about 8 minutes.

In a 9-by-13-inch glass or ceramic baking dish, lay the onion slices in an even layer. Drizzle with 2 tablespoons olive oil, and season with ¼ teaspoon of the salt. Layer the tomatoes over the onions. Place the halibut fillets on top. Drizzle with the remaining 2 tablespoons oil, and season with the remaining ¼ teaspoon salt. Stick a thyme sprig on each piece of fish.

Cover tightly with foil, and bake until the tomatoes release their juices, about 10 to 15 minutes. Remove foil, and bake until the onions are caramelized in places and the fish is cooked through, about 10 minutes more. Serve hot.

SWORDFISH BAGNARA STYLE

Pesca Spada Bagnara

The Calabrian coast is where the magnificent swordfish that migrate to this corner of the Tyrrhenian Sea every year are most plentiful. Make sure you buy fresh swordfish for this recipe.

Serves 6

2 pounds swordfish steak, 1¼-inch thick, with skin
½ cup extra-virgin olive oil
1 lemon, thinly sliced
5 tablespoons small capers, drained
4 plump cloves garlic, peeled and thinly sliced
1 teaspoon kosher salt
1 tablespoon dried oregano
1½ tablespoons chopped fresh Italian parsley

Heat the oven to 425 degrees. You will need a 4-quart baking dish, 10 by 15 inches, or similar size; a roasting pan large enough to hold the baking dish inside it (on the rack); and a sturdy flat metal baking/roasting rack to fit inside the roasting pan. Cut the swordfish steak into six serving pieces. Pour the olive oil into the baking dish, and scatter in the lemon slices, capers, and garlic. Turn the lemon slices over to coat them with oil, and gather them to one side of the dish. Season the swordfish pieces on both sides with salt, lay them in the dish in one layer, coat with oil on all surfaces. Distribute the lemon slices on top.

Meanwhile, bring a pot of water to the boil. Set the baking rack in the big roasting pan, and pour in boiling water to the depth of an inch. Put the dish of swordfish on the rack in the roasting pan, and tent the big pan with a large sheet of aluminum foil. Arch the sheet over the fish, and press it against the sides of the roasting pan. Carefully set the covered pan in the oven, and bake just until the swordfish is cooked through, 10 to 12 minutes.

Remove the foil, and lift the baking dish from the pan and out of the oven. Immediately crumble the oregano over the hot swordfish and into the pan juices, then sprinkle the parsley over everything. Serve right away, placing each piece of swordfish in a warm shallow bowl and spooning some of the cooking juices over it.

SEARED TUNA WITH FENNEL

Tonno Scottato in Padella al Finocchio

The fennel can be made ahead and reheated, but don't crust and sear the tuna until the last minute. If you can't find fennel powder, you can make your own by grinding fennel seeds in a spice grinder. This recipe can easily be multiplied if you have a crowd to feed. The tuna can be grilled rather than seared, if you prefer; just make sure the grill is not so hot that it burns the bread crumbs. The most important aspect of this dish is the freshness of the tuna.

Serves 6

FENNEL

¼ cup extra-virgin olive oil
4 cloves garlic, crushed and peeled
3 medium fennel bulbs, trimmed, cored, and cut
    into 2-inch chunks
1 teaspoon kosher salt
⅓ cup drained capers in brine
2 tablespoons chopped fresh Italian parsley

TUNA

¾ cup fine dried bread crumbs
2 tablespoons chopped fresh Italian parsley
1 teaspoon fennel powder (store-bought or made by
    milling fennel seeds in a spice grinder)
1 teaspoon kosher salt
6 tablespoons extra-virgin olive oil
Six 6-to-8-ounce tuna steaks, about 1-inch thick
Lemon slices, for garnish

For the fennel, in a large straight-sided skillet, heat the olive oil over medium heat. When the oil is hot, add the garlic. Let the garlic sizzle for a minute, then add the fennel and season with the salt. Toss to coat the fennel in the oil. Cover the skillet, and let the fennel sweat (without coloring), until it is just tender, about 10 to 12 minutes.

Uncover, stir in the capers, and cook, stirring occasionally, until the fennel is tender and caramelized (adjust the heat as necessary to keep it from burning), about 10 to 15 minutes more. Stir in the parsley, and keep warm while you sear the tuna.

For the tuna, in a shallow bowl, combine the bread crumbs, parsley, fennel powder, and ½ teaspoon salt. Drizzle with 2 tablespoons of the oil and toss to coat the crumbs in oil. On a rimmed sheet pan, drizzle the tuna with 2 tablespoons olive oil, and season with the remaining ½ teaspoon salt. Turn to coat the tuna in the oil.

Add the remaining 2 tablespoons oil to a large nonstick skillet over medium-high heat. Press the tuna into the crumbs, patting so they adhere. Sear the tuna in the skillet on both sides, until the crumbs are crispy but the tuna is still rare inside, about 2 minutes per side. Serve the tuna on a bed of the fennel, garnished with lemon slices.

SEARED SALMON PAILLARDS WITH ARUGULA SALAD

Paillard di Salmone Scottato con Insalata di Rucola

This dish cooks in minutes and makes a lovely light lunch entrée for a small gathering. Sear the salmon ahead of time and serve it at room temperature if you have a bigger crowd and want to serve it family style or on a buffet. My grandkids love it served on toasted bread as a sandwich.

Serves 4

SALMON

1¼-pound piece center-cut skinless salmon fillet
2 tablespoons extra-virgin olive oil
1 teaspoon kosher salt

SALAD

2 tablespoons freshly squeezed lemon juice
1 teaspoon Dijon mustard
½ teaspoon kosher salt
¼ cup extra-virgin olive oil
8 cups loosely packed baby arugula
¼ cup chopped fresh chives

Slice the salmon on the bias into eight equal thin slices (you can pop the salmon into the freezer 15 minutes before slicing to make this easier). In a large bowl, gently toss the salmon with the olive oil and salt.

In another large bowl, for the salad, whisk together the lemon juice, mustard, and salt. Whisk in the oil in a slow, steady stream to make a smooth dressing.

For the salmon, heat a large nonstick skillet over high heat. When the skillet is hot, add the salmon in one layer. Sear until the underside is crispy, about 1 minute. Flip, and sear the second side, about 1 minute. Remove the salmon to four serving plates.

Add the arugula and chives to the bowl with the dressing, toss, and mound on top of the salmon.

CABBAGE ROLLS STUFFED WITH SALMON

Involtini di Verza Farciti al Salmone

This dish is very good for a buffet and for large parties, because it can be made a day in advance. Just reheat gently with the lid on before serving, adding a little water if the rolls have soaked up all of the cooking liquid.

Serves 6

ROLLS

1 teaspoon salt, plus more for the cooking pot
1 medium head savoy cabbage
1 cup Arborio or other short-grain rice
3 tablespoons extra-virgin olive oil
1 pound skinless salmon fillet, cut into ½-inch dice
1 bunch scallions, white and green parts, chopped (about 1 cup)
1 cup fine dried bread crumbs
½ cup drained capers in brine
3 tablespoons chopped fresh Italian parsley

SAUCE

2 tablespoons unsalted butter
3 tablespoons extra-virgin olive oil
6 cloves garlic, crushed and peeled
2 anchovy fillets, chopped
2 tablespoons tomato paste
Juice of 1 lemon
2 cups dry white wine
2 cups chicken stock (page 148)
½ teaspoon salt, plus more to taste

For the rolls, bring a large pot of salted water to boil. Remove twelve (or thirteen or fourteen for good measure, if you can get them from one head of cabbage) large outer cabbage leaves, keeping them as intact as possible. Add the leaves to the boiling water, and

simmer until they are droopy and flexible, about 8 to 10 minutes. Drain and cool. Once they're cool, flip the leaves so that the ridged side is facing up. With a paring knife, trim away the ridge so the leaves are mostly flat. Finely shred the remaining, inner cabbage, and reserve.

In a small saucepan, bring 2 cups water and ½ teaspoon salt to boil. Add the rice, and simmer until it's al dente and all of the water is absorbed, about 13 to 14 minutes. Spread the rice on a sheet pan to cool.

In a medium nonstick skillet, heat the 3 tablespoons olive oil over medium-high heat. When the oil is hot, add the salmon, and season with the remaining ½ teaspoon salt. Toss to coat the salmon in the oil, then add the scallions. Cook until the salmon is browned and the scallions wilt, about 2 to 3 minutes. Remove from the heat, and scrape into a bowl to cool.

Once the salmon is cooled, mix in the cooled rice, the bread crumbs, capers, and parsley. Mix with your hands to form a cohesive stuffing.

Lay the cabbage leaves, ridged side down, on your work surface (they'll form a natural cupped shape, which will confirm which side should be facing up). Divide the filling among the cabbage leaves, centered crosswise but more toward the bottom. Fold the

(recipe continues)

sides in, and roll up each leaf, encasing the filling. Set the rolls aside, seam side down, while you make the sauce.

For the sauce, in a large Dutch oven, melt the butter in the olive oil over medium heat. When the butter is melted, add the garlic and anchovies, and cook until they're sizzling, about 1 minute. Add the reserved shredded cabbage, stir, and cook until wilted, about 7 to 8 minutes. Clear a space in the pan, and add the tomato paste. Cook and stir the tomato paste in that spot until it is toasted and darkens a shade or two, about 2 minutes. Mix the tomato paste into the cabbage, and add the lemon juice, white wine, and stock. Bring to a simmer, season with the salt, and nestle the rolls in the sauce. Cover, and cook until the cabbage is just tender, about 30 minutes. Uncover, and cook until the cabbage is very tender (but the rolls still hold their shape) and the sauce is thick and flavorful, about 30 minutes more. Serve hot.

TROUT WITH MUSHROOMS

Trota in Padella con Funghi

Ask your fishmonger to butterfly and debone the trout for you, because it is tedious work. Run your fingers over the flesh to make sure all of the bones are out. You can leave the head on or remove it before cooking, depending on which you prefer. Fish heads and bones give more flavor to the sauce. If you want to double the recipe, sauté as many trout as will fit in the pan at a time, set them on a tray, and keep them in a warm oven until you make the sauce. When ready to serve, plate the hot trout from the oven and pour the sauce over them.

Serves 4

TOPPING

¼ cup extra-virgin olive oil

3 medium leeks, white and light-green parts, halved lengthwise and sliced ½ inch thick

1 tablespoon fresh thyme leaves, chopped

12 ounces mixed mushrooms, sliced (about 4½ cups)

2 stalks celery, chopped

½ teaspoon kosher salt

Pinch crushed red pepper flakes

Grated zest of 1 lemon

¼ cup chopped fresh Italian parsley

TROUT

Four 1-pound trout, boned and butterflied

3 tablespoons extra-virgin olive oil, plus more for the sheet pans

½ teaspoon kosher salt

2 tablespoons fine dried bread crumbs

1 lemon, thinly sliced

Juice of 1 lemon (use the one you zested)

1 cup dry white wine, plus more as needed

2 tablespoons chopped fresh Italian parsley

2 tablespoons unsalted butter, cut into pieces

Preheat oven to 425 degrees. For the topping, heat the olive oil in a large skillet over medium-high heat. When the oil is hot, add the leeks, and cook until they begin to wilt, about 4 minutes. Sprinkle with the thyme, and cook until fragrant, about 1 minute. Add the mushrooms and celery, and season with the salt and red pepper flakes. Cover, and cook until the vegetables are softened, about 15 minutes.

Uncover, increase the heat, and boil away any liquid left in the pan. Scrape the topping into a bowl, and stir in the lemon zest and parsley.

For the trout, rub the fish all over with the olive oil, and season with the salt. Brush two rimmed sheet pans with olive oil, and put two trout, skin side down and open like a book, on each. Divide the topping among the trout, and sprinkle with the bread crumbs. Lay the lemon slices in the spaces in the pan. In a spouted measuring cup, combine the lemon juice, wine, and parsley. Pour this into the spaces in the pan, adding more wine as needed so the liquid fills the entire bottom of both pans. Dot the tops of the trout with the butter, and bake until the topping is browned and the trout are cooked through, about 20 to 22 minutes.

MIXED SEAFOOD STEW

Brodetto di Pesce Misto

This is a great dish to serve family style—just set it in a bowl in the center of the table with a serving spoon. Alongside, serve a pile of grilled or crusty bread or a bowl of hot polenta. It is perfect for a casual dinner party among friends.

Serves 6 to 8

1 pound extra-large shrimp, peeled and deveined (about 30)
1½ teaspoons kosher salt
All-purpose flour, for dredging
½ cup extra-virgin olive oil, plus more for drizzling
1 pound sea scallops, side muscle or "foot" removed
6 cloves garlic, crushed and peeled
8 leafy sprigs fresh thyme
2 cups dry white wine
Juice of 1 lemon
¼ teaspoon crushed red pepper flakes
24 littleneck clams, scrubbed
1 pound mussels, scrubbed and debearded if necessary
1 bunch scallions, white and green parts, chopped (about 1 cup)
¼ cup chopped fresh Italian parsley
1 to 2 tablespoons fine bread crumbs
Crusty bread, for serving

Season the shrimp with ½ teaspoon of the salt. Spread some flour on a rimmed sheet pan, and dredge the shrimp in the flour, tapping off the excess. Heat 2 tablespoons of the oil in a large Dutch oven over medium-high heat, and add the shrimp. Cook, turning once, until seared on both sides, about a minute per side. Remove to a plate.

Add 2 more tablespoons oil to the pot. Season the scallops with ½ teaspoon salt. Dredge the scallops in flour, and brown on both sides, like the shrimp, about 1 minute per side. Remove to the plate with the shrimp.

Pour out any oil left in the pot, and wipe it clean with a paper towel. Over medium-high heat, add the remaining ¼ cup olive oil. When the oil is hot, add the garlic and thyme, and cook until sizzling, about 1 minute. Add the wine, lemon juice, and red pepper flakes, and bring to a simmer. Dump in the clams, and cover the pot. Simmer just until they begin to open, about 3 minutes. Add the mussels, season with the remaining ½ teaspoon salt, and cover again. Cook about 3 to 4 minutes more, and discard any that haven't opened.

Add the shrimp, scallops, scallions, and parsley. Cook and toss just until the shrimp and scallops are heated through, about 3 minutes.

With a spider, transfer the seafood to a serving bowl, leaving the cooking juices behind. Bring the juices to a boil, and sprinkle in a tablespoon of the bread crumbs. Bring to a simmer, and cook until sauce is thickened, adding up to 1 tablespoon more bread crumbs if it is still too loose. Drizzle in a little olive oil, pour all of the juices over the seafood, and serve right away with crusty bread.

A Surprise Party

Throwing a surprise party takes careful planning. Don't slip up and spill the beans! The cooking gets a bit more complicated if the person you are trying to surprise lives with you or is a constant visitor. You certainly want to consider making foods that can keep well in the refrigerator and that are easily uncovered, dressed, and served. Maybe start with some caponata (page 39), carrot and chickpea dip (page 37), marinated mushrooms (page 43), spicy giardiniera (page 45), Italian deviled eggs (page 49), and crostata with mushrooms and onion (page 76). A platter or two of cured meats, such as prosciutto, mortadella, or salami, is always an easy and welcome starter (see page 94 for advice on putting together a delectable charcuterie plate). Choose items that can be made in advance and hidden out of sight, such as a layered casserole with beef, cabbage, and potatoes (page 310), goulash (page 311), braised beef rolls stuffed with barley (page 312), lamb and fennel stew (page 321), and monkfish in tomato sauce with green olives and capers (page 255). Certainly include baked pastas, such as stuffed shells (page 221), and lasagna with ricotta and mozzarella (page 224). These all can be made ahead of time, and then popped into the oven shortly before the party is set to begin.

And, of course, if it's a birthday, don't forget a birthday cake—the most important part! A delicious chocolate sponge cake with sour cherries and chocolate zabaglione mousse filling (page 336) and the almond torte with chocolate chips (page 335) keep well and are sure to delight any birthday boy or girl. Augment the cake with fruits, cookies, and nuts that can be stored with cellophane or aluminum foil on top of a bedroom dresser and kept well hidden.

Poultry and Meat

If you are going to have a large party where meat will be the star, fire up your grill, get your oven going, or pull out a big braising pot—and make sure your guests are good eaters. For a larger dinner party a chicken roasted with pomegranate in the oven (page 279), braised veal shank (ossobuco, page 288), and roasted pork shoulder with roasted vegetable sauce (page 296) can be timed so they are perfectly cooked and ready to come out of the oven just when you need to serve them at the table. For a more intimate dinner, chicken dishes cooked in a skillet work well, such as chicken and sausage bites (opposite) or veal scaloppine with green olives and zucchini (page 291). Since they need to be closely monitored while cooking, they are easier to master for a smaller group that can join you in the kitchen as you cook. A particular Italian favorite is a mixed grill (page 314), which might include Maremma-style steak (page 309), chicken liver spiedini (page 281), and grilled sausage. Lots of vegetables and salads are good to serve with these dishes, whereas with braised dishes such as beef and root vegetables braised in red wine (page 316), pork shoulder with Genovese sauce (page 298), and lamb and fennel stew (page 321), I like to serve some polenta.

CHICKEN AND SAUSAGE BITES WITH APPLE CIDER VINEGAR SAUCE

Bocconcini di Pollo e Salsicce all'Aceto di Mele

No matter whom you are hosting, this is a recipe that all your guests will love. If you have a small family gathering, it is easy to make on top of the stove; if you have a bigger crowd, use the oven, multiplying the ingredients by two or three for larger groups. When you are finished browning everything, put it all in a roasting pan, season with salt and crushed red pepper, add the rosemary, vinegar, and honey, and set in a 400-degree oven for 20 minutes or so, or until the sauce is reduced to a glaze and the sausages and chicken are cooked through.

Serves 6 to 8

1½ pounds boneless, skinless chicken breast
1 teaspoon kosher salt, plus more to taste
2 tablespoons unsalted butter
2 tablespoons extra-virgin olive oil
1 pound sweet Italian sausage (about 4 links), each link cut in thirds crosswise
4 cloves garlic, crushed and peeled
2 medium onions, cut into 1-inch wedges left attached at the root
¼ teaspoon crushed red pepper flakes
1 sprig fresh rosemary
½ cup apple cider vinegar
1 tablespoon honey
3 tablespoons chopped fresh Italian parsley

Slice the chicken breasts into ¾-inch strips on the bias, and season with ½ teaspoon of the salt. Add the butter and olive oil to a large nonstick skillet over medium-high heat. When the butter is melted, add the chicken and brown all over, about 2 to 3 minutes; remove it to a plate.

When all of the chicken is out of the skillet, add the sausage and garlic. Cook, turning the sausage, until it is browned all over, about 4 to 5 minutes.

Add the onions, and cook, turning the wedges, until they're caramelized on the edges, about 8 minutes. Season with the remaining ½ teaspoon salt and the crushed red pepper.

Add back the chicken, tuck in the rosemary sprig, and pour in the vinegar and honey. Cover the skillet, and simmer until the onions have wilted and the chicken and sausage are cooked through, about 4 to 5 minutes.

Uncover, increase the heat, and boil until the sauce is reduced to a glaze, about 1 to 2 minutes. Stir in the parsley, season with salt if necessary, and serve.

CHICKEN BREAST AND LIVERS WITH MARSALA

Petto e Fegatini di Pollo Marsala

Combining the chicken breasts and livers makes this dish full of flavor. Of course, you can always opt to leave out the livers, in which case you should double the mushrooms.
To clean the livers, halve them and trim away all fat and sinew. Wash and dry them very well, so they don't splatter when you're browning them.

Serves 6

3 large boneless, skinless chicken breasts (about 1½ pounds)
4 tablespoons unsalted butter
2 tablespoons extra-virgin olive oil
1½ teaspoons kosher salt
All-purpose flour, for dredging
12 ounces chicken livers, halved, cleaned, and cut into 1-inch chunks
1 pound mixed mushrooms (white, shiitake, cremini, oyster, etc.), thickly sliced
8 fresh sage leaves
½ cup dry white wine
½ cup dry Marsala
1 cup chicken stock (page 148)
2 tablespoons chopped fresh Italian parsley

Halve the chicken breasts crosswise on the bias. With a meat mallet, pound the breasts between sheets of plastic wrap to an even thickness of about ½ inch.

In a large skillet, melt 2 tablespoons of the butter in the oil over medium-high heat. Season the chicken with ½ teaspoon salt. Spread some flour on a plate, and lightly dredge the chicken in the flour, tapping off the excess. Brown the chicken on both sides, about 1 to 2 minutes per side, and remove to a plate.

Season the chicken livers with ½ teaspoon salt, and dredge in the flour as well. Brown all over, about 2 to 3 minutes. Remove to the plate with the chicken breasts.

Add the remaining butter to the skillet. When it melts, add the mushrooms and sage, and season with the remaining ½ teaspoon salt. Cook, stirring occasionally, until the mushrooms brown and soften, about 5 to 6 minutes.

Add the wine and Marsala. Bring to a boil, and cook until reduced by half, about 2 minutes. Add the stock, and slide the chicken breasts and livers back into the pan. Simmer until the chicken and livers are cooked through, about 7 minutes. Stir in the parsley, and serve.

CHICKEN PARMIGIANA WITH FRESH TOMATO SAUCE

Pollo alla Parmigiana con Pomodoro Fresco

In this rendition of chicken Parmigiana, the chicken cutlets are not fried but baked, and they are not doused with sauce. Hence, they remain light and delicious. The diced fresh tomatoes bake together with the Taleggio, making a savory, cheesy tomato dressing for each cutlet. It is an easy dish to make for a crowd, because you can multiply by two or three, or as much as you have space for in your oven. Large trays of baked chicken Parmigiana are perfect to serve at children's parties or when hungry teenagers come to visit.

Serves 6 to 8

2 cups fine dried bread crumbs

1½ cups grated Grana Padano

¼ cup chopped fresh Italian parsley

2 teaspoons dried oregano, preferably Sicilian on the branch

1 teaspoon kosher salt

½ cup plus 2 tablespoons extra-virgin olive oil

3 large eggs

All-purpose flour, for dredging

6 boneless and skinless chicken breasts (about 2 pounds)

1½ pounds ripe plum tomatoes, seeded and cut into ¼-inch dice

½ pound Taleggio, rind removed, cheese diced into ½-inch cubes

Preheat oven to 400 degrees. Line two rimmed sheet pans with parchment (or use two glass or ceramic casseroles). In a large (8-quart) bowl, toss together the bread crumbs, 1 cup of the grated cheese, the parsley, dried oregano, and ½ teaspoon of the salt. Drizzle in ½ cup of the olive oil, and toss to coat the crumbs in the oil. Spread the crumbs on a rimmed sheet pan.

Beat the eggs in a large shallow bowl. Spread some of the flour on a plate. Slice the chicken breasts on the bias, and cut into two or three pieces each (depend-

ing on how large they are). Pound the chicken breasts with a meat mallet between sheets of plastic wrap to an even thickness of about ½ inch.

Working with one piece at a time, dip the chicken in flour, then egg, then the bread crumb mixture, turning and pressing to coat thoroughly in the crumbs. Lay the breaded pieces on the parchment-lined pans. Bake the chicken until the coating is crisp all over, about 15 minutes.

Meanwhile, in a large bowl, toss together the diced tomatoes, Taleggio, remaining ½ teaspoon salt, and 2 tablespoons oil.

Once the chicken is browned on both sides, pull it out to finish with the topping tomatoes and cheese. Increase oven temperature to 425 degrees. Spoon the tomato mixture evenly on top of each piece of chicken. Sprinkle evenly with the remaining ½ cup grated cheese, return to oven, and bake until the top is crusty and the sauce is bubbly, about 8 to 10 minutes more.

CHICKEN ROLLS WITH KALE PESTO

Involtini di Pollo Farciti con Pesto di Cavolo Nero

This recipe makes more pesto than you will need; it's difficult to make just a small amount in the food processor. The extra will keep in the refrigerator for several days, or in the freezer for several months. It's perfect on pasta or sandwiches, or stirred into soups. Or try it in the ziti recipe on page 214.

Kale has become quite popular lately. Part of the Brassica *species, kale can sometimes be sweet, sometimes spicy, and is always slightly bitter. Although I like the Tuscan kale of my Italian heritage, different varieties—such as curly kale, Siberian kale, and Ragged Jack—can be used in this recipe as well as in other kale recipes throughout this book.*

Serves 8

1 medium bunch Tuscan kale (*cavolo nero*), tough stems removed, leaves coarsely chopped (about 1 pound)

4 cups loosely packed fresh Italian parsley leaves

3 cloves garlic, crushed and peeled

2½ teaspoons kosher salt

1 cup extra-virgin olive oil

¼ cup grated Grana Padano

8 boneless, skinless chicken breasts (about 2½ pounds)

4 tablespoons unsalted butter

All-purpose flour, for dredging

1 pound cremini mushrooms, trimmed and thickly sliced

6 fresh sage leaves

½ cup dry white wine

1 cup chicken stock (page 148)

In a food processor, combine the kale, parsley, garlic, and 1½ teaspoons of the salt. Pulse to make a coarse paste. With the machine running, pour in all but 2 tablespoons of the olive oil in a slow, steady stream. Process to make a smooth pesto. Scrape 1 cup of the pesto into a medium bowl (store the rest for another time). Stir in the grated cheese.

With a meat mallet, pound the chicken breasts between sheets of plastic wrap to an even thickness of about ½ inch. Season the cutlets with ½ teaspoon of the salt. Spread the pesto on the chicken, and roll up tightly, securing the rolls closed with toothpicks.

Heat a large skillet over medium heat, and add the remaining 2 tablespoons olive oil and 2 tablespoons of the butter. Spread some flour on a plate, and lightly dredge the rolls in flour, tapping off the excess. Brown the rolls all over, about 4 minutes, then remove to a plate.

When all of the rolls are out of the skillet, add the mushrooms, sage leaves, and remaining ½ teaspoon salt. Cover, and cook until the mushrooms give up their juices, about 5 minutes. Uncover, increase the heat, and cook, stirring occasionally, until they're caramelized, about 4 minutes more.

Add the wine, bring to a boil, then add the stock. Nestle the chicken rolls in the sauce, and bring to a simmer. Simmer until the rolls are just cooked through, about 7 to 8 minutes.

Remove the rolls to a platter, and remove toothpicks. Bring the sauce to a boil, and simmer to reduce to your liking. Whisk in the remaining 2 tablespoons butter, pour this over the chicken, and serve.

CHICKEN WITH TUNA SAUCE

Pollo Tonnato

When preparing this dish, don't discard the oil from the can of tuna. Taste it, and if it is not too fishy or rancid, use it in making the tonnato sauce. All of the components of the salad can be made ahead and refrigerated; just arrange the platter at the last minute. This is a great dish for a buffet; the recipe can be doubled easily.

Serves 6 as a main course or 10 as an appetizer

CHICKEN

1 large carrot, cut into chunks
2 stalks celery, cut into chunks
1 small onion, halved
2 fresh bay leaves
1 teaspoon kosher salt
2½ pounds boneless, skinless chicken breasts

SAUCE

Two 5-ounce cans Italian tuna packed in olive oil,
    oil drained and reserved
¼ cup drained capers in brine
¼ cup cornichons
3 tablespoons red wine vinegar
2 tablespoons Dijon mustard
2 anchovy fillets
⅓ cup olive oil, or less, as needed
Kosher salt, to taste

SALAD

6 stalks celery, julienned
2 large carrots, julienned
2 tablespoons extra-virgin olive oil
1 tablespoon red wine vinegar
½ teaspoon kosher salt

For the chicken, combine the carrot, celery, onion, bay leaves, salt, and 3 quarts water in a medium Dutch oven. Bring to a simmer, add the chicken, and continue to simmer until it is just cooked through, about 10 to 12 minutes. Let cool completely in the poaching liquid, then remove and refrigerate the chicken until it's cold. Reserve 1 cup of the cooking liquid and half of the carrots and celery.

For the sauce, combine the tuna, capers, cornichons, vinegar, mustard, anchovies, and the reserved poached vegetables in a blender. Add about ½ cup cooking liquid, and blend until smooth. Remove the plastic insert in the blender top, and, with the blender running, add ⅓ cup olive oil, including the reserved oil from the tuna can, unless it is not up to par, in a slow, steady stream to make a thick dressing (a little thicker than pancake batter). If the dressing is still too thick, add more poaching liquid a little at a time, and blend again. Season with salt, and refrigerate until ready to use.

For the salad, plunge the celery and carrot into a bowl of ice water until the pieces crisp and curl, about 15 to 20 minutes. Pat very dry, and put in a large bowl. Drizzle with the oil and vinegar, and season with the salt. Toss well.

To serve, spoon a bed of sauce on a platter or individual plates. Thinly slice the chicken against the grain, and arrange in an overlapping circle over the sauce. Mound the salad on top. Serve any extra dressing on the side.

ROASTED GUINEA HEN WITH BALSAMIC GLAZE

Faraona Arrosto al Balsamico

The blend of balsamic vinegar and honey to baste the guinea hen gives the bird a beautiful mahogany glaze and a delicious sweet-tart taste. This glazing technique can be used for most birds; if you can't find guinea hens, use two small organic chickens instead.

This dish makes for a festive presentation, perfect for a special dinner. Set the two birds on a cutting board or plate, decorate with some rosemary sprigs, and present them to the table; then take them back to the kitchen, carve, and serve on two platters, family style.

Serves 6

Two 2½-pound guinea hens
2 teaspoons kosher salt
Freshly ground black pepper
4 sprigs fresh rosemary
4 sprigs fresh sage
¼ cup extra-virgin olive oil
2 medium onions, coarsely chopped
1 cup chopped celery
1 cup chopped carrot
2 fresh bay leaves
2 cups chicken stock (page 148)
3 tablespoons balsamic vinegar
1 tablespoon honey

Preheat oven to 425 degrees. Remove all visible fat and the neck and giblets from the hens. Rinse the hens under cold water, and pat them dry with paper towels. Season the birds generously with the salt and pepper, inside and out. Stick one rosemary sprig and one sage sprig in the cavity of each bird.

In a heavy roasting pan or very large ovenproof skillet, heat the oil over medium heat. Add the onions, celery, carrot, the remaining rosemary and sage, and the bay leaves, and cook, stirring, until the onions are wilted, about 6 minutes. Smooth the vegetables into an even layer, and nestle the prepared hens, breast side up, over them. Roast, basting with enough of the chicken stock to keep the vegetables well moistened, until the vegetables and hens are golden brown, about 1 hour. The leg joint should wiggle somewhat freely.

Spoon off enough of the roasting juices to measure 1 cup, not including fat. Stir in the balsamic vinegar and honey until the honey is dissolved. Baste the hens. Return the hens to the oven, and roast, continuing to baste occasionally with the honey mixture, until the hens are a rich mahogany color and the leg joint moves easily when you wiggle it, about 25 minutes. (If you are using a meat thermometer, it should register 165 degrees when inserted into the thickest part of the thigh, away from the bone.)

Remove the hens from the oven, and cover them with a tent of aluminum foil to keep them warm. Strain the vegetables and pan juices through a sieve into a small saucepan, pressing as much of the vegetable solids through the sieve as possible. Skim the fat from the surface of the sauce, and bring the sauce to a simmer while carving.

To carve the birds: Remove the wings by cutting through the joint that attaches them to the body. With a long, thin knife, carve out the breast meat from each side and cut thin slices of the breast meat,

(recipe continues)

including some of the skin with each slice. Arrange the breast slices on a platter. Separate the legs from the body by cutting around the joint that connects the leg to the backbone. This will be easier if you first hold the leg by the tip of the drumstick and pull it away from the body, allowing you to see the joint that connects the leg to the backbone. Cut the legs in half at the knee joint. Arrange the leg pieces on the platter. Spoon some of the sauce over the bird, and pass the remaining sauce separately.

ROASTED CHICKEN WITH POMEGRANATE

Pollo Arrosto al Melograno

Moving the hot pans in and out of the oven while preparing this dish requires caution: make sure you have a good grip and thick oven mitts. You can also prepare this recipe with one larger roasting chicken, adding to the cooking time by about 25 percent, depending on the size.

Serves 6

Two 2½-pound whole chickens
1 teaspoon kosher salt
¼ teaspoon freshly ground black pepper
3 tablespoons extra-virgin olive oil
1 cup chicken stock (page 148)
1 cup pure pomegranate juice
6 tablespoons Grand Marnier
4 tablespoons unsalted butter
2 tablespoons fresh rosemary leaves
2 tablespoons brandy or cognac

Heat oven to 425 degrees. With kitchen shears, cut out the backbones from the chickens, starting at the neck and cutting along both sides of the backbone. Open and lay each chicken flat, skin side down, on the cutting surface. Press the chicken open and, with a paring knife, cut into the white cartilage that covers the top of the breastbone. Bend the two sides of the chicken backward; the bone will pop up. With your fingers detach the breastbone from the meat. Remove the central breastbones and the smaller attached ribs, using your fingers and a paring knife. Season both sides of the chicken halves with the salt and pepper, and rub them with the olive oil.

Place two very large cast-iron or other heavy ovenproof skillets over medium-high heat. When they're hot, place the chicken halves, skin side down, in the skillets; they should fit comfortably side by side, without overlapping. Cook until the skin is well browned, 5 to 7 minutes. Resist the temptation to peek for at least the first few minutes; the skin is much less likely to stick if it is allowed to brown and crisp. Turn the chicken pieces over, freeing the skin with a metal spatula if it sticks in places, and cook until the second side is brown, about 5 minutes.

Place the skillets in the oven, and roast, turning the chickens twice, about 20 minutes. Check at the leg joint. It should be thoroughly cooked; there should be no pink juices. Remove the skillets from the oven, and spoon off all fat. Divide the stock, juice, Grand Marnier, butter, rosemary, and brandy between the two skillets, and swirl to combine. Baste the chicken and return to the oven to roast, basting the chickens frequently and turning them once, until the meat in the thickest part between the leg and thigh reads 165 degrees on an instant-read thermometer.

Set the chickens on a cutting board and with a chef's knife cut them in half or quarters. Transfer the cut chickens to plates. Combine the sauce from both pans in one pan, and place it over medium heat. Simmer the sauce until syrupy, about 2 to 3 minutes. Strain the sauce through a fine sieve, and spoon the sauce over the chickens.

ITALIAN CHICKEN "STIR FRY"

Pollo alla Stir Fry

This stir-fry has the convenience of being finished in the oven, so you have a few minutes to spare to get your guests to the table. You can vary the vegetables, based on the season. It is a great dish for a family-style dinner, and also fits well on a buffet table; I even like it for brunch.

Serves 6 to 8

½ cup extra-virgin olive oil
1 medium onion, sliced ½ inch thick
2 bell peppers (1 red, 1 yellow), cut into ½-inch strips
2 teaspoons kosher salt
1 cup frozen peas, thawed (or use fresh if in season)
1 cup peeled frozen fava beans, thawed (or use fresh if in season; see page 40 for instructions)
3 cloves garlic, crushed and peeled
1 pound mixed mushrooms (white, cremini, shiitake, oyster, etc.), thickly sliced
1 tablespoon fresh thyme leaves
1½ pounds boneless, skinless chicken breasts, cut into 1-inch chunks
All-purpose flour, for dredging the chicken livers
8 ounces chicken livers, trimmed of all fat and sinew and cut into ½-inch chunks

Preheat oven to 400 degrees. In a large skillet, heat 2 tablespoons of the oil over medium-high heat. Add the onion and peppers, and season with ½ teaspoon salt. Toss and cook until onions are golden on the edges and beginning to wilt, about 3 to 4 minutes.

Add the peas and favas, and toss and cook until heated through, about 3 minutes more. Transfer all to a large roasting pan.

Add 2 more tablespoons olive oil to the same skillet, over medium-high heat. Add the garlic, and let it sizzle a minute. Add the mushrooms and thyme, and season with ½ teaspoon salt. Cook and stir until the mushrooms give up their liquid, then reduce the liquid away and brown, about 5 minutes. Add to the roasting pan.

In the same skillet, heat 2 more tablespoons olive oil. Season the chicken breasts with ½ teaspoon salt. Brown all over, about 2 to 3 minutes. Add to the roasting pan.

Spread some flour on a plate. Return the skillet to the heat, and add the remaining 2 tablespoons oil. Season the chicken livers with the remaining ½ teaspoon salt, and dredge lightly in the flour. Brown all over, about 2 minutes, and add to the roasting pan. Give everything a toss to combine, and roast in the oven until everything is nicely browned, about 10 minutes for rare and 15 minutes for well-done chicken livers. Serve right away.

CHICKEN LIVER SPIEDINI

Spiedini di Fegatini di Pollo

Chicken liver is flavorful, easy to cook, and inexpensive, but not used often enough in the kitchen, in my opinion. This recipe offers an easy way to do just that. Make sure the liver is fresh, and preferably from an organic free-range chicken.

Serves 4 as an entrée, or more as part of a grilling buffet

2 teaspoons kosher salt, plus more for the cooking pot
1½ pounds shiitake mushrooms, stems trimmed
¼ cup red wine vinegar
2 medium red onions, cut into chunks about the same size as the livers
6 tablespoons extra-virgin olive oil
1½ pounds chicken livers, fat and sinews trimmed, cut in half
2 lemons, 1 cut into 8 slices, 1 juiced
16 large fresh sage leaves
2 tablespoons chopped fresh Italian parsley

Bring a large pot of salted water to boil. Preheat a grill to medium heat. Soak eight wooden skewers in water for 15 minutes (or use metal skewers). Add the shiitake caps to the boiling water, and simmer just until they are floppy around the edges, about 2 to 3 minutes. Remove with a spider, and pat very dry on kitchen towels.

Add the vinegar to the water, and bring to a simmer. Add the red onions, and simmer until they just begin to wilt, about 2 to 3 minutes. Drain and pat very dry, and place with the shiitakes. Put the shiitakes and onions in a large bowl, and toss with 2 tablespoons oil and ½ teaspoon salt.

In another bowl, toss the chicken livers with 2 tablespoons of the oil and 1 teaspoon salt. Thread the livers on the skewers, alternating with the mushrooms and onions, including one lemon slice and two sage leaves on each skewer.

Grill the skewers over medium heat, turning to all sides, until the livers are just cooked through, about 10 minutes for rare to 15 minutes for well done. Remove to a platter. In a small bowl, whisk together the remaining 2 tablespoons olive oil, juice of 1 lemon, ½ teaspoon salt, and the parsley. Drizzle the dressing over the skewers, and serve.

TURKEY BREAST WITH APRICOTS

Petto di Tacchino con Albicocche

This is a fabulous dish for those special dinners when you do not feel like dealing with a whole turkey. It cooks much faster, and the recipe can be doubled, using two whole breasts, if you have a big crowd.

Serves 8

8 ounces dried apricots

½ cup bourbon

7-pound whole bone-in turkey breast (if your
    butcher has a neck or giblets, take those, too)

2 tablespoons unsalted butter, softened

2½ teaspoons kosher salt, plus more to taste

3 tablespoons extra-virgin olive oil

3 medium carrots, cut into ½-inch chunks

3 stalks celery, cut into ½-inch chunks

1 large onion, cut into 1-inch chunks

4 sprigs fresh rosemary

4 cups chicken stock (page 148)

Preheat oven to 375 degrees. In a medium bowl, combine the apricots and bourbon. Let soak 10 minutes. Remove the apricots, reserving the bourbon. Finely chop half of the apricots, and leave the other half whole.

Rub the softened butter over and under the skin of the turkey breast, and season all over with 1½ teaspoons salt.

In a roasting pan, heat the olive oil over medium heat. When the oil is hot, add the carrots, celery, and onion, and cook, stirring occasionally, until they begin to brown and soften, about 6 minutes. (If you have the neck or giblets, add them with the vegetables to brown, too.) Add the chopped apricots, and season with the remaining teaspoon salt. Pour in the reserved bourbon, and add the rosemary. Add the stock, bring to a simmer, and cook until reduced slightly, about 5 minutes.

Fit a rack in the roasting pan, over the vegetables, and set the turkey on it, skin side up. Throw the whole apricots into the sauce around the turkey. Cover with foil, and roast 45 minutes.

Uncover, and roast, basting the turkey breast occasionally, until the thickest part of the breast reads 165 degrees on a meat thermometer. Let turkey rest on a cutting board while you finish the sauce.

For the sauce, pluck out the whole apricots and set them aside. Pour the rest of the sauce into a medium saucepan, and mash with a potato masher (or put through a food mill into the saucepan). Let the sauce sit for a minute, and skim any fat from the top. Bring the sauce to a simmer, and stir in the whole apricots.

Slice the turkey, and arrange it on a platter. Spoon half of the sauce over the sliced turkey. Serve the extra sauce on the side.

TURKEY MEATLOAF WITH MUSHROOM SAUCE

Polpettone di Tacchino con Salsa di Funghi

Meatloaf, polpettone *in Italian, is always a crowd pleaser. This turkey version is lighter than most recipes, but just as delicious. It can be prepared in advance and baked before your guests arrive. Any leftovers reheat well when cut into slices and simmered in the mushroom sauce until hot. This is a favorite among my grandkids, and also works great for a potluck dinner.*

Serves 8 to 10

MEATLOAF

3 cups crustless day-old bread cubes

1 cup milk

3 pounds ground turkey

2 large eggs, beaten

2½ cups panko bread crumbs

1 cup grated Grana Padano

1 cup finely chopped red bell pepper

1 cup finely chopped scallions, white and light-green parts

⅓ cup chopped fresh Italian parsley

2 teaspoons kosher salt

2 tablespoons extra-virgin olive oil

SAUCE

¼ cup extra-virgin olive oil

2 large shallots, chopped

1¾ pounds mixed mushrooms (white, cremini, shiitake, oyster, etc.), thickly sliced (about 8 cups)

8 fresh sage leaves

1½ teaspoons kosher salt

2 tablespoons tomato paste

1 cup dry white wine

2 cups chicken stock (page 148)

3 tablespoons unsalted butter, cut into bits

3 tablespoons chopped fresh Italian parsley

For the meatloaf, preheat oven to 375 degrees. In a medium bowl, combine the bread cubes and milk, and toss. Let sit until the milk is absorbed, about 10 minutes. Squeeze out any excess milk, and put the squeezed-out bread in a large bowl.

To the large bowl, add the turkey, eggs, panko, grated cheese, bell pepper, scallions, parsley, and salt. Mix with your hands to distribute the ingredients evenly. Brush a large roasting pan with 1 tablespoon of the olive oil. Form the meat mixture into a loaf in the roasting pan, and brush with the remaining tablespoon olive oil. Loosely cover the roasting pan with foil, and bake until the meatloaf is set on the outside, about 40 minutes. Uncover, and bake until cooked through (the center of the loaf will read 165 on a meat thermometer), about 45 to 50 minutes more. Let the meatloaf rest, covered with foil to keep warm, while you make the sauce.

For the sauce, in a large skillet, heat the olive oil over medium heat. Add the shallots, and cook until they begin to soften, about 4 minutes. Add the mushrooms and sage, and season with the salt. Cover, and let the mushrooms sweat until tender, about 10 minutes.

Uncover, and increase the heat to reduce away the liquid and brown the mushrooms, about 1 to 2 minutes. Clear a space in the pan, and add the tomato paste. Cook and stir the tomato paste in that spot until it is toasted and darkens a shade or two, about 1 minute. Stir the tomato paste into the mushrooms, and add the wine. Simmer to reduce the wine by half, then add the stock. Simmer to blend the flavors and reduce the stock a bit, about 5 minutes. Right before serving, whisk in the butter until the sauce is smooth. Stir in the parsley. Slice the meatloaf, and serve the sauce on the side.

DUCK LEG AND RICE PILAF

Cosce d'Anatra con Riso al Pilaf

This very flavorful dish is a favorite of mine because you can prepare it in advance and then leave it to finish in the oven as your guests are arriving. Perfect for an intimate dinner, it also works well in the center of the table for family-style dining. Once the dish is cooked, cut the duck legs at the drumstick joint to create smaller pieces for easier service, return them to the rice, and serve.

Serves 4 to 6

4 bone-in duck legs (about 10 to 11 ounces each)
1¼ teaspoons kosher salt, plus more to taste
2 stalks celery, cut into ½-inch chunks
1 large carrot, cut into ½-inch chunks
1 medium onion, cut into ½-inch chunks
Grated zest and juice of 1 large lemon
1 lemon, halved
1 red bell pepper, cut into ½-inch chunks
¾ cup halved pitted green olives
5 cups chicken stock, or as needed (page 148)
2 cups long-grain white rice
¼ cup chopped fresh Italian parsley

Preheat oven to 400 degrees. With a sharp knife, separate the duck drumsticks from the thighs. Trim off any excess fat or skin from the duck, and cut the skin into ½-inch pieces.

For the cracklings, in a large shallow Dutch oven (or something like a paella pan), heat the duck skin over medium-low heat and begin to render the fat slowly. Stir as you go, so the fat renders evenly and the skin crisps all over, removing the pieces to a paper towel as they become brown and crisp, about 8 minutes.

Pour out all but ¼ cup of the duck fat (if you don't get ¼ cup, add olive oil). Heat the fat over medium heat. Season the duck pieces with ¼ teaspoon kosher salt. Brown the duck in the fat on all sides, 8 minutes.

Add the celery, carrot, and onion, and season with the remaining teaspoon of salt. Add the lemon juice and zest, cover, and cook until the onion begins to wilt, about 6 minutes.

Add the bell pepper and olives and 1 cup stock. Bring to a simmer, and cook until pepper is almost tender and stock is entirely reduced away, about 5 minutes.

Add the rice, and stir to coat it in the fat. Let it toast for a minute or two, then pour in the remaining 4 cups stock. Turn the duck pieces skin side up. Sprinkle with the crisp duck cracklings. Cover, and bake until rice is al dente, about 20 minutes. Uncover, and bake 5 minutes more to crisp the top. Squeeze the juice of the remaining lemon over all, and sprinkle with the parsley. Remove from oven, cut the duck legs here, if desired, and return to rice. Toss, and serve hot.

What Wine to Serve?

Choosing wine can be as simple or as complicated as you like. Wine at a meal is usually paired with each course, but it is not unusual to go through a whole meal with a single sparkling wine, such as champagne or prosecco, or a favorite white or red. Selecting a wine is a personal and economic choice. For a stand-up reception or a buffet, a good sparkling wine such as prosecco, a good white wine, and a good red should be offered throughout the evening. Let the guests choose which they prefer. For an elegant sit-down dinner, it is impressive to offer a different wine with every course; start with a champagne or prosecco before dinner, followed by a white, then perhaps a rosé, followed by red wine, paired to the flavors of each dish of the meal served. As a rule of thumb, white wine goes well with light appetizers, fish, some pastas, and light chicken preparations; red wine pairs well with more robust flavors, usually meats like a more intensely flavorful chicken preparation, veal, pork, beef, and game. A good dessert wine is always a glorious finish. If you are a wine aficionado, then the choice can really be fun; otherwise, if you take your menu to your local wine shop, they will gladly recommend wines within your budget.

If you are making or printing a menu for your meal, which is an added touch that your guests will appreciate, make sure you include the wine, with the producer and the vintage noted. Specify the wine underneath the course it is served with. For smaller dinner parties, wine can make for a good topic of conversation, so take the time to do a little bit of research about what you are serving, such as learning about the wine maker and the region it comes from.

BRAISED VEAL SHANK

Ossobuco alla Milanese

This is one of my favorites, and it is always on the menu at our restaurant Becco in the theater district in Manhattan. You will likely have to special-order veal shanks cut to this thickness from your butcher, so be sure to plan in advance. This cut is the shank of the front leg of a calf, and when it is cooked it becomes fork-tender, which is why it is important to tie it with some kitchen twine, so it does not fall apart in the pot. Ossobuco is best when cooked a few hours or even a day or two in advance so that it soaks up the flavors of the sauce. This dish feels luxurious, and it is a bit expensive, but it makes a rich main course for a sit-down dinner that you can prepare in advance, so you can enjoy your guests. This recipe can easily be doubled for larger parties.

Serves 6

VEAL

About 8 cups chicken stock (page 148)
6 veal shanks cut 3 inches thick (about 1 pound each)
2 fresh bay leaves
4 whole cloves
1 sprig fresh rosemary
10 juniper berries
2 teaspoons kosher salt
All-purpose flour, for dredging the meat
½ cup vegetable oil
¼ cup extra-virgin olive oil
2 cups finely chopped onions
½ cup shredded carrot
½ cup finely chopped celery
1 tablespoon tomato paste
1 cup whole canned Italian San Marzano tomatoes, crushed by hand
2 cups dry white wine
1 orange, zest removed with a vegetable peeler, and juiced
Zest of 1 lemon, removed with a vegetable peeler
Freshly ground black pepper, to taste

GREMOLATA

2 tablespoons finely chopped fresh Italian parsley
2 plump cloves garlic, finely chopped
Finely grated zest of 1 lemon

Put the stock in a medium saucepan, and warm it over low heat. Stand the shank pieces up on a flat end. Cut six lengths of twine, each about 2 feet long, and wrap one around the outside of each ossobuco, in the middle (the meat will look as though it's wearing a very tight belt). Tie the twine securely, and trim the ends. Cut a small square of cheesecloth, and wrap in it the bay leaves, cloves, rosemary sprig, and juniper berries. Tie the packet with twine.

Season the veal with ½ teaspoon of the salt. Put some flour in a shallow bowl, and dredge the veal all over in it. Heat the vegetable oil in a large Dutch oven over medium-high heat. When the oil is hot, brown the veal all over, turning to brown all sides, about 8 minutes. Remove the veal to a plate as it browns.

When all the veal is browned, carefully pour the

(recipe continues)

hot vegetable oil out of the empty pan, leaving the crusted bits of meat on the bottom. Pour in the olive oil, set the pot over medium-high heat, and add the onions, carrot, and celery. Stir them around for a minute or two, scraping the pan to release the caramelized bits. Drop in the cheesecloth herb sachet, season with the remaining 1½ teaspoons salt, and cook, stirring, until the vegetables are sizzling and wilting, about 4 minutes. Clear a space in the pan, and add the tomato paste. Cook and stir the tomato paste in that spot until it is toasted and darkens a shade or two, about 1 minute, then stir it into the vegetables. Add the crushed tomatoes, stir well, and bring to a boil. Raise the heat to high, pour in the wine, and cook for a couple of minutes at a boil, to evaporate the alcohol. Pour in the orange juice and about 6 cups of the hot stock; drop in all the strips of citrus zest, and bring the liquids to a boil. Return the ossobuco to the saucepan, side by side so they're evenly immersed in the sauce. Add more hot stock if necessary, just to cover the tops of the ossobuco with liquid. Cover the pan, and lower the heat so the sauce is perking steadily. Cook for an hour or so, covered, checking that the sauce has not reduced too much and is still covering the meat (add stock if needed).

Turn the ossobuco over in the pan. Cook, uncovered, for another hour or more at a bubbling simmer, adjusting the heat as necessary to maintain the slow but steady concentration of the sauce. As the braising-liquid level gradually drops, carefully turn the shanks again, so no parts dry out. Cook for 2 to 3 hours in all, until the meat at its thickest part is tender enough to pierce with a fork with only slight resistance, and the sauce is thick, reduced well below the tops of the shank pieces. Season with fresh pepper to taste. Turn off the heat. Lift the shanks from the pot with sturdy tongs, letting the sauce drain off, and place them on a large platter. Cut off the twine, and discard the sachet.

Strain the sauce through a sieve, pressing on the solids, and return it to the pot to keep warm. (If it is too thin, quickly reduce it over high heat.) Stir together the chopped parsley, garlic, and lemon zest for the gremolata just before serving, for freshness. Rewarm the veal in the sauce, and turn to coat. To serve, spoon sauce over the veal on a platter, and sprinkle lightly with gremolata (about ½ teaspoon per serving). Serve with small spoons for scooping the delicious marrow from the bones, and pass the remaining gremolata at the table.

VEAL SCALOPPINE WITH GREEN OLIVES AND ZUCCHINI

Scaloppine di Vitello con Olive e Zucchine

This is a quick and easy way to serve veal for a dinner party. All of the ingredients can be prepped ahead of time, and take under 10 minutes in a skillet to cook when you're ready to serve. You can also make this with thinly pounded scaloppine of pork tenderloin or chicken breast. Usually to get a more uniform size of scaloppine it is best to have your butcher slice them for you.

Serves 4 to 6

1¼ pounds of veal leg scaloppine
¼ cup extra-virgin olive oil
7 cloves garlic, crushed and peeled
1 teaspoon kosher salt
1 pound medium zucchini, cut into thick
   3-by-½-inch matchsticks
Pinch crushed red pepper flakes
1 cup large pitted green olives, slivered
2 tablespoons drained capers in brine

With a meat mallet, pound the scaloppine between sheets of plastic wrap, to an even thickness of ¼ inch.

In a large bowl, toss together the veal, 2 tablespoons of the oil, three of the garlic cloves, and ½ teaspoon salt. Let marinate 15 to 20 minutes at room temperature.

Heat the remaining 2 tablespoons olive oil in a large skillet over medium-high heat. When the oil is hot, add the remaining four garlic cloves, and let them sizzle a minute. Add the zucchini, and season with the remaining ½ teaspoon salt and the red pepper flakes. Cook and toss until the zucchini begins to wilt, about 3 to 4 minutes. Add the olives and capers, and toss to combine. Cook and toss until the zucchini is tender, about 2 minutes more. Remove the skillet from the heat but keep it warm.

Heat another large skillet over medium-high heat. When it's hot, sear the veal in batches (you don't need to add any additional oil) until it's browned and just cooked through, about 2 minutes per side. Set aside and keep the scaloppine warm. Once all of the veal is done, spoon the zucchini onto a warm platter and top with the veal. Serve immediately.

VEGETABLE-STUFFED POACHED BREAST OF VEAL

Cima Genovese

This veal breast stuffed with a vegetable frittata is a traditional dish from Liguria, in northern Italy. Cut into slices that look like a vegetable mosaic and topped with some traditional green sauce, it is fit for every table, whether served as an appetizer, as a main course, or on a buffet table. It might seem to require a lot of work, but I promise, the many compliments it earns you will make it worthwhile.

Serves 8 to 10

VEAL

½ cup extra-virgin olive oil

1 medium carrot, cut into 2-by-¼-inch sticks

1 medium zucchini (about 7 ounces), cut into 2-by-¼-inch sticks

1 medium red bell pepper, cut into 2-by-¼-inch sticks

3 ounces fresh spinach, stemmed

½ cup shelled fresh peas

6 large eggs

½ cup milk

4 ounces prosciutto, sliced ⅛ inch thick, julienned

5 teaspoons kosher salt

Freshly ground black pepper, to taste

1 breast of veal, about 6½ pounds, boned and butterflied by your butcher

4 large hard-boiled eggs

1 medium onion, sliced

1 medium carrot, sliced

3 fresh bay leaves

SALSA VERDE

2 hard-boiled eggs, yolks and whites separated, finely chopped

¾ cup extra-virgin olive oil

½ cup red wine vinegar

½ cup finely chopped roasted red bell peppers

½ cup finely chopped cornichons

½ cup very thinly sliced scallions

¼ cup finely chopped red onion

¼ cup chopped fresh Italian parsley

2 tablespoons chopped fresh chives

2 tablespoons drained tiny capers in brine

¼ teaspoon mustard powder

Kosher salt, to taste

For the veal, in a large skillet, heat the olive oil over medium heat. Add the julienned vegetables, spinach, and peas, and cook, tossing lightly, until softened, about 5 minutes. In a small bowl, lightly beat the raw eggs and the milk together. Add to the skillet, and cook, stirring, until the eggs are scrambled loosely. Off the heat, stir in the prosciutto, and season with 1 teaspoon salt and pepper to taste. Spoon the mixture into a colander set over a bowl, and allow it to cool to room temperature.

Cut a piece of butcher's twine long enough to reach completely around the breast of veal three times lengthwise, keeping in mind that the meat will be thicker when it is stuffed, and thread the twine into a trussing needle. On a flat surface, open the veal as you would a book, with the longer side facing you. Season the surface with 1 teaspoon salt and pepper to taste, then spread the drained egg mixture over one side of the veal breast, leaving a 1-inch border along the edges. Arrange the hard-boiled eggs end to end over the length of the filling. Fold the other half of the veal over the filled side, as you would close a book, and tightly stitch the open edges together, drawing the twine through the meat at 1-inch intervals. Wrap the veal breast tightly in a double thickness of cheesecloth, and tie the package crosswise at 2-inch intervals with more butcher's twine.

Fill a deep pot, large enough to hold the veal comfortably, halfway with cold water. Add the remaining 1 tablespoon salt, the sliced onion, sliced carrot, and bay leaves, and bring to a simmer. Slip the veal roll into the water, and adjust the heat to maintain a gentle simmer until the veal feels tender when pierced with a skewer, about 2¼ hours. Transfer the drained veal to a roasting pan, and set a second, smaller roasting pan, a loaf pan, or the like on top of it. Place weight of about 4 pounds, such as a couple of large cans of tomatoes, in the second pan, and allow the stuffed veal to cool to room temperature.

While the veal cools, make the salsa verde. In a medium bowl, stir together all of the ingredients except the salt. Season with salt, and refrigerate until you slice the veal.

To serve, unwrap the cooled stuffed veal, remove the stitches, slice as you would a jelly roll, and spoon the salsa around the meat.

OVEN-BRAISED PORK CHOPS WITH APPLES, ONIONS, AND DRIED CHERRIES

Costolette di Maiale con Mele, Cipolle, e Ciliegie

This delicious and festive recipe is easily doubled for a larger group—you can bake it in two skillets or transfer it all to a large roasting pan. With the onions and fruits like built-in side dishes, it is always a nice big pan roast to bring out to the table for a holiday meal.

Serves 4

½ cup dried cherries

½ cup dry white wine

4 center-cut bone-in pork chops, about 1¼ inches thick (about 3 pounds total)

1 teaspoon kosher salt

3 tablespoons extra-virgin olive oil

4 cloves garlic, crushed and peeled

2 medium onions, each cut into 6 wedges through the root end

2 large Golden Delicious apples, peeled, cored, and each cut into 6 wedges

8 large fresh sage leaves

¼ cup white wine vinegar

2 tablespoons honey

Preheat oven to 425 degrees. Put the cherries and wine in a bowl, and let the cherries soak 10 minutes to soften.

Season the pork chops with ½ teaspoon of the salt. Heat a large ovenproof skillet over medium-high heat, and add the olive oil. When the oil is hot, add the chops and brown on both sides, about 2 minutes per side.

Add the garlic. Once it is sizzling, tuck the onions and apples into the spaces around the chops, and cook, moving them around as needed, until golden, about 5 minutes. Scatter the sage leaves in the spaces in the pan, and season with the remaining ½ teaspoon salt.

Stir the vinegar and honey into the cherries and wine, and pour this into the pan. Bring to a simmer, and put the skillet on the bottom rack of the oven. Bake, turning the chops, apples, and onions twice during baking, until the pork is cooked through and the juices have reduced to a glaze, about 20 minutes.

To serve, remove the chops to a platter or plates. If the juices are still too thin, reduce them on the stove a bit. Spoon the glazed apples and onions over the chops, and serve.

ROASTED PORK SHOULDER WITH ROASTED VEGETABLE SAUCE

Spalla di Maiale Arrosto al Sugo di Verdure

Pork shoulders (also called butts or Boston butts) are terrific roasts, tastier than pork loin, in my opinion, and definitely less expensive. To feed a big crowd, ask your butcher to cut a larger butt for you, or cook two smaller ones in a single very big roasting pan. Be sure to increase the vegetables, seasonings, cooking liquids, and cooking time proportionally with your meat.

Serves 6 to 8

ROAST

5-to-7-pound bone-in pork shoulder roast, exterior fat trimmed to ¼ inch

1½ teaspoons kosher salt

2 tablespoons extra-virgin olive oil

PAN AND SAUCE

4 medium onions, cut into ½-inch chunks

2 medium carrots, cut into ½-inch chunks

2 medium leeks, white and light-green parts, cut into ½-inch chunks

3 stalks celery with leaves, cut into ½-inch chunks

¼ cup dried porcini mushrooms, crumbled or chopped (about ½ ounce)

1 teaspoon whole black peppercorns

6 whole cloves

1 tablespoon fresh rosemary leaves

2 fresh bay leaves

3 tablespoons extra-virgin olive oil

1 teaspoon kosher salt, plus more to taste

1½ cups dry white wine

3 cups chicken stock (page 148)

For the roast, arrange a rack in the middle of the oven, and preheat to 400 degrees. Rinse and dry the butt, leaving the entire layer of fat on the top. Place it in a roasting pan, and sprinkle the salt on all sides. Pour on the olive oil, and rub it all over the roast. Set the meat, fat side up, in the center of the pan.

For the sauce, scatter all the chopped vegetables, the porcini, peppercorns, cloves, rosemary, and bay leaves into the pan around the meat. Drizzle with the olive oil, and season with the salt, tossing the vegetables around to combine. Pour the white wine and broth into the pan. The liquid should come up to about an inch on the sides of the meat; if not, add water as needed.

Set the pan in the oven, and roast for an hour; then stir the vegetables and rotate the pan back to front.

Roast for another hour or a little more (depending on the size of the roast). The internal temperature should be 170 degrees on an instant-read thermometer, and the meat should be browned all over with dark edges; the top (especially the fat) should be crisp and caramelized. There will still be a considerable amount of juices in the pan, and the vegetables should be cooked through and lightly browned. The roast is ready to serve now, unless you want to glaze it, in which case raise the oven temperature to 425 degrees and cook for an additional 15 minutes.

To make the sauce and finish the roast, lift the pork out of the roasting pan with a large spatula, and rest it on a platter. Set the roast on a warm corner of the stove, covered loosely with foil.

Remove the bay leaves, and then, with a potato masher, crush the cooked vegetables in the juices, breaking them up into little bits. Set a sieve in a medium saucepan, and pour everything from the pan into the sieve, including any flavorful caramelized bits that can be scraped up. Press the vegetables and other solids against the sieve with a big spoon to release their liquid, and then discard them. Let the liquid settle, and when the fat rises, skim it off. Set the saucepan over high heat; bring the juices to a boil and let them reduce to 3 cups, uncov-

ered. (Add water before reducing if needed to make 3 cups.)

For further browning of the meat, return the roast to the roasting pan. When the oven is at 425 degrees, set the pan on a higher rack, baste with some sauce, and roast until browned and crusty, about 10 to 15 minutes, checking the meat frequently and turning the pan if browning unevenly.

Let the roast rest for 10 minutes before serving. Insert a long knife blade into the meat so it rests, then draw the knife blade along the bone, following its contours, and the meat will lift off. Arrange the boneless pork on a warm serving platter.

To finish the sauce, cook the strained roasting juices until they have reduced by half, or to a consistency you like. Moisten the roast with some of the sauce, and pass the rest of the sauce.

PORK SHOULDER WITH GENOVESE SAUCE

Spalla di Maiale con Salsa Genovese

This pork shoulder makes a great dish for any crowd and is also a wonderful addition to any buffet table. This recipe makes enough to sauce 2 pounds of pasta. If you're serving a smaller group, any leftover sauce will freeze very well. It is an easy sauce to make. Once you put it in the pot, it will cook by itself—just stir now and then, so it does not stick. The sauce needs about 3 hours, but the end product is worth it.

Serves 8 to 12

6 tablespoons extra-virgin olive oil, plus more for drizzling

3½-pound bone-in pork shoulder, exterior fat trimmed to ¼ inch

1 tablespoon kosher salt, plus more for the pasta water

4 pounds onions, sliced ¼ inch thick

1 pound carrots, cut into chunks

6 cloves garlic, crushed and peeled

2 tablespoons tomato paste

4 fresh bay leaves

2 pounds cavatappi or other tube pasta

1 cup grated Grana Padano

Heat 4 tablespoons of the olive oil in a large Dutch oven over medium heat. Season the pork all over with 1 teaspoon of the salt. When the oil is hot, add the pork, and gently brown all over, about 10 minutes. Remove to a plate.

Add the remaining 2 tablespoons oil and the onions. Cook and stir until they begin to wilt, about 8 minutes.

In a food processor, combine the carrots and garlic, and process to make a *pestata,* or paste, of the vegetables. Scrape the *pestata* into the onions, and cook until it begins to dry out, about 6 minutes. Clear a space in the pan, and add the tomato paste. Cook and stir the tomato paste in that spot until it is toasted and darkens a shade or two, about 1 minute, then stir it into the onions. Drop in the bay leaves, and season with the remaining 2 teaspoons salt. Put the pork on top, reduce the heat to low, and cover. Let cook, checking occasionally to make sure the onions aren't scorching, until the onions have turned into a silky sauce and the pork is very tender, about 3 hours. The secret to the success of this sauce is low-temperature long cooking time. The cooking juices will be released by the onions and meat, so stirring periodically is a must.

Bring a large pot of salted water to boil for the pasta. Remove the bay leaves from the Dutch oven, and shred the meat with two forks, discarding fat and bone. Bring the pork and its sauce back to a simmer.

Add the pasta to the pot, and cook until al dente. Remove the pasta with a spider directly to the sauce, and add a drizzle of olive oil. Toss to coat the pasta, adding a little pasta water if it seems dry. Off heat, sprinkle with the grated cheese, toss, and serve.

ROASTED PORK LOIN WITH CABBAGE AND DRIED CHERRY SAUCE

Filetto di Maiale al Forno con Cappucci e Salsa di Ciliegie

This is an easy, flavorful, and elegant dinner course. Pork loin filet is easy to cook and slice, and the cabbage and cherry sauce are simple to prepare; once you have all the ingredients ready, you can have dinner in 1 hour. This recipe can easily be multiplied for bigger crowds, as well as made in advance and reheated for serving. Just keep in mind not to overcook the meat when reheating.

If you can't find fennel powder, you can make your own by grinding fennel seeds in a spice grinder.

Serves 6 to 8

PORK

2-to-2½-pound boneless pork loin, tied to keep its shape
2 teaspoons kosher salt
2 teaspoons fennel powder (store-bought or made by milling fennel seeds in a spice grinder)
4 tablespoons unsalted butter
2 tablespoons extra-virgin olive oil
4 cloves garlic, crushed and peeled
1 medium onion, sliced
1 large head green cabbage, cored and shredded
2 fresh bay leaves
3 sprigs fresh thyme
½ cup dry white wine
½ cup dried cherries

CHERRY SAUCE

2 cups dried cherries
1½ cups dry white wine
1½ cups chicken stock (page 148)
2 fresh bay leaves
1 teaspoon fresh thyme leaves
2 tablespoons balsamic vinegar

2 tablespoons unsalted butter
½ teaspoon kosher salt

For the pork, preheat oven to 375 degrees. Season the pork all over with 1 teaspoon salt and 1 teaspoon fennel powder. Heat a large Dutch oven over medium heat. Melt 2 tablespoons of the butter in the olive oil. When the butter is melted, sear the pork all over, about 6 minutes total, then remove to a plate.

When the pork is out, melt the remaining 2 tablespoons butter in the Dutch oven, and add the garlic. Once the garlic is sizzling, add the onion and cook until wilted, about 4 minutes. Add the cabbage, bay leaves, and thyme, and season with the remaining salt and fennel powder. Cook until the cabbage just begins to wilt, about 5 minutes. Add the white wine, and bring to a simmer. Add 1 cup water. Set the pork on top of the cabbage, and cover the pot. Roast 20 minutes.

After 20 minutes, uncover, stir in the dried cherries, and continue to roast until a thermometer inserted into the center of the pork reads 145 degrees,

(recipe continues)

about 25 to 30 minutes more. Let rest 10 minutes before slicing.

Meanwhile, for the sauce, in a medium saucepan, combine the dried cherries, white wine, chicken stock, bay leaves, and thyme. Bring to a simmer, and cook until cherries are very soft, about 20 minutes. Let cool slightly, and remove bay leaves. Pour into a blender, and add the vinegar, butter, and salt. Carefully blend until smooth. Return to the saucepan, and reheat over low heat while you finish the pork.

Once the pork has rested, remove the strings and thinly slice. Serve the pork on a bed of the cabbage, with the sauce on the side.

PORK SCALOPPINE WITH OLIVES AND CELERY

Scaloppine di Maiale con Olive e Sedano

This dish is best when made right before serving, but you can prep all of the ingredients earlier in the day. Once that is done, the dish comes together in one pan in less than 20 minutes, making it a good choice for weeknight entertaining.

Serves 6

2 pork tenderloins (about 2 pounds total)
1 teaspoon kosher salt
All-purpose flour, for dredging
4 tablespoons unsalted butter
2 tablespoons extra-virgin olive oil
1 cup finely chopped celery (about 4 stalks)
2 cloves garlic, crushed and peeled
1 cup pitted green olives (such as Cerignola), sliced or slivered
¼ cup drained capers in brine
½ teaspoon celery seeds
½ cup dry white wine
Juice of 1 lemon
1 cup chicken stock (page 148)
2 tablespoons chopped fresh Italian parsley

Slice the pork on the bias into ½-inch-thick medallions. Season all over with ½ teaspoon of the salt. Spread some flour on a plate for dredging.

In a large skillet over medium-high heat, melt 2 tablespoons of the butter in the olive oil. When the butter has melted, brown the pork on both sides, in batches, about 2 minutes per side, removing the pork to another plate as it browns.

Pour the fat from the skillet. Over medium heat, melt the remaining 2 tablespoons butter. Add the celery and garlic, and cook until the celery begins to soften around the edges, about 4 minutes. Add the olives, capers, and celery seeds. Once everything is sizzling, add the wine and lemon juice. Bring to a boil, add the stock, and simmer to reduce by about a third, about 3 to 4 minutes.

Return the pork to the pan, and simmer until just cooked through, about 3 to 4 minutes. Stir in the parsley, and serve.

PANCETTA WITH FENNEL-FLAVORED EGGS AND APPLES

Uova all'Essenza di Finocchio con Mele

This is an ideal breakfast or brunch dish. Serve with lots of crusty bread to soak up the juices from the apples, pancetta, and eggs. If you cannot find fennel powder, it is easy to make by grinding fennel seeds in a spice grinder. Keep it in a glass jar; it will come in handy to add a subtle fennel flavor to your rubs and marinades.

Serves 6

PANCETTA AND APPLES

Six ¼-inch-thick slices pancetta (8 ounces total)
1 tablespoon extra-virgin olive oil
2 tablespoons cider vinegar
2 tablespoons unsalted butter
2 medium Golden Delicious apples, cored and cut crosswise into 6 rings each
2 tablespoons maple syrup

FENNEL EGGS

2 tablespoons extra-virgin olive oil
6 large eggs
¼ teaspoon kosher salt
¼ teaspoon fennel powder
2 tablespoons grated Grana Padano

For the pancetta and apples, lay the pancetta in one layer in a large skillet over medium heat, and drizzle with the olive oil. Cook until the pancetta has rendered its fat and is crisp, turning as needed, about 5 to 6 minutes. Remove to a paper-towel-lined plate to drain. Drain off all but a thin layer of fat from the pan.

Over medium heat, add the vinegar and butter, and stir to combine. Add the apple rings and cook, moving them around in the pan, until they are tender and golden, about 4 minutes.

Add the pancetta back to the skillet, and drizzle the maple syrup over all. Cook, turning the pancetta and apples, until evenly glazed, about 2 minutes. Keep warm while you make the eggs.

For the eggs, set a large (12-inch) nonstick skillet over a burner that's still off. Swirl the pan with the olive oil, and gently break all the eggs to fill the pan, taking care not to break the yolks. Sprinkle with the salt and fennel powder. Sprinkle the grated cheese over all.

Cover the skillet, and turn the flame to medium low. Cook until the whites are set and the yolks are done to your liking, about 7 to 8 minutes for still-runny yolks.

To serve, set the apples and pancetta on a warm plate, and top with a cooked egg.

SAUSAGES AND APPLES

Salsicce e Mele al Tegame

This flavorful one-pot meal is perfect for when big crowds are coming, because the recipe can easily be doubled. It is great for family-style dining or buffets.

Serves 6 to 8

¼ cup extra-virgin olive oil
12 links sweet Italian sausage without fennel seeds (about 2½ pounds)
2 medium onions, halved, then quartered at the root end
1½ teaspoons kosher salt
8 fresh sage leaves
¼ cup cider vinegar
4 Golden Delicious apples, cored and cut into 8 wedges each

Heat a large shallow Dutch oven or very large skillet over medium heat. Add the oil. When the oil is hot, add the sausages and brown all over, about 5 to 7 minutes.

Add the onions and 1 teaspoon salt. Stir to coat the onions in the oil. Cover the skillet, and let the onions brown and wilt, stirring occasionally, about 5 minutes.

Scatter in the sage leaves, and add the vinegar and ¾ cup hot water. Bring to a simmer, cover, and cook until onions are wilted, about 5 minutes.

Add the apples, remaining ½ teaspoon salt, and 1 cup water. Bring to a simmer, set the cover ajar, and cook until apples are tender, about 10 to 15 minutes.

Uncover the pan, increase the heat to get the juices bubbling, and simmer until the juices reduce and glaze the sausages, apples, and onions, about 2 to 3 minutes. Serve right away.

ROASTED POTATOES WITH SAUSAGE

Salsicce e Patate al Forno

Since everything is already cut into serving-sized pieces, you can set this rustic dish right out in the roasting pan and let guests serve themselves. It is great for those days when you are not sure how many will show up for dinner! It's also a good dish to add to your buffet table. Make some extra; any leftovers can be chopped up for a frittata or sandwich filling the next day. My family adores this dish.

Serves 8 to 12

5 tablespoons extra-virgin olive oil

10 links sweet Italian sausage without fennel seeds, cut in thirds crosswise (about 2 pounds)

1½ pounds russet potatoes, unpeeled, cut into 1-to-2-inch chunks

3 small bell peppers (red, yellow, and orange), stemmed, seeded, and cut into 1-to-2-inch chunks

3 small onions, cut into 1-inch wedges but left attached at the root end

3 or 4 hot pickled cherry peppers, halved and seeded (or leave seeds in for more heat)

6 cloves garlic, crushed and peeled

4 sprigs fresh rosemary

¼ cup red wine vinegar

2 teaspoons kosher salt

1 bunch scallions, white and green parts, chopped (about 1 cup)

Preheat oven to 425 degrees. Heat 2 tablespoons of the olive oil in a large skillet over medium heat. When the oil is hot, add the sausages and brown all over, about 6 to 7 minutes. Put the sausages in a large roasting pan.

Add 1 tablespoon oil to the skillet, and add the potatoes over medium heat. Brown all over, about 4 minutes, then add to the roasting pan. Repeat with the bell peppers, then the onions, adding 1 tablespoon of oil to the skillet each time.

Once all of the vegetables are in the roasting pan, add the pickled cherry peppers, garlic, and rosemary to the skillet, and get everything sizzling. Add the vinegar and ¾ cup water, and bring to a boil. Scrape up any browned bits from the bottom of the pan with a wooden spoon, and pour the mixture from the skillet over the contents of the roasting pan. Season all with the salt, and toss. Cover the roasting pan with foil, and roast until the vegetables are just tender, about 30 minutes.

Uncover, and roast until the vegetables are very tender and glazed, tossing occasionally, about 15 minutes more. Add the scallions, toss, and serve.

STUFFED CABBAGE LEAVES

Foglie di Cavolo Cappuccio Farcite

Stuffed cabbage is a dish we cannot take off the menu in our restaurant Lidia's Kansas City. The stuffed cabbages can be made a day or two ahead, and they freeze well. But when you reheat them, do so over a medium flame or in the oven, adding a little water if they are dry. This is a perfect dish for family gatherings or buffet tables. The recipe can be doubled with no difficulty; just make sure you have a large enough casserole dish to cook everything comfortably. Otherwise, cook in two pans.

Serves 8

1 large head green cabbage (about 4½ pounds)
1 cup white wine vinegar
7 tablespoons extra-virgin olive oil
2 large onions, chopped
¾ cup long-grain white rice
6 cups chicken stock (page 148)
One 35-ounce can whole San Marzano tomatoes, crushed by hand
2½ teaspoons kosher salt
¼ teaspoon freshly ground pepper
1 pound ground beef
1 pound ground pork
1 large egg, beaten
1 cup fine dried bread crumbs
⅓ cup chopped fresh Italian parsley

With a paring knife, core the cabbage. Bring a large pot of water to a boil, add the vinegar, and place the cabbage in the pot, weighed down to keep it submerged. Cook until the leaves soften, about 12 minutes; remove the cabbage, and cool under running water.

Carefully remove sixteen whole leaves from the cabbage, saving the remainder for other uses, and set them aside to drain on paper towels. In a medium saucepan, heat 3 tablespoons of the oil over medium heat, add ½ cup of the onions, and cook until translucent, about 3 minutes. Stir in the rice, add 1 cup of the chicken stock, and bring to a simmer. Cover, and cook over low heat 7 minutes. Set aside to cool.

In a large Dutch oven, heat the remaining olive oil over medium heat. Add the tomatoes and remaining 5 cups stock. Season with ½ teaspoon of the salt and the pepper. Let simmer.

In a large bowl, combine the ground meats, egg, bread crumbs, reserved rice, parsley, and the remaining 2 teaspoons salt and some pepper, mixing well. Divide the mixture into sixteen equal portions, and roll each into a sausagelike cylinder about 2½ inches long. Working with one cabbage leaf at a time, place a cylinder of stuffing perpendicular to the stem. Roll the leaf around the stuffing, forming a snug fit, and tuck in both ends of the leaf to enclose the stuffing completely. Repeat with the remaining cabbage leaves and stuffing. Arrange the cabbage rolls side by side in two layers in the casserole with the tomato sauce, gently shake the pan so the sauce spreads evenly, and return to a simmer. Gently stir cabbage rolls from time to time to prevent them from sticking to the bottom of the pan and scorching. Reduce the heat to low, and simmer gently until the cabbage is very tender and the sauce is thick and flavorful, about 1½ hours. Cover partially during the last 30 minutes. To serve, spoon the tomato sauce over the cabbage rolls.

Ring in the New Year Right

There are endless ways in which to host a New Year's Eve party, from serving just appetizers and finger foods to doing something a little more elaborate and setting up a buffet or a sit-down dinner. I say, ring in the new year with a great meal and a splurge.

I like to begin a bit informally, with a family-style spread on the table. Platters of smoked or pastrami salmon, shrimp and mixed bean salad (page 122), octopus and potato salad (page 254), or Prosciutto di Parma "purses" (page 36) set a very festive tone and are perfectly accompanied by prosecco or spumante. If I want to do a course of *primi* Italian style, I serve a baked pasta that can be prepared in advance, such as lasagna with ricotta and mozzarella (page 224) or baked stuffed shells (page 221). For the main course, I like to go with something that makes a big splash at the table. Roasted chicken with pomegranate (page 275), oven-braised pork chops with apples, onions, and dried cherries (page 295), beef tenderloin with roasted vegetables and porcini sauce (page 318), and Maremma-style steak (page 309) are some of my favorite meat entrées to serve. If you want to stay a bit lighter, a whole roasted fish, such as salmon, or roasted lobster with fennel (page 253) would be equally good and impressive. Then, of course, there are the side dishes. Some of my favorites are a raw and cooked salad (page 116), asparagus and leeks in lemon vinaigrette (page 104), and skillet Brussels sprouts with lemon sauce (page 158). The meat or fish should be presented to the table for a round of applause before being portioned and served. Take your bow when appropriate! Since the oven is going, make roasted pear, blueberry, and grape compote (page 331), served with a scoop of vanilla ice cream, for a wonderful finale.

An Italian tradition still in full practice is to serve some cotechino and lentils after midnight—a good omen for the new year. The cotechino, a flavorful and rich sausage from the Modena area, signifies a tasty and fulfilling life in the next year, and the lentils represent an abundance of coins—that is, money. Usually, just a small tasting is served and the rest eaten for lunch on New Year's Day. Cotechino sausage can be bought in Italian specialty shops like Eataly; boil it according to the directions on the package. Try my lentils with butternut squash (page 157) to serve with it.

MAREMMA-STYLE STEAK

Bistecca alla Maremmana

At Felidia, we do several dishes that serve two or more, which are brought to the table and carved tableside for the guests. This is one of the most popular. Whether in the restaurant or at home, everybody loves a good steak, and this is a particularly impressive one. Even though the Italians in general are not big steak-eaters, the area of Tuscany around Florence is famous for its mammoth steaks, known as bistecca alla fiorentina. *Maremma is a very rustic county in Tuscany—to the west, toward the Tyrrhenian Sea—where a substantial number of cattle are raised. The cut of meat used here is a Porterhouse, which is similar to a T-bone steak but with a larger cross-section of the tenderloin (filet mignon) along one side of the T. Either will yield good results, but choose a prime steak that has been aged properly for 2 to 3 weeks, and make sure it is cut evenly in thickness, with some of the protective outer fat left on.*

Serves 6

1 tablespoon fresh rosemary leaves
2 teaspoons coarse sea salt
2 tablespoons extra-virgin olive oil, plus more for
    serving
1 Porterhouse steak, 2½ to 3 inches thick, about
    3 pounds, at room temperature

Finely chop the rosemary leaves with a chef's knife, and place in a mortar with the salt. With a pestle, crush and grind them together into a coarse rub. Continue grinding with the pestle as you drizzle in the olive oil, until the mixture has thinned to spreading consistency. Cover, and set aside.

Preheat a gas or charcoal grill to medium heat. Lay the steak on the grill, and grill the first side for 8 to 10 minutes, until the meat is well browned and marked. Turn onto the other side, and cook for another 8 to 10 minutes. Set the steak on its edges, letting it stand or holding it with tongs, and grill the edges until browned, about 5 minutes total. Insert an instant-read thermometer into the center of the meat. It's rare to medium rare if it reads 120 degrees and feels springy to the touch. If it is below 120 (and

it may be, depending on the thickness of the steak and the heat of your grill), continue to grill, flipping and checking the temperature every 2 minutes.

When done, set the steak on a platter or carving board, and immediately brush it with the rosemary paste, coating it lightly on all surfaces. Let the steak rest for 10 minutes, allowing the natural juices and the seasonings to permeate the entire cut.

To serve, cut the large loin and tenderloin meat sections away from the T-bone. Once you have the two pieces of meat, slice each piece on a slight bias into ½-inch-thick strips, keeping the slices together, and reposition the sliced piece of meat back on the T-bone in the original position. Pour any juices released in carving over the meat, and drizzle with a bit of extra-virgin olive oil.

LAYERED CASSEROLE WITH BEEF, CABBAGE, AND POTATOES

Casseruola di Manzo, Cavolo Cappuccio, e Patate

This is a wonderful dish from the Italian Alps. It is easy, delicious, and, once you have done the preparation, a one-pot complete meal that can be brought, still bubbling from the oven, to a family-style meal. Just set a coaster and a spoon and plop the hot casserole down. This recipe can easily be multiplied, made in multiple baking vessels, and spread along the table.

Serves 8 or more

12 large fresh sage leaves
¼ cup fresh rosemary leaves
8 plump cloves garlic, crushed and peeled
⅔ cup extra-virgin olive oil
1 tablespoon kosher salt
2 pounds red potatoes, sliced ½ inch thick
4-pound boneless beef shoulder roast (preferably top blade or top chuck shoulder roast)
1 stick (8 tablespoons) unsalted butter, softened
1 head savoy cabbage, about 2½ pounds, cored and sliced into ½-inch shreds
2 cups dry white wine
1 pound Italian Fontina, shredded

Preheat oven to 375 degrees. In a food processor, combine the sage, rosemary, garlic, ¼ cup of the olive oil, and ½ teaspoon of the salt into a fine-textured paste. Put the potato slices in a large bowl; sprinkle with 1 teaspoon salt, 2 tablespoons olive oil, and 1 tablespoon of the paste (*pestata*). Toss well to coat the slices with the seasonings.

Slice the beef across the grain into ¾-inch-thick slices (if using a top blade roast, slice it crosswise). Put the meat slices in a second large bowl, and add 1 teaspoon salt, 2 tablespoons olive oil, and 2 tablespoons of the paste.

Brush a 10-by-15-inch (or slightly larger) baking dish with the remaining olive oil and 2 tablespoons of the butter. Arrange half of the potato slices in a single layer on the pan bottom, spread half the cabbage shreds evenly over the potatoes, and season with ¼ teaspoon salt. Distribute all the beef slices in a single layer over the cabbage and press down on the beef. Dot the top of the beef with 2 tablespoons of butter. Lay the remaining potato slices on top of the beef slices, spread the rest of the cabbage evenly over the slices, and season with the remaining ¼ teaspoon salt. Stir all of the remaining *pestata* into the white wine, pour this all over the cabbage shreds, and dot the top with the rest of the butter.

Tent the baking dish with a sheet of aluminum foil, arching it above the food so it doesn't touch and pressing it against the sides of the pan. Bake until the meat and vegetables are all very tender and almost all of the liquid has been absorbed, about 2 to 2½ hours.

Increase oven temperature to 425 degrees. Remove the foil, and sprinkle the shredded Fontina over the top of the potatoes and cabbage (which will have sunk down in the pan). Bake another 20 minutes or so, until the Fontina has melted, bubbled, and browned into a crusty topping. Let the casserole rest for 10 minutes. Set the roasting pan on a trivet at the table, and serve family style.

BEEF AND POTATO GOULASH

Goulash di Manzo e Patate

You can use sweet Hungarian paprika or spicy Spanish smoked paprika in this recipe. The difference in flavor is just what's in the name: one is mild and sweet, the other spicy with a smoky flavor. The goulash can be fully prepared a day or two ahead of time, just reheat gently before serving. If you're making it ahead, slightly undercook the potatoes and onions so they don't overcook when you reheat. This is a great recipe for family gatherings; it can be doubled easily. Just make sure you have a wide enough Dutch oven so the ingredients are not so overcrowded that the potatoes break. The dish is also welcome on a buffet table, and any leftovers freeze well. For casual affairs, I like to put the pot in the middle of the table on a trivet and let people help themselves.

Serves 8 to 12

4 pounds boneless beef chuck roast, cut into 2-inch chunks

1 tablespoon kosher salt, plus more to taste

All-purpose flour, for dredging

4 ounces thickly sliced pancetta, chopped

6 cloves garlic, crushed and peeled

⅓ cup extra-virgin olive oil

¼ cup tomato paste

2 tablespoons sweet paprika

1 teaspoon ground cumin

4 fresh bay leaves

Zest of 1 lemon, grated

2½ pounds russet potatoes, peeled and cut into 2-inch chunks

3 medium onions, cut into 6 wedges each, through the root end

Bring 8 cups water to a bare simmer in a saucepan, and keep it simmering. Season the beef with 2 teaspoons salt. Spread some flour on a rimmed sheet pan, and toss the beef to coat it lightly, tapping off the excess.

In a mini–food processor, pulse the pancetta and garlic to make a smooth paste, or *pestata*. Heat a large Dutch oven over medium heat, and add the oil. When the oil is hot, add the beef in two batches, and brown all over, about 6 to 8 minutes per batch. Remove the beef to a plate as it browns.

Once all of the beef is out, scrape the garlic and pancetta *pestata* into the pot. Cook and stir until the fat is rendered, about 4 minutes. Clear a space in the pan, and add the tomato paste. Cook and stir the tomato paste in that spot until it is toasted and darkens a shade or two, about 1 to 2 minutes.

Put the beef back in the pot. Sprinkle with the paprika and cumin, and season with the remaining teaspoon of salt. Stir to distribute the tomato paste, and add 4 cups of the hot water. Drop in the bay leaves and lemon zest, cover, and simmer until the beef just begins to become tender, about 1 hour, adding 2 cups more water after 30 minutes.

After 1 hour, add the potatoes and onions and the remaining 2 cups of hot water. Cover, and simmer until the beef and vegetables are very tender, about 45 to 50 minutes more; uncover during the last 20 minutes or so, to thicken and reduce the sauce. Remove the bay leaves, season with salt, and serve.

BRAISED BEEF ROLLS STUFFED
WITH BARLEY

Involtini di Manzo Farciti al Farro

Allow for two beef rolls per guest if this is the only entrée, or one per guest as part of a larger buffet. The rolls can be made and braised a day ahead. Remember that you only need ¼ cup uncooked barley to make 1 cup cooked. You could also use another hearty grain in its place, such as farro or brown rice. Cook the grain al dente (slightly undercooked) for this recipe: it will cook further inside the rolls.

Serves 6 or more

FILLING

2 tablespoons extra-virgin olive oil
1 small carrot, finely diced
1 stalk celery, finely diced
½ small onion, finely diced
½ teaspoon kosher salt
1 cup cooked barley
2 tablespoons unsalted butter, cut into pieces
½ cup grated Grana Padano

ROLLS AND SAUCE

2¾-pound piece beef bottom round
1½ teaspoons kosher salt, plus more to taste
18 to 24 medium spinach leaves
3 tablespoons extra-virgin olive oil
2 small onions, quartered at the root
2 medium carrots, cut into 2-inch chunks
2 stalks celery, cut into chunks
3 tablespoons tomato paste
2 cups dry white wine
¼ cup dried porcini mushrooms, rinsed (about ½ ounce)
4 whole cloves
4 cups chicken stock (page 148)

For the filling, add the olive oil to a medium skillet over medium heat. When the oil is hot, add the carrot, celery, and onion, and season with the salt. Cook and stir until the vegetables have begun to soften, about 5 minutes. Add the barley and the butter, and toss to melt the butter and coat the barley. Remove from the heat, let cool, and stir in the grated cheese.

For the rolls, slice the beef against the grain into twelve slices (it will be easier to slice if very cold). With a meat mallet, pound the slices to an even thickness of about ¼ inch.

Lay the slices out flat on your work surface, and season both sides with 1 teaspoon salt. Cover the tops of the slices with three or four spinach leaves per slice, pressing to adhere. Form the filling into balls, and put one at the bottom of the short end of each roll. Tuck the corners in, and roll each up the long way, to form a compact roll. Secure each one closed with one or two toothpicks.

For the sauce, add the olive oil to a large Dutch oven over medium heat. When the oil is hot, add the rolls, and brown all over, in batches if necessary, about 4 minutes per batch. Remove the rolls to a plate as they brown.

Add the onions, carrots, and celery, and cook until the edges begin to brown, about 4 minutes.

Clear a space in the pan, and add the tomato paste. Cook and stir the tomato paste in that spot until it is toasted and darkens a shade or two, about 1 minute. Stir the tomato paste into the vegetables.

Add the wine, porcini, cloves, and remaining ½ teaspoon salt, and bring to a simmer. Return the rolls to the pot, and add 2 cups of the stock. Cover, and simmer until the beef is very tender, about 2 hours total, adding the remaining 2 cups stock about halfway through.

To serve, remove the rolls to a deep platter, and remove and discard the toothpicks. Put the carrots on the platter as well. Fish out the cloves, pass the rest of the sauce and solids through a food mill or sieve, and rewarm in a saucepan. Season the sauce with salt if necessary, and pour over the rolls to serve.

La Grande Grigliata—Barbecue Italian Style

Grigliata mista is a staple on summer menus in Italy. A platter of mixed grilled meats, which usually includes steak, lamb chops, sausage, and chicken and is served with a salad, is one of the most popular things to serve during the hot Mediterranean summers. In coastal areas, the *grigliata mista* often features a mix of fish and seafood instead of meat, with squid, shrimp, and white fish being the staples.

Italians love to grill their vegetables as much as they do their proteins. Season peppers, eggplants, and mushrooms with some olive oil and salt, grill them gently over medium heat before cooking your meat or fish, and pile them on serving platters, covered with aluminum foil to keep warm.

While you have the grill going, throw on some slices of bread for bruschetta. The grilled bread makes for perfect hors d'oeuvres; just top with some diced tomatoes dressed with olive oil, salt, and some shredded basil.

The key to good grilling is knowing your grill. How hot does it get, and how well does it maintain the heat? You also need to know what gets cooked at high heat and quickly, such as a thick steak, and what needs a lower temperature and a longer cooking time, such as chicken on the bone. Patience is of the essence: grilled items should not be flipped too often, particularly if you're cooking whole fish, which will begin to break and fall apart if moved around too much on the grill.

Most grilled meats in Italy are seasoned with salt, pepper, and herbs, such as rosemary. Let them sit for 20 to 30 minutes before they go on the grill. Italians rarely use marinades or barbecue sauce, but occasionally a dried rub is applied to meats. The rub is usually made of some salt, rosemary, and wild fennel powder or dry porcini powder.

An Italian *grigliata* should be informal, with the grilled vegetables, salads, bread, and piping-hot platters of meat or fish put out on a serving table so your guests can help themselves. The traditional finale is almost always seasonal fruits, and if you want to add that extra touch, throw some peaches, apricots, or figs on the grill.

BEEF AND ROOT VEGETABLES BRAISED IN RED WINE

Brasato Manzo e Verdure Invernali al Vino Rosso

This hearty one-pot meal is perfect for a dinner party, especially in the fall or winter. It is great for family-style dinners, too, and can be made a day or two in advance—it reheats well. You can easily substitute whatever you have on hand for the vegetables; just keep in mind that the cooking time may need to be adjusted. I use red wine here, which gives the stew a lot of body, but white wine is good as well. This recipe is also very good using game meat instead of beef. Boar and venison are excellent prepared this way; just keep in mind that the game meat might be tougher and take longer to cook. Add more stock when cooking, and check the doneness of the meat by inserting a fork. If the fork penetrates the meat easily and slides out cleanly, that is an indication that the meat is likely done.

Serves 8 to 10

6-pound boneless beef bottom round roast, tied
6 cups chicken stock (page 148)
½ cup dried porcini mushrooms (about 1 ounce)
¼ cup extra-virgin olive oil
2 teaspoons kosher salt, plus more to taste
3 ounces thickly sliced pancetta, coarsely chopped
1 medium onion coarsely chopped, plus 2 medium onions cut into 2-inch chunks
1 medium carrot, cut into chunks
4 fresh bay leaves
2 sprigs fresh rosemary
2 sprigs fresh sage
One 6-ounce can tomato paste
One 750ml bottle dry red Italian wine
2 pounds rutabaga or turnips, peeled and cut into 1-to-2-inch chunks

To tie the boneless beef bottom round you will need a long piece of butcher's twine. Tie the twine tight around the large part of the roast with a square knot. With your index finger, hold the twine down about 1 inch from the first knot. With your other hand, wrap the twine around the meat. Press the twine under the twine held by your index finger, pull it tight, pass under once more, and repeat the same procedure 1 inch lower. Repeat until finished. Cut the excess twine and secure the knot.

Preheat oven to 350 degrees. In a medium saucepan, heat the stock to just simmering. In a spouted measuring cup, ladle 1 cup of the stock over the dried porcini and let soak 5 minutes. Keep the rest of the stock simmering.

In a large Dutch oven heat the oil over medium heat. Season the beef all over with 1 teaspoon salt. Brown the beef all over, about 8 minutes, then remove.

In a food processor, combine the pancetta, the coarsely chopped onion, and the carrot. Process to make a smooth paste or *pestata*. Scrape the *pestata* into the pot once the beef has been removed, and cook until the fat is rendered, about 4 to 5 minutes. Add the bay leaves, rosemary, and sage. Clear a space in the pan, and add the tomato paste. Cook and stir the tomato paste in that spot until it is toasted and darkens a shade or two, about 2 to 3 minutes. Add the wine, stir the tomato paste into it, and pour in the porcini and stock, leaving any grit from soaking in the bottom of the cup. Season with the remaining teaspoon salt. Add 3 cups hot stock, and put the roast in the pan. Cover, and bake 1½ hours.

After 1½ hours, add the remaining 2 cups stock, the rutabagas or turnips, and the 2 onions cut into chunks. Cover the pot, and continue to bake until the meat and vegetables are very tender, about 1 to 1½ hours more.

Remove the meat to a cutting board, and remove the strings. Discard the bay leaves and herb sprigs from the sauce. Bring the sauce to a boil, reduce to your liking, and season with salt if necessary. Thinly slice the meat against the grain, return it to the sauce to moisten it, and serve.

BEEF TENDERLOIN, ROASTED VEGETABLES, AND PORCINI SAUCE

Filetto di Manzo con Verdure al Forno e Salsa di Funghi Porcini

This is a preparation for an elegant meal and therefore requires a bit more attention. But once done it is fantastic. The sauce can be prepared and the vegetables can be partially cooked in advance, but the filet should be seared at the last minute. As delicious as the beef tenderloin is in this recipe, you can substitute a pork loin—just make sure to adjust the cooking temperature accordingly.

Serves 8 to 10

SAUCE

3 cups chicken stock (page 148)
1 cup loosely packed dried porcini mushrooms
   (about 2 ounces)
2 tablespoons extra-virgin olive oil
1 small onion, coarsely chopped
1 medium carrot, coarsely chopped
3 cups dry white wine
2 sprigs fresh rosemary
3 fresh bay leaves
2 tablespoons honey
½ teaspoon kosher salt, plus more to taste
3 tablespoons unsalted butter, chilled, cut into
   pieces

BEEF AND VEGETABLES

1½ pounds carrots, cut into 1-inch chunks
1½ pounds new red potatoes, halved
1 pound white boiling onions, peeled, and halved
   through the root
7 tablespoons extra-virgin olive oil
1 tablespoon plus 1 teaspoon kosher salt
1 whole boneless beef tenderloin roast, about 3 to
   3½ pounds, tied (see page 316)
1½ pounds button mushrooms, trimmed

Preheat oven to 425 degrees. Warm the stock in a small saucepan, remove from heat, and add the porcini. Let soak and soften 10 minutes, then strain, reserving the soaking liquid and the porcini.

In a large saucepan, heat the olive oil over medium heat. When the oil is hot, add the onion and carrot, and cook until the onion begins to wilt, about 4 minutes. Add the wine, rosemary, bay leaves, honey, and ½ teaspoon salt. Add the soaked porcini, and pour in the soaking liquid, leaving any grit from soaking behind. Cover, and simmer to blend the flavors, about 20 minutes. Uncover, and cook until vegetables are very soft and sauce has reduced by about a third, about 10 to 15 minutes more. Pass the sauce through a sieve, pressing on the solids, and return it to the saucepan. Keep warm.

For the beef, in a large bowl, toss the carrots, potatoes, and onions with ¼ cup olive oil and 1½ teaspoons salt. Dump the vegetables into a roasting pan large enough to hold them in one layer. Roast on the bottom rack of the oven until the vegetables begin to color, about 15 minutes.

While the vegetables roast, brush the beef with 1 tablespoon of the oil and 2 teaspoons of the salt. Heat a large skillet over medium-high heat. Sear the beef until it's brown all over, about 8 minutes.

Remove the roast to the cutting board, and add the remaining 2 tablespoons oil to the skillet. Add the button mushrooms, and season with the remaining ½ teaspoon salt. Brown the mushrooms all over, about 5 minutes.

After the potatoes, onions, and carrots have roasted 15 minutes, stir in the button mushrooms and place the seared roast on top of the vegetables.

Roast, stirring the vegetables occasionally, until the roast reads 125 degrees on an instant-read thermometer for medium rare, about 20 minutes. Remove the roast to a cutting board, and let rest 5 minutes.

Rewarm the sauce over low heat, and whisk in the butter pieces. Season with salt if necessary. Remove the strings, and thinly slice the beef. Serve the beef on a bed of the vegetables with the sauce on the side.

ROASTED LAMB SHOULDER WITH CARROTS AND PARSNIPS

Spalla d'Agnello Arrosto con Carote e Pastinaca

Lamb shoulder roasts generally come rolled and tied. If yours is, untie and unroll it to give yourself a flat piece of meat about 2 inches thick. This recipe is a nice way to do roast lamb and vegetables all at the same time, and makes a hearty family meal when you pile the roasted vegetables on a platter or two, slice the roasted lamb, and set it on top. Collect all the remaining sauce in the roasting pan, and drizzle it over the meat. This recipe is easily doubled; just make sure you have a large enough roasting pan so the meat and vegetables aren't crowded, or use two roasting pans.

Serves 6 to 8

1½ pounds large carrots, cut into 2-inch chunks

1½ pounds parsnips, cut into 2-inch chunks

4 stalks celery, cut into 1 inch chunks

½ cup dried porcini mushrooms, coarsely chopped (about 1 ounce)

2 fresh bay leaves

1 tablespoon chopped fresh thyme leaves

1 tablespoon chopped fresh sage leaves

1½ teaspoons kosher salt, plus more to taste

3 tablespoons extra-virgin olive oil

3½-pound boneless lamb shoulder roast, trimmed of excess fat

2 cups chicken stock (page 148)

1 cup dry white wine

2 tablespoons red wine vinegar

1 bunch scallions, white and light-green parts, chopped (about 1 cup)

Preheat oven to 425 degrees. In a large stainless-steel roasting pan, combine the carrots, parsnips, celery, porcini, bay leaves, thyme, sage, and ½ teaspoon salt. Drizzle with 2 tablespoons of the olive oil, and toss well. Season the lamb with the remaining teaspoon salt, and rub with the remaining tablespoon oil. Set on top of the vegetables, and pour the stock and wine into the pan. Cover tightly with foil, and roast for 1 hour.

Uncover, and give everything a stir. Roast, uncovered, until the lamb is very tender, about 1 hour to 1 hour and 15 minutes more. Remove the lamb to a cutting board to rest.

Set the roasting pan on the stovetop, and reduce the sauce to your liking, stirring constantly so the vegetables don't burn. The finished sauce should glaze the vegetables. When the sauce is reduced, add the vinegar and scallions, and give everything a quick final boil. Remove the bay leaves, and season the sauce with salt if necessary. Thickly slice the lamb against the grain, and return it to the sauce to warm it before serving.

LAMB AND FENNEL STEW
Agnello Brasato con Finocchio

Have your butcher cut the lamb shoulder into pieces for you, with the bone still attached—it will add flavor and moisture to the finished stew. This is a delicious, easy, and economical one-pot meal for the family, or double the recipe for a party or buffet. It can be prepared a day in advance; any leftovers will freeze well.

Serves 8

All-purpose flour, for dredging
4 pounds lamb shoulder on the bone, cut into 2-to-3-inch chunks
1 tablespoon kosher salt, plus more to taste
3 tablespoons extra-virgin olive oil
2 medium onions, chopped
4 fresh bay leaves
2 tablespoons tomato paste
1 teaspoon celery seeds
One 28-ounce can whole San Marzano tomatoes, crushed by hand
2 large fennel bulbs, trimmed, cored, and cut into 2-inch chunks
3 tablespoons chopped fresh Italian parsley

Heat 6 cups water over low heat in a small saucepan, and keep it hot. Spread some flour on a plate. Season the lamb all over with 2 teaspoons salt, and dredge the pieces in flour, tapping off the excess. Heat a large Dutch oven over medium heat. Add the oil. When the oil is hot, sear the lamb in batches until brown all over, about 8 to 10 minutes. Remove the pieces to a plate as they brown.

When all of the lamb is out of the pot, add the onions and bay leaves, and cook until they begin to soften, about 5 minutes. Clear a space in the pan, and add the tomato paste. Cook and stir the tomato paste in that spot until it is toasted and darkens a shade or two, about 1 minute. Stir the paste into the onions, and sprinkle with the celery seeds and remaining 1 teaspoon salt. Add the tomatoes, slosh out the can with 2 cups of the hot water, and add that to the pan. Cover, and simmer 45 minutes.

After 45 minutes, uncover and add 2 cups more hot water and the fennel. Cover, and continue to simmer, adding more water as needed to keep the meat almost covered. Continue to cook until the meat is tender, about 45 minutes to an hour more.

Remove the lamb to a deep platter, remove bay leaves, and bring the sauce to a boil to reduce it to your liking. Stir in the parsley, pour the sauce over the lamb, and serve.

Setting the Mood by Setting the Table

The way you set your table is indicative of the mood and setting you want to create for your event. It begins with the table or tables you use—round or square or oblong—the tablecloths, and the color of your place mats, if you use them. The centerpieces, be they fresh flowers, fruits, or simple candles, all help to set the tone. Your settings of cutlery and glassware will be an indication early on whether there will be multiple courses and different wines served.

My preference is for comfortable elegance: a nice tablecloth and cloth napkins to match, with a homemade centerpiece of flowers and branches from my garden, which I love to mix with seasonal fruits and vegetables. For glasses, I use an elegant, simple cut for white and red wine, and distinctly different ones for water. I do not like to clutter the table with too much cutlery, just enough to accommodate the food I have chosen to serve. I do the dessert setup when the table is clear and I'm ready to serve.

I like to start my event by serving the antipasto as a buffet, which allows the guests to mingle and leaves the table setting untouched for the sit-down part of the meal. Asking everyone to be seated for a plated course of pasta or soup brings us all together and gives the event a slightly more formal feel. I then serve the main course individually plated, but the *contorni* or side dishes, usually vegetables, are served family style, encouraging my guests to share and pass the food around, creating even more of a sense of familiarity among them. For a big dinner crowd, I will sometimes serve the main course family style, on platters, as well.

For dessert, I like to revert to a buffet, with lots of cookies and fresh fruit to give everyone a chance to mingle again and to take as little or as much of their favorites before sitting down together to enjoy. There are times when particularly important people come to dinner, or the occasion warrants a more formal setting; for these I take out my best tablecloth, silverware, crystal, and old china, but it is not my preferred way to have a dinner at my house.

Whether the event is formal or casual, it is always important to set the table properly. You may want to start with a charger plate underneath the dinner plate if it is a truly elegant affair. This is followed by the plate for the next plated course, such as soup or pasta. Choose a favorite napkin fold, and place it directly on or to the left of the plate. The knife goes on the right, with the cutting edge facing inward, and the spoon to the right of the knife. The forks go on the left, with the fork first to be used the farthest away from the plate and the main-course fork next to it. The dessert fork or spoon is brought to the table just before dessert is served, fork left, spoon right. There are some variations, particularly if you have an antipasto knife or a fish fork and knife. Glasses are placed toward the right of the plate, at about two o'clock, with the bigger, red wine glass the farther from the plate, then the smaller, white wine glass closer to the plate, which will be used first, and then the water glass next to the white wine glass.

A table well set is a clear indication to your guests that you are pleased and excited to have them and that you look forward to cooking for and eating with them.

Desserts

Italy has one of the largest repertoires of desserts, yet Italian desserts and sweets are less often consumed after a meal, but, rather, in a separate social setting. A *passeggiata,* leisurely stroll, after a meal in Italy usually includes a social interlude with a sweet. On Sunday afternoons, Italians generally have their meal at home and then meet for some *dolci e caffè.* It is an easy way to share some time with people you are fond of without having to do much work to entertain. Continuing this tradition, I find that a dessert party or gathering is a great way to celebrate an occasion.

Many desserts can be prepared in advance, such as my almond torte with chocolate chips (page 335), pear and chocolate tart (page 344), or apple cherry strudel (page 346). Simply put them out buffet style with serving utensils, allowing your guests to take what they want in whatever amount they want to gobble down. A mix of cakes, tarts, and fresh fruits, as well as cooked fruits such as baked pineapple (page 330) and spoon desserts like berry tiramisù (page 349) and coffee panna cotta (page 351), is always a good idea; of course, also include something chocolatey, such as chocolate orange truffles with different coatings (page 355). Add some good espresso, coffee, and tea, and then sit back and enjoy being with your guests! Instead of serving individually plated desserts at a dinner party, a buffet-style sampling is also a good way to end a dinner. Just set a nicely decorated table with the dessert choices, china, and service utensils, and let your guests help themselves.

POLENTA WITH HONEY AND BERRIES

Polenta Croccante e Dolce con Frutti di Bosco

Three cups hot polenta (about half the recipe on page 193) poured into a 13-by-9-inch baking pan, when chilled, can be portioned into twelve slices, with some scraps for the cook to nibble on. An assortment of berries is good for the warmer months; some maple sugar and poached fruits are perfect for winter. When I was a young girl, polenta was often eaten with sugar or honey as dessert, and this remains one of my favorite ways to eat it even now.

Serves 6 as dessert or 3 as breakfast

1 cup strawberries, stemmed and halved, or
    quartered if large
1 cup blueberries
1 cup blackberries or raspberries
3 tablespoons honey
2 tablespoons dark rum, cognac, or brandy
2 tablespoons unsalted butter
12 slices chilled cooked polenta, about
    3 by 2 by ½ inch each
Confectioners' sugar, for dusting
6 fresh sprigs mint, for garnish

Preheat oven to 200 degrees. In a large bowl, combine the berries, honey, and rum, and toss well. Let them stand, tossing once or twice, while preparing the polenta.

In a large heavy nonstick skillet, melt half the butter over medium heat. When the butter is foaming, add half the polenta slices in a single layer. Sauté the polenta, turning once, until golden brown on both sides, 8 to 10 minutes. Transfer the polenta to a baking sheet, and keep warm in the oven. Repeat with the remaining butter and polenta.

Divide the polenta among serving plates. Spoon some of the berries and their syrup over each serving, and sprinkle with the confectioners' sugar. Decorate the plates with the mint sprigs, and serve.

BAKED PINEAPPLE

Ananas al Forno

Most desserts are vegetarian, and this one is easily also vegan if you substitute vegetable or coconut oil for the butter and serve it without ice cream. The pineapple can be baked ahead of time, and rewarmed in the oven or on the stovetop in a skillet. Without the ice cream, this will serve four as a warm fruit dessert—my favorite.

Serves 8

3 tablespoons unsalted butter, softened
1 cup loosely packed light-brown sugar
⅔ cup bourbon
Juice of 1 orange
1 pineapple, peeled, cored, and cut into 8 rings
Vanilla ice cream, for serving

Preheat oven to 375 degrees. Spread the butter on the bottom of a 9-by-13-inch baking dish, and sprinkle with half of the brown sugar. Pour the bourbon and orange juice all around, to soak up the brown sugar. Arrange the pineapple rings on top, and sprinkle with the remaining brown sugar.

Bake on the bottom rack of the oven, basting the pineapple with the pan juices occasionally, and turning the rings once or twice, until tender and glazed, about 50 minutes. (If the pineapple is cooked and the pan juices are still too runny, you can reduce them in a skillet while you keep the pineapple warm in the oven.)

To serve, put the pineapple rings in shallow serving bowls, and serve a scoop of ice cream over the top of each.

ROASTED PEAR, BLUEBERRY, AND GRAPE COMPOTE

Pere, Mirtilli, ed Uva al Forno

The compote can be made a day ahead and warmed just before serving. It is also good as a topping for gelato, ice cream, or a slice of pound cake. One or two other fruits can be added to the pears, but they will remain the star, since they retain their shape in baking. This is my go-to dessert when I have a big dinner party. First of all, I love cooked fruit, and, second, this is so easy to prepare beforehand and then plate when dessert time rolls around that it makes entertaining easy.

Serves 6 to 8

2 cups prosecco
½ cup sugar
½ cup blueberry jam
Juice of 2 lemons
½ teaspoon pure vanilla extract
4 ripe Bosc pears, quartered and cored but unpeeled
3 cups seedless green grapes
1 pint blueberries
2 Savoiardi (ladyfingers) per guest, for serving
Whipped cream, for serving

Preheat oven to 425 degrees. In a 9-by-13-inch baking dish, stir together the prosecco, sugar, jam, lemon juice, and vanilla. Add the pears, and toss to coat. Cover the dish tightly with foil, and bake until juices are bubbly and pears are just beginning to become tender, about 20 to 30 minutes, depending on their ripeness.

Uncover, and stir in the grapes. Bake until they begin to soften, about 15 minutes more.

Stir in the blueberries, and bake until all of the fruit is very soft and the juices have thickened, about 15 minutes more.

Let cool so the juices thicken a bit, about 15 minutes. Spoon into serving bowls, and garnish each portion with Savoiardi and whipped cream.

CHOCOLATE HAZELNUT BREAD PARFAIT

Pane Inzuppato al Cioccolato e Nocciole

Bread and chocolate was a special treat for me when I was a child, and sometimes Grandma would turn it into a simple, luscious dessert like this one. The beauty of this recipe is the recycling of the old bread into something new and tasty. These parfaits can be made a few hours in advance and kept in the refrigerator until ready to serve.

Serves 6 to 10, depending on size of parfaits

6 ounces semisweet chocolate, chopped
2¾ cups heavy cream, 1½ cups of it chilled for
   whipping
¼ cup hazelnut liqueur
8 ounces thinly sliced day-old country bread, crusts
   removed, cut into large chunks (about 2 to
   3 inches)
1 cup chocolate-hazelnut spread, such as Nutella
1 cup toasted coarsely chopped skinned hazelnuts

In a double boiler (or a bowl set over simmering water), combine the chocolate and 1 cup cream over low heat. Once the chocolate melts, remove from heat and whisk until smooth. Whisk in the liqueur, and pour into a shallow baking dish. Add the bread, and turn to coat. Let the slices sit, turning occasionally, until they're soaked and softened, about 10 minutes, depending on how hard the bread is.

In the same double boiler, melt the chocolate-hazelnut spread with ¼ cup of the cream. When it's warmed, whisk until smooth. Stir in half of the chopped nuts.

Whip the remaining 1½ cups chilled cream to soft peaks.

To assemble, fit the soaked bread into the bottom of parfait cups or wineglasses, adding any soaking juices that remain (6 to 10 portions, depending on your serving size). Drizzle with the chocolate-hazelnut sauce. Top with whipped cream and a final sprinkling of nuts. Serve immediately.

BLUEBERRY AND RICOTTA PARFAIT

Ricotta con Mirtilli

If you don't want to make your own ricotta, you can substitute a good-quality fresh version from the supermarket, but this is so easy to do, you'll want to give it a try. If using store-bought ricotta, you will need about 1¼ to 1½ cups.

This is a perfect make-ahead dish, because all of the components can be prepared a day in advance. Refrigerate the ricotta and blueberries, and store the almonds in an airtight container. This combination is delightful, but you can substitute other berries, such as straw-berries or raspberries, if you want.

Serves 4

RICOTTA
2 quarts milk (preferably organic)
1 cup heavy cream (preferably organic)
½ teaspoon kosher salt
3 tablespoons lemon juice

BLUEBERRIES
1 pint blueberries
½ cup blueberry jam
⅓ cup sugar
Grated zest and juice of 1 lemon (about 3 tablespoons)
1 fresh bay leaf

ALMONDS
1 tablespoon unsalted butter, plus more for the baking sheet
1 cup sugar
¾ cup slivered almonds

Sponge cake or pound cake, cut into fingers, for serving

For the ricotta, line a large sieve with a double thickness of damp cheesecloth, and set this over a bowl. Combine the milk, cream, and salt in a medium heavy-bottomed saucepan, and slowly bring to a boil.

Add the lemon juice, and reduce the heat to the lowest setting. Stir gently until the mixture begins to curdle, about 2 minutes. Remove from heat, and let sit without stirring for 10 minutes.

Pour the mixture through the cheesecloth, and let drain 1 hour. What's left in the cloth is the ricotta. Chill until ready to use.

For the blueberries, in a medium saucepan, combine the blueberries, jam, sugar, lemon juice and zest, and bay leaf. Simmer until the blueberries break down and the sauce thickens, about 8 to 10 minutes. Cool to room temperature, and refrigerate until ready to use.

For the almonds, butter a baking sheet, or line the baking sheet with a silicone baking mat. In a small saucepan, combine the sugar and ¼ cup water, and bring to a simmer. Without stirring, cook until the sugar is a deep caramel color, swirling the pan occasionally to mix, about 4 to 5 minutes. Remove from the heat, stir in the butter and almonds, and mix well. Spread in a thin layer on the baking sheet, and let cool completely. Break into shards once cooled.

To assemble the parfaits, divide the ricotta among four parfait cups or wineglasses. Spoon the blueberry sauce on top. Sprinkle with the candied almonds, and add a cake finger on the side. Serve immediately.

ALMOND TORTE WITH CHOCOLATE CHIPS

Torta di Mandorle con Gocce di Cioccolato

This cake is delicious as is, but can also be served with a dusting of confectioners' sugar, whipped cream, or zabaglione (page 336). It's great for breakfast or brunch, as well as dessert.

Serves 10 or more

10 ounces (2½ sticks) unsalted butter, softened, plus more for the baking pan

1¾ cups all-purpose flour, plus more for the baking pan

½ teaspoon baking powder

¼ teaspoon kosher salt

1 cup sugar

5 large eggs

Grated zest of 1 lemon

1 teaspoon pure almond extract

2 cups almond flour or almond meal

1 cup semisweet chocolate chips

½ cup lightly toasted sliced blanched almonds

Preheat oven to 350 degrees. Butter and flour the bottom and sides of a 10-inch springform pan. Sift together the all-purpose flour, baking powder, and salt onto a piece of parchment.

In a mixer fitted with the paddle attachment, cream the butter and sugar at medium-high speed until light and fluffy, about 2 minutes. At medium speed, add the eggs one at a time, mixing each in thoroughly before adding the next, and scraping down the sides of the bowl as needed. Beat in the lemon zest and almond extract, then raise the speed to high and beat the batter until very light, a minute or more. At low speed, mix in half of the sifted flour mixture, beating just until it is incorporated; beat in half the almond flour. Scrape the bowl, and mix in the remaining flour and almond flour. Beat briefly at medium speed to make a smooth batter. At low speed, mix in the chocolate chips just until evenly distributed. Scrape the batter into the prepared pan, and spread it in an even layer. Scatter the sliced almonds all over the top.

Bake, rotating the pan halfway through the baking time, until the cake is golden brown on top and a knife inserted in the center comes out clean, about 45 minutes. Cool the cake in the pan for about 10 minutes on a wire rack. Run the blade of a paring knife around the edge of the cake, then open the spring and remove the side ring. Cool the cake completely before serving. Cut it into wedges, and serve.

CHOCOLATE SPONGE CAKE WITH SOUR CHERRIES AND CHOCOLATE ZABAGLIONE MOUSSE FILLING

Torta "Rigó Jancsi"

This cake takes a bit of work—and it should be assembled at least 6 hours to a day ahead—but you don't have to worry about it once it's put together, freeing you to do last-minute tasks before your gathering. Amarene are wild cherries preserved in syrup. Fabbri is a very good brand.

Serves 8 to 10

CHOCOLATE SPONGE CAKE

Unsalted butter, softened, for the cake pan
2 cups all-purpose flour, plus more for the cake pan
½ cup unsweetened cocoa powder
¼ teaspoon baking powder
¼ teaspoon baking soda
6 large eggs
1½ cups granulated sugar

CHERRY SYRUP

½ cup sweet Marsala
2 tablespoons confectioners' sugar
1½ cups amarena cherries, with their liquid, reserving ½ cup (cherries only) for decoration

FILLING

8 ounces very good quality semisweet or bittersweet chocolate, chopped
1 teaspoon unflavored gelatin
3 tablespoons cold water
7 egg yolks, at room temperature
½ cup granulated sugar
½ cup dry Marsala
1½ cups chilled heavy cream
2 tablespoons unsweetened cocoa powder

For the cake, preheat oven to 375 degrees. Butter the sides and bottom of a 10-inch-round, 3-inch-high cake pan. Sprinkle the sides and bottom with flour, making sure to coat the entire surface, and tap out the excess.

In a small bowl, sift together the 2 cups flour, the cocoa, baking powder, and baking soda.

In a medium bowl set over a large saucepan of simmering water in double-boiler style, beat the eggs and sugar together until the mixture has warmed and the sugar has dissolved, about 3 minutes. Using a handheld electric mixer, beat the egg-sugar mixture at high speed until doubled in volume, about 5 minutes. Remove the bowl from the heat. With a rubber spatula, fold the dry ingredients into the egg mixture.

Pour the batter into the prepared cake pan, and bake until a wooden skewer or cake tester inserted into the center of the cake comes out clean and the cake's surface springs back when lightly pressed, about 25 minutes. Let it stand on a wire rack until completely cool, 1 to 2 hours, before removing from the pan.

Meanwhile, for the syrup, in a small saucepan, stir the sweet Marsala and confectioners' sugar over low

(recipe continues)

heat until the sugar is completely dissolved. Remove from the heat, add the amarena cherries and their liquid, and set aside.

For the zabaglione filling, in a small heatproof bowl set over a pan of gently simmering water, melt the chocolate, stirring often to melt evenly. Remove the pan from the heat, and leave the bowl of chocolate over the water to keep it warm. Meanwhile, sprinkle the gelatin over 3 tablespoons cold water in a small bowl. Let stand until softened, about 10 minutes.

In a medium heatproof bowl set over a pan of simmering water, whisk the egg yolks, sugar, and dry Marsala until smooth. Continue beating (switching to an electric handheld mixer, if you like) until the mixture is pale yellow and fluffy and falls in thick ribbons when the whisk or beaters are lifted, about 8 minutes if you are whisking by hand or about 4 minutes if you are using an electric mixer. It is important to whisk continuously, or the egg-yolk mixture will curdle. Scrape the softened gelatin into the egg mixture, and stir until the gelatin is dissolved. With a rubber spatula, fold the melted-chocolate mixture into the egg mixture. Let the mixture stand until cool, about 10 minutes.

Meanwhile, in a medium bowl, beat the heavy cream with an electric mixer until it forms stiff peaks when the beaters are lifted. With a rubber spatula, fold the whipped cream into the chocolate-egg mixture until no traces of white are visible.

To assemble the cake, with a long, thin serrated knife, slice the chocolate sponge cake horizontally into three even layers. Set the bottom layer into a 10-inch springform pan, and brush it with about a third of the cherry syrup—it will be quite moist. Scatter half the cherries over the cake layer. Spoon half the chocolate zabaglione filling over the cherries. Repeat with the next layer of the cake, cherries and syrup, and chocolate mousse filling, reserving 1 cup of the mousse for the top layer. Moisten the cut side of the top cake layer with the remaining syrup, and place it, cut side down, over the filling. Press very gently. Spread the remaining mousse evenly over the cake. Cover the pan securely with plastic wrap, and refrigerate until the filling is firm, at least 6 hours or up to one day.

To serve, release the side of the springform pan and remove it. With a cake spatula dunked in warm water, smooth the mousse on the top and sides of the cake. Decorate with the reserved cherries. Cut the cake into wedges with a thin, serrated knife.

HEAVENLY CAKE

Torta Angelica

This is an easy-to-make dessert that is delicious and light. Have the cake ready and the berries marinating before your guests arrive, and just assemble when you're ready to serve it. Any leftover cake is just as good toasted for breakfast.

Serves 8

CAKE

½ cup extra-virgin olive oil, plus more for the cake pan

1½ cups all-purpose flour, plus more for the cake pan

2 teaspoons baking powder

2 large eggs

2 cups confectioners' sugar

Grated zest of 1 orange

1 teaspoon pure vanilla extract

¼ teaspoon salt, plus a pinch for the egg whites

4 egg whites

ASSEMBLY

2 cups quartered fresh strawberries

½ cup sweet dessert wine, such as sweet Malvasia or Torcolato

1 cup chilled heavy cream

For the cake, preheat oven to 350 degrees. Lightly grease an 8-inch springform cake pan with olive oil. Sprinkle the inside of the pan with flour, and rotate the pan to coat the sides and bottom evenly. Tap out any excess flour. Sift the 1½ cups flour and the baking powder onto a piece of parchment.

In a mixer fitted with the paddle attachment, beat the whole eggs and the confectioners' sugar at medium speed until creamy, smooth and doubled in volume. Add the orange zest, vanilla, and ¼ teaspoon salt, and beat well to distribute. Alternate adding a little at a time of the ½ cup olive oil and the flour mixture, stirring gently after each addition, beginning and ending with the flour. In a clean mixer bowl fitted with the whisk, whip the egg whites with a pinch of salt until they hold stiff peaks when the beaters are lifted from them. Add about a fourth of the whites to the batter, and with a rubber spatula gently fold them in, scraping the mixture from the bottom of the bowl over the whites. Fold in the remaining whites in the same way.

Pour the batter into the prepared pan, and bake until the top is a deep golden brown and springs back quickly when pressed with your finger, about 40 minutes. Cool the cake on a wire rack about 20 minutes. Run a thin-bladed knife around the edges of the pan, and release the sides of the pan. Cool the cake completely before serving.

While the cake is baking, in a small bowl, toss the strawberries with the wine, and let sit at room temperature so the berries give up their juices. Whip the cream to soft peaks, and keep chilled.

To serve, slice the cake into eight wedges. Brush each slice with some of the wine juices from the berry bowl, and spoon the berries and remaining juice over top. Dollop whipped cream on each portion, and serve.

CHOCOLATE RICOTTA CHEESECAKE

Torta di Ricotta al Cioccolato

This cheesecake can be served chilled or at room temperature. I prefer it at room temperature, drizzled with some chocolate sauce and a dollop of whipped cream, or topped with my favorite fruit jam and whipped cream. This is one of the desserts at our restaurant Becco, where we serve it topped with fresh strawberries tossed in strawberry jam.

Serves 8

Unsalted butter, softened, for the baking pan
Fine dried bread crumbs, for the baking pan
4 ounces bittersweet chocolate
½ cup heavy cream
¼ cup unsweetened cocoa
5 large eggs
1 cup sugar
¼ teaspoon kosher salt
4 cups ricotta
Grated zest of 1 small orange

Preheat oven to 375 degrees. Coat the bottom and sides of an 8-inch springform pan with butter, and sprinkle with the bread crumbs to coat, tapping out the excess.

In a double boiler (or a bowl set over simmering water), gently melt the chocolate in the cream. When the chocolate is melted, remove it from the heat and whisk in the cocoa until smooth.

In a mixer fitted with the paddle attachment, beat the eggs, sugar, and salt at high speed until light and smooth, about 2 minutes. Add the ricotta and orange zest, and mix until smooth, about 1 minute. Add the chocolate mixture, and mix again until smooth, about 1 minute.

Spread the mixture in the prepared pan, and bake until set (the very center will still be just a bit jiggly), about 1 hour to 1 hour and 10 minutes. Cool on a rack completely before running a knife around the edges of the pan to unmold.

UPSIDE-DOWN RHUBARB CAKE

Crostata Invertita al Rabarbaro

This cake can be served with whipped cream, vanilla ice cream, or a dollop of crème fraîche. You should prepare and mix the rhubarb and sugar a day before so the rhubarb releases its juices. So make sure to plan ahead.

Serves 8 to 10

RHUBARB

2 pounds rhubarb, washed, trimmed, and cut into
1-inch pieces
¾ cup sugar

CAKE

1 stick unsalted butter, softened, plus more for
greasing the pan
1 cup plus 2 tablespoons sugar
1¾ cups all-purpose flour
2 teaspoons baking powder
Pinch salt
2 large eggs
½ teaspoon pure vanilla extract
1 cup milk

For the rhubarb, in a large bowl, toss together the rhubarb and sugar. Cover, and refrigerate 8 hours. Drain through a sieve or colander, reserving the juices.

Put the rhubarb and ½ cup of its juice in a skillet, and simmer until you have about 4 cups softened rhubarb, about 3 minutes. (Don't overcook; the rhubarb should still keep its shape.) Drain, reserving the juices, and let both juices and rhubarb cool completely.

For the cake, preheat oven to 375 degrees, setting a rack in the lower third. Grease a 10-inch cake pan with the extra butter, and sprinkle the bottom (but not the sides) of the pan with 2 tablespoons of the sugar. Spread the drained rhubarb in an even layer on the bottom. Sift the flour, baking powder, and salt onto a piece of parchment paper.

In a mixer fitted with the paddle attachment, combine the remaining 1 cup sugar and 1 stick butter. Beat at medium speed until smooth and light, about 2 to 3 minutes. Scrape down the sides of the bowl, and beat in the eggs one at a time, still at medium speed. Add the vanilla, and beat at high speed for 2 minutes or so, to lighten and smooth the batter.

Scrape down the sides, and, at low speed, mix in the dry ingredients in three additions, alternating with the milk, beginning and ending with the flour. Beat at high speed for about a minute, until light and completely smooth. Spread the batter evenly over the rhubarb.

Bake on the lower rack in the oven until a cake tester comes out clean and the top of the cake is golden brown, about 45 minutes. Remove the cake, and cool on a rack for about an hour. The pan should be comfortable to hold but still slightly warm when you invert it.

While the cake cools, put the reserved rhubarb juice in a small saucepan, bring it to a boil, and cook until syrupy, about 3 to 4 minutes.

To unmold the cake, run the blade of a paring knife around the side of the slightly warm pan. Cover the cake top with a round serving plate and, holding tight, flip the pan and plate upside down to invert. Slice the cake into wedges, and serve with a drizzle of the rhubarb syrup.

PEACH ALMOND CAKE

Torta di Pesche

This cake is great as is, or you can dust it with some powdered sugar, or top it with a dollop of a mixture of whipped and sour cream. It is also delicious for breakfast or brunch.

Serves 8 to 10

3 tablespoons butter, softened, plus more for the pan
4 ripe peaches
2 tablespoons Amaretto or brandy
1 tablespoon lemon juice
¾ cup plus 1 tablespoon sugar
2 cups unbleached flour
2 teaspoons baking powder
¼ teaspoon freshly grated nutmeg
¼ teaspoon salt
2 large eggs
2 tablespoons milk
¼ teaspoon pure almond extract
¼ cup sliced almonds
2 tablespoons smooth apricot jam

Preheat oven to 350 degrees. Grease a 10-inch springform pan with butter. Slice the unpeeled peaches into eighths; there should be 2 cups of sliced fruit, so add or subtract peaches accordingly. In a bowl, mix the peaches, Amaretto, lemon juice, and 1 tablespoon of the sugar, coating the peaches well, and let marinate for 10 minutes. Sift the flour, baking powder, nutmeg, and salt together onto a piece of parchment.

In a mixer fitted with the paddle attachment, beat the eggs with the milk and almond extract at medium speed until smooth. Add the remaining sugar, and beat until light, about 2 minutes. Add the sifted dry ingredients, and mix just to combine. Drop in the softened butter in pieces, and mix just until a smooth batter is formed.

Scrape and press the dough into an even layer in the prepared pan. Arrange the peaches (leaving the juices behind in the bowl, reserving them), skin side down, in a radiating pattern, and press them lightly into the dough. Sprinkle with the almonds. Bake until cooked through and golden on top, about 30 to 35 minutes. Let cool until slightly warm on a cooling rack.

Meanwhile, in a small saucepan, combine the peach juices and apricot jam. Simmer until syrupy, about 2 minutes. Brush the syrup over the warm cake, cut into wedges, and serve.

PEAR AND CHOCOLATE TART

Crostata di Pere e Cioccolata

This tart is basically pears baked in chocolate pudding. It is just as good as it sounds, and makes for a striking presentation topped with some whipped cream. I am sure it will become one of your favorites.

Serves 10 to 12

CARAMEL

⅔ cup sugar

TART

16 amaretto cookies, crumbled
½ cup unsweetened cocoa powder
¼ cup sugar
⅓ cup milk
2 large eggs, plus 1 egg yolk
1 tablespoon dark rum
½ teaspoon baking powder
¾ cup plus 2 tablespoons heavy cream
3 ripe Bosc pears, peeled, cored, and thinly sliced

For the caramel, stir the sugar and 2 tablespoons water together in a medium skillet. Cook over medium heat, stirring occasionally, until the sugar is melted and the syrup is boiling. Once it boils, don't stir, just swirl occasionally so the caramel cooks evenly. Simmer until the syrup begins to turn a medium amber color, about 7 to 8 minutes. Pour the caramel immediately into a 10-inch round heatproof pie dish or shallow casserole.

Preheat oven to 325 degrees. Choose a roasting pan large enough to hold the pie plate, and place it on the center rack of the oven. Heat a kettle of water to boiling.

Put the crumbled cookies in a blender, and blend in bursts until finely ground. Pour in the cocoa and sugar, and pulse to mix with the cookies. Pour in the milk, eggs, yolk, rum, and baking powder, and blend at low speed, stopping occasionally to scrape down the sides of the blender, until smooth. Pour in the heavy cream, and blend just enough to incorporate it. Scrape into a mixing bowl and stir in the pears.

Pour the chocolate-pear mixture into the prepared dish, and set the dish in the roasting pan. Pour in enough of the boiling water from the kettle to come halfway up the side of the pie plate. Bake until firm in the center and lightly browned on top, about 40 minutes.

Remove from the oven, and let cool in the water bath until you can safely remove it. Cool on a rack to room temperature, then refrigerate until chilled. To serve, run a thin knife around the edge of the custard to loosen. Invert a plate large enough to hold the tart comfortably, then, in one quick motion, flip the tart over and set the plate down. The tart may take several seconds to work itself loose from the dish. After it does so, gently lift off the dish, and serve the tart cut into wedges.

APPLE CHERRY STRUDEL

Strudel di Mele con Ciliegie Secche

Strudel seems like a lot of effort, but this dough is quite flexible and easy to work with. I strongly recommend making this recipe with a family member or friend. It will be much easier—and more fun! The dough can be made in advance, and it can easily be frozen; just defrost before rolling it. You might need a little extra flour on the working surface as you roll it out. The strudel can be made earlier in the day. If you'd like to serve it warm, gently reheat it, uncovered, in a 350-degree oven for about 10 to 15 minutes. It's delicious served with vanilla ice cream and the cherry sauce below (which can also be made ahead and reheated).

Serves 10 or more

DOUGH

2 cups all-purpose flour, plus more for working the dough

3 tablespoons extra-virgin olive oil

½ teaspoon kosher salt

FILLING

5 large Golden Delicious apples, cored, peeled, and sliced ¼ inch thick (about 7 to 8 cups)

10 ounces dried cherries

¾ cup sugar

Grated zest and juice of 1 large lemon

2 tablespoons dark rum

½ teaspoon ground cinnamon

ASSEMBLY

6 tablespoons unsalted butter, softened

1 cup fine dried bread crumbs

½ cup sugar, plus more for sprinkling

½ teaspoon ground cinnamon

Heavy cream, for brushing

CHERRY SAUCE

1 cup orange juice

½ cup cherry jam

For the dough, in a food processor, combine the flour, oil, and salt. Pulse a few times to incorporate. With the machine running, pour in ½ cup water, and process to make a smooth, silky dough, about 30 to 40 seconds. If the dough is still crumbly, add more water, a tablespoon at a time, to get a smooth dough that forms a ball on the blade, or add a bit more flour if it is too wet. Turn the dough onto a floured work surface and knead until very smooth and elastic, about 3 minutes. Wrap in plastic, and let rest at room temperature for 2 hours or overnight in the refrigerator. (If you do refrigerate the dough, let it come to room temperature again before rolling.)

For the filling, in a large bowl, combine the apples, dried cherries, sugar, lemon zest and juice, rum, and cinnamon. Let stand 20 minutes, tossing occasionally.

When you're ready to assemble, preheat oven to 375 degrees. Line a baking sheet with parchment paper. In a small skillet, melt 2 tablespoons of the butter over medium-low heat. When the butter is melted, add the bread crumbs, and cook, tossing often, until crisp and golden, about 4 minutes. Scrape into a bowl to cool, then mix in the sugar and cinnamon.

To roll the dough, sprinkle your work surface (at least 3 feet square) with flour. Roll the dough from the center to the edges into a very thin square about 20 by 20 inches. As the dough gets thinner, you can alternate rolling and stretching with your hands to coax it into the shape you want. If the dough tears a little, press it together to patch it. The finished square should be very thin—you should be able to see the shadow of your hand through it. (To help with rolling, at this point you can put the dough on a thin tablecloth or a sheet if you like, though you can also roll as is.)

Brush the surface of the dough with the remaining 4 tablespoons softened butter, leaving a 1-inch border around the edges. Sprinkle the crumbs on top of the butter, leaving the same border. Drain the filling (but save the juices!). Mound the filling on the lower third of the dough, leaving a 2-inch border on the bottom and 2 inches on each side.

Fold the bottom over the filling and press the dough on each side closed gently so the filling doesn't come out as you roll. (If you're using a cloth under the strudel, lift that as a guide to help you roll; otherwise ask for another set of hands to help you.) Roll the strudel, holding the filling in as you go, to make a lumpy-looking log shape. If it tears as you roll, just patch it up and continue rolling. Roll the strudel, seam side down, onto the baking sheet. Twist the loose dough on the ends to close them up, then use them to coax the strudel into a crescent shape, and tuck them under to seal completely.

Brush the strudel all over with the heavy cream, and sprinkle with sugar. With a sharp paring knife, cut six or so slits in the top of the strudel, to allow steam to escape.

Bake, rotating the pan from front to back halfway through baking, until the strudel is crispy and deep golden brown and the filling can be seen bubbling through the slits, about 40 to 45 minutes. Let it cool in the pan about 10 minutes, then use 2 large spatulas to remove from the parchment and cool on a wire rack.

While the strudel cools, make the sauce. In a small saucepan, combine the reserved filling juices, the orange juice, and the cherry jam. Simmer over medium heat until thickened and syrupy, about 10 minutes. Let cool until just warm (or rewarm if you made it ahead).

To serve, slice the strudel and serve with the warm sauce.

BERRY TIRAMISÙ

Tiramisù ai Frutti di Bosco

Tiramisù is a common dessert on the menus of Italian restaurants and in Italian homes. It is certainly a favorite in our restaurants, but it is easy to make at home as well. This dessert is best made a day ahead, to allow the flavors to combine. Any combination of berries—or even just one kind—will make a marvelous tiramisù.

Serves 10 or more

BERRIES

4 cups blueberries
6 cups thickly sliced strawberries
¾ cup granulated sugar
Grated zest of 1 orange
2 cups orange juice
1 cup chunky blueberry jam
¼ cup dark rum
¼ cup superfine sugar

ASSEMBLY

2 cups ricotta, at room temperature
Two 8-ounce containers mascarpone, at room
   temperature
¼ cup superfine sugar
1½ teaspoons pure vanilla extract
42 Savoiardi (ladyfingers)

For the berry sauce, in a medium saucepan, combine 2 cups blueberries, 2 cups strawberries, the granulated sugar, orange zest and juice, jam, and rum. Bring to a simmer, and cook to make a slightly syrupy sauce, about 10 to 15 minutes. Pour into a shallow pan (where you will be soaking the Savoiardi), and let cool.

Put the remaining 2 cups blueberries, remaining 4 cups strawberries, and the superfine sugar in a medium bowl. Toss to combine, and let sit at room temperature 10 minutes.

In a mixer fitted with the paddle attachment, mix the ricotta and mascarpone at medium speed for a few seconds to combine, then add the superfine sugar and vanilla. Beat at medium-high speed until light and smooth, about 2 minutes.

To assemble, soak half of the Savoiardi in the cooked berry sauce until moistened, rolling them around to coat thoroughly. Tightly fit these Savoiardi in the bottom of a deep 9-by-13-inch glass or ceramic dish. Spoon a few spoonfuls of the remaining cooked berry sauce over the Savoiardi. Spread half of the ricotta mixture in an even layer over the Savoiardi.

Layer a little more than half of the uncooked berries (you just want an even layer) over the mascarpone. Soak the remaining Savoiardi in the cooked berry sauce, and arrange in a tight layer over the fresh berries. Spread the remaining mascarpone over this in a smooth layer. Cover, and chill overnight for best results. Combine the remaining fresh berries and any cooked berry sauce left from soaking the Savoiardi, cover, and chill overnight.

To serve, cut squares of the tiramisù and serve with a little of the leftover berries and sauce.

CHOCOLATE CUSTARD WITH AMARETTO COOKIES

Bonet

This dessert can be prepared up to 2 days ahead. To get all of the caramel topping to unmold with the custard, dip the bottom in very hot water for 30 seconds to a minute, to loosen it. Amaretto cookies give this custard a delicious almond flavor, but any crumbly cookies you have will do just fine.

Serves 8

2¼ cups sugar
2 cups heavy cream
1 cup milk
¼ cup unsweetened cocoa powder
1 tablespoon instant espresso granules
3 large eggs, plus 3 large egg yolks
1 cup finely crushed amaretto cookies (about 20 cookies)

Preheat oven to 350 degrees. Put a kettle of water on to boil. In a medium skillet, moisten 1¼ cups sugar with ¼ cup water. Cook over medium heat until the sugar is melted and the syrup is boiling. Once it boils, simmer without stirring—just swirl occasionally so the caramel cooks evenly. Cook until the syrup begins to turn a medium amber color, about 10 to 12 minutes. Pour the caramel immediately into a 9-by-5-by-3-inch loaf pan, and carefully swirl to coat the caramel about halfway up the sides.

In a medium saucepan over medium heat, combine ¾ cup sugar, the cream, milk, cocoa powder, and espresso granules. Heat until bubbles form around the edges, then whisk until everything is dissolved and the mixture is an even color. Strain into a large, spouted measuring cup.

Meanwhile, in a large bowl, whisk the eggs, yolks, and remaining ¼ cup sugar until smooth and pale yellow. Pour in the hot cream mixture slowly, whisking constantly. Whisk in the amaretto crumbs.

Pour the custard mixture into the caramel-lined mold, and place the mold in a 9-by-13-inch glass or ceramic baking dish. Add boiling water to come halfway up the sides of the pan. Bake until the custard is set, with just a bit of jiggle left in the center, about 1 hour to 1 hour and 10 minutes.

Remove from the oven, and let cool in the water bath until you can safely remove it. Cool on a rack to room temperature, then refrigerate until chilled. To unmold, run a paring knife around the edge of the custard. Dip the bottom of the mold in hot water for 30 seconds. It should loosen very easily. Place a flat oval platter at least a couple of inches longer than the mold facedown over the custard. Holding the mold and platter firmly together, invert them with one quick motion. Wait a moment for the melted caramel to begin to seep onto the platter, then gently lift the mold. Serve the *bonet* cold, cut into 1-inch-thick slices; use a cake spatula to lift the top plate.

COFFEE PANNA COTTA

Panna Cotta al Caffè

This simple dessert couldn't be easier to prepare and is best when made a day ahead. You can garnish with chocolate-covered espresso beans or crumbled chocolate biscotti. In this recipe, the flavorings are the coffee and Sambuca, but you can use the base recipe and flavor it with whatever you want. Or omit the coffee granules and Sambuca entirely to make a plain vanilla version.

Serves 8

1 cup milk
1 tablespoon powdered gelatin
2½ cups heavy cream
¾ cup sugar
3 tablespoons instant espresso granules
1 tablespoon Sambuca or other anise-flavored
    liqueur
1 teaspoon pure vanilla extract
Pinch kosher salt

Heat the milk until just warm to the touch. Sprinkle in the gelatin, and let it dissolve, about 5 minutes.

In a medium saucepan, combine the cream and sugar over low heat. Cook, stirring, just until the sugar is dissolved and the cream bubbles around the edges, about 4 minutes.

Remove the pot from the heat, and add the milk mixture, coffee granules, Sambuca, vanilla, and salt. Stir until the coffee and gelatin are dissolved and the mixture is completely smooth.

Pour into eight 5-ounce ramekins, and chill until set, overnight.

To unmold, dip the bottoms of the ramekins in hot water for a few seconds, and loosen the edges with a paring knife. Invert a serving plate over a ramekin and flip, tapping on the bottom to loosen the panna cotta and drop it onto the plate.

SOFT ICE CREAM WITH NOUGAT

Semifreddo al Torrone

A semifreddo is a delicious and creamy rendition of an Italian ice cream, easy to make—no need for an ice-cream machine—and to serve. I love to add fruits and nuts to give a variety of flavors.

Torrone—or nougat—is loved by Italians, and it gives this semifreddo a gelateria *(traditional Italian ice-cream shop) quality and taste. Be sure to buy hard torrone for this dessert—the soft kind is impossible to chop and won't give the crunch that makes this recipe a treat. For best results, freeze overnight.*

Serves 8 to 10

5 large eggs, separated
1 cup superfine sugar
½ cup dry white wine
1 tablespoon brandy or cognac
2 cups chilled heavy cream
1 cup finely chopped torrone or other hard nougat candy with nuts

Line a 9-by-5-by-3-inch loaf pan snugly with plastic wrap. In the top of a double boiler, or in a large heatproof bowl over a pan of simmering water, whisk the egg yolks, ½ cup of the superfine sugar, and the white wine until smooth. Continue beating (switching to a handheld electric mixer if you prefer) until the mixture is pale yellow and fluffy and falls in thick ribbons when the whisk or beaters are lifted, about 8 minutes if you are whisking by hand or about 4 minutes if you are using an electric mixer. Whisk continuously, or the egg yolk will cook and the mixture will appear curdled. Remove the top of the double boiler from the heat, and set it in a large bowl of ice water. Whisk constantly until it's chilled, and then whisk in the brandy.

In a large bowl, whisk the heavy cream until it holds stiff peaks when the whisk is lifted. (You can also whisk it in an electric mixer with the whisk attachment.)

In a clean mixer bowl fitted with the whisk attachment, whisk the egg whites until foamy. While continuing to beat, gradually add the remaining ½ cup superfine sugar, and beat until the whites are glossy and form stiff peaks when the beaters are lifted.

Add about a fourth of the beaten egg whites to the chilled white wine mixture, and with a rubber spatula gently fold them in, scraping the wine mixture from the bottom of the bowl over the whites. Fold in the remaining whites in the same way. Fold the lightened wine mixture and the torrone into the whipped cream in the same way.

Transfer the mixture to the lined loaf pan, and smooth the surface with a spatula. Rap the pan on the counter a few times to remove any air bubbles. Cover securely with plastic wrap, and freeze overnight. (Semifreddo, if tightly wrapped, will keep up to one week in the freezer.)

To serve, remove the top layer of plastic wrap and invert the pan onto a platter large enough to hold the semifreddo. Tap the bottom of the pan sharply to loosen the frozen mixture. Remove the plastic wrap, and with a long, thin knife cut the semifreddo into slices. (You can warm the knife in hot water first to make slicing easier.)

CHOCOLATE ORANGE TRUFFLES WITH DIFFERENT COATINGS

Tartufi di Cioccolato all'Arancia

The orange flavor is subtle here, but you can match coatings to accent it or play off it. Use one or all of the suggested coatings here, or come up with some of your own. Truffles are a great dessert idea when you want a decadent last bite without a lot of fuss. You can round out the course with fresh fruit in season to end the meal on a light note.

Makes about 36

TRUFFLE MIXTURE

¾ cup heavy cream
1 tablespoon grated orange zest
8 ounces bittersweet chocolate, finely chopped
4 ounces semisweet chocolate, finely chopped
1 tablespoon Grand Marnier or other orange
    liqueur
1 tablespoon butter, cut into pieces
¼ teaspoon pure vanilla extract

COATING SUGGESTIONS

½ cup unsweetened cocoa powder
1 cup finely chopped pistachios
1 cup finely chopped toasted almonds
1 cup chopped toasted coconut
½ cup instant espresso powder

In a small saucepan, combine the cream and orange zest. Bring to a bare simmer, just until bubbles form around the edges.

Put the chocolate in a medium glass bowl. Slowly pour in the hot cream. Let sit for a few minutes, until most of the chocolate appears to be melted, then add the liqueur, butter, and vanilla, and beat vigorously until smooth and shiny. Let sit at room temperature until set but still soft, about 1 to 2 hours.

Line a baking sheet with parchment. Use two small spoons to make thirty-six dollops of truffle mixture on the baking sheet, and refrigerate until firm, about 30 minutes to 1 hour.

You can roll the truffles in just one or any combination of the ingredients here, according to taste. Prepare the coatings of your choice and put them in small shallow bowls. Rolling will be a little less messy if you wear disposable kitchen-prep gloves or oil your hands with a little vegetable oil. Roll the truffles in your hands to form balls, and roll them, one at a time, in the coating of your choice, pressing gently as you roll to make the coating stick.

Put the truffles, without letting them touch each other, on wax paper in an airtight container, and refrigerate until ready to serve. (They can be made up to 2 days ahead; just be sure to store them tightly covered.)

CHOCOLATE CROSTOLI

Crostoli al Cioccolato

Crostoli, fried sweet dough pieces that look like crispy ribbons, were and still are the traditional cookie of the holidays. The crostoli can be made ahead of time, but give them a final dusting of cocoa and confectioners' sugar just before serving, so they look fresh from the fryer.

Makes about 36

6 tablespoons unsalted butter, softened
½ cup granulated sugar
½ teaspoon kosher salt
¼ cup milk
1 large egg, plus 1 large egg yolk
¼ cup orange juice
Grated zest of 2 oranges
2¼ cups all-purpose flour, plus more for rolling the
    dough
½ cup cocoa powder
Vegetable oil, for frying
¼ cup confectioners' sugar

In a food processor, blend the butter, sugar, and salt until smooth. Add the milk, egg and yolk, orange juice, and zest, and process everything together until smooth. Scrape down the sides of the bowl. Add the flour and ¼ cup of the cocoa, and pulse until the dough comes together. Clean the bowl again, and pulse a few more times to mix thoroughly. Scrape the dough out onto a lightly floured work surface, and knead briefly into a soft, smooth ball. (If it is sticky, knead in more flour in small amounts.) Wrap the dough tightly in plastic, and chill 1 hour (or up to 1 day).

Cut the chilled dough in half, and work with one piece at a time. Flatten the dough on a lightly floured work surface, and roll it out into a rough square approximately 16 by 16 inches. With a fluted cutter, trim the edges and divide it into fourteen strips about 1¼ inches wide. Cut all the strips in half to form twenty-eight ribbons, each about 7 inches long (they will shrink after you cut them).

One at a time, tie each ribbon into a simple overhand knot. Place the knotted crostoli on a baking sheet lined with parchment, leaving room between them so they don't stick to each other. Roll out the second piece of dough; cut and tie the same way.

Meanwhile, pour vegetable oil in a deep frying pan and heat to 360 degrees. Fry the crostoli in two or three batches until crisp and cooked all the way through, about 4 minutes per batch, turning occasionally. Drain on a paper-towel-lined baking sheet. Repeat with the remaining batches. To serve, combine the confectioners' sugar and remaining ¼ cup cocoa in a fine strainer, and dust the crostoli through the strainer, turning them to coat both sides.

FIG AND HAZELNUT BUTTER COOKIES

Biscotti con Nocciole e Marmellata di Fichi

These cookies can be made a day ahead. Store them in an airtight container between layers of parchment so they don't stick together. You can play around with combinations of jam and nuts for the filling, as you like.

Makes about 48

2½ cups all-purpose flour
½ teaspoon kosher salt
2 sticks unsalted butter, softened
1 cup sugar
1 large egg
1 teaspoon pure vanilla extract
⅓ cup fig preserves
⅓ cup coarsely chopped toasted skinned
  hazelnuts

Sift the flour and salt together. Beat butter and sugar with an electric mixer until very pale and fluffy, about 4 minutes, then beat in the egg and vanilla extract. At low speed, mix in the flour mixture until a dough forms. Wrap dough in plastic, and chill until firm, about 1 hour.

Preheat oven to 350 degrees with racks in the top and bottom thirds. Line two large baking sheets with parchment paper. Pinch off heaping-teaspoon-sized pieces of dough, and roll them into balls. Place balls on the prepared baking sheets, about 2 inches apart, and flatten them slightly with the palm of your hand. Bake them until they are puffed but not browned, about 8 minutes.

Remove baking sheets from oven, and carefully make a small crater in the middle of each cookie, using a teaspoon-sized measuring spoon. Fill each crater with ¼ to ½ teaspoon preserves, and sprinkle some chopped hazelnuts into the preserves. Finish baking the cookies until they are golden brown on the bottom and edges, about 8 minutes more. Cool the cookies on the baking sheets for 5 minutes, then transfer them to racks and cool completely. Store in airtight containers at room temperature.

CHUNKY CHERRY BREAD PUDDING

Budino di Pane e Ciliegie

Bread pudding is one of my favorite desserts to make. It's not syrupy-sweet, which I like, and once you have the basic recipe you can change the fruits and flavorings based on whatever you have at hand. I also love the idea of not wasting but recycling day-old bread.

Serves 8

1 tablespoon unsalted butter, softened

1 cup plus 2 tablespoons sugar

½ teaspoon ground cinnamon

6 large eggs

2 cups heavy cream

1 cup milk

¼ teaspoon kosher salt

1 teaspoon pure vanilla extract

6 cups brioche or other rich egg bread, day-old, cut into ½-inch cubes

1 cup halved pitted Bing cherries, fresh or frozen (thawed if frozen)

6 tablespoons chunky cherry preserves

½ cup sliced almonds

Preheat oven to 350 degrees. Bring a kettle of water to boil and keep it hot. Coat the bottom and sides of a 2-quart oval or rectangular baking dish with the softened butter. Sprinkle 2 tablespoons of the sugar on the buttered surfaces; tilt and shake the pan so it's sugared. Stir together another ¼ cup of the sugar with the cinnamon in a small bowl.

Whisk the eggs in a large bowl until thoroughly blended. Gradually pour in the cream, milk, the remaining ¾ cup sugar, the salt, and vanilla. Whisk until smooth. Stir the bread cubes into the custard, pushing them down so they're all submerged, and stir in the cherries. Let the bread soak for 15 minutes.

Spoon the pudding into the baking dish, and drop teaspoonfuls of the preserves on top, distributing evenly, then scatter the almonds on top. Finally, sprinkle with the cinnamon sugar. Put the pudding dish inside a roasting pan, and set the pan in the oven. Pour the boiling water to come halfway up the sides of the baking dish. Bake the pudding until the top is golden brown and crusty and the custard is set, about 1 hour to 1 hour and 10 minutes. (A knife blade inserted into the custard should come out clean.) Remove from the oven, and let the pudding cool in the water bath until you can safely remove it. Serve warm.

The Strong Finish—Italian After-Dinner Drinks

Although Italians enjoy wine with their meals, they love to linger after eating with a grappa or an amaro. The choices of after-dinner drinks today are many, ranging from Cognac to anisette to Sambuca, but some old favorites remain as staples. Grappa is the most common after-dinner drink; the art of making it has evolved to include grappa made from single varietals, sometimes aged in wood or infused with herbs.

The tradition of drinking amari, my favorites, or bitter after-dinner drinks such as Averna, Lucano, and Montenegro, is long-standing; these liqueurs are fantastic after a big meal, to aid digestion or just to savor. The bitters are usually distilled alcohol with infusions of many herbs, barks, and vegetables such as artichokes, as well as citrus fruits, and spices heated, steamed, and infused into the alcohol. The best way to enjoy an amaro is straight up or over one or two ice cubes.

Italians also enjoy a good number of cordials or after-dinner liqueurs. Cordials and liqueurs are alcoholic beverages that are sweet and have a pronounced flavor that could be of fruit, herbs, seeds, coffee, or flowers. They are taken with coffee after dinner sometimes instead of dessert (or with coffee even when just getting together). A favorite Italian American liqueur is Sambuca, a licorice-flavored cordial, often served with a coffee bean floating in it. Then there are the endless varieties of sweet, flavored after-dinner drinks, such as limoncello, distilled alcohol with lemon peel and sugar; nocino, a walnut-flavored liqueur; Frangelico, a hazelnut-flavor liqueur; Amaretto, an almond-flavored liqueur; Strega, made with wildflowers and herbs; and anisette, an anise-flavored liqueur, among many others.

Index

(Page references in *italics* refer to illustrations.)

A Note About the Authors

Lidia Bastianich is an Emmy award–winning public television host, best-selling cookbook author, restaurateur, and owner of a flourishing food and entertainment business. Lidia has married her two passions in life—her family and food—to create multiple culinary endeavors with her two children, Joseph and Tanya.

Lidia's cookbooks, coauthored with her daughter, Tanya, include *Lidia's Mastering the Art of Italian Cuisine, Lidia's Commonsense Italian Cooking, Lidia's Favorite Recipes, Lidia's Italy in America, Lidia Cooks from the Heart of Italy,* and *Lidia's Italy*—all companion books to the Emmy-winning and three-time-nominated television series *Lidia's Kitchen, Lidia's Italy in America,* and *Lidia's Italy.* Lidia's series air internationally in Mexico, Canada, the Middle East, Croatia, the United Kingdom, and Spanish-speaking South American countries. Lidia has also published *Lidia's Family Table, Lidia's Italian-American Kitchen, Lidia's Italian Table,* and *La Cucina di Lidia.*

Lidia is the chef/owner of four acclaimed New York City restaurants—Felidia, Becco, Esca, and Del Posto—as well as Lidia's Pittsburgh and Lidia's Kansas City along with her daughter, Tanya. She is also founder and president of Tavola Productions, an entertainment company that produces high-quality broadcast productions. In 2014, three Tavola productions—*Lidia's Kitchen, Lidia Celebrates America*, and Amy Thielen's *Heartland Table* on the Food Network—were nominated for James Beard Awards. *Lidia Celebrates America: Home for the Holidays* won the James Beard Award in 2016 for Best Special. Together with Tanya and Lidia's son-in-law, Corrado, Lidia also has developed a line of pastas and all-natural sauces, LIDIA'S.

With her son, Joe Bastianich, Mario Batali, and Oscar Farinetti, Lidia opened Eataly, the largest artisanal Italian food and wine marketplace, in New York City, Chicago, Boston, and São Paulo, Brazil. A second New York location opened in 2016; the Los Angeles location will open in 2017 and Toronto in 2018.

Lidia's first children's book, *Nonna Tell Me a Story: Lidia's Christmas Kitchen*, was inspired by her five grandchildren and was accompanied by an animated one-hour special for public television. The second installment in the series, *Lidia's Family Kitchen: Nonna's Birthday Surprise,* was released in spring 2013, and the third was released in January 2015.

Lidia is a founding member of Les Dames D'Escoffier and of Women Chefs and Restaurateurs, two nonprofit organizations of women leaders in the food and hospitality industries. She is also on the board of Arrupe College, a higher-education program for underprivileged students, founded by Loyola University Chicago. Lidia gives freely of her time and knowledge and is active in community service activities and special events on behalf of several foundations and public television.

Tanya Bastianich Manuali's visits to Italy as a child sparked her passion for the country's art and culture. She dedicated herself to the study of Italian Renaissance art during her college years at Georgetown, and earned a master's degree from Syracuse University and a doctorate from Oxford University. Living and studying in many regions of Italy for several years, she taught art history to American students in Florence, although she met her husband, Corrado Manuali, who is from Rome, in New York.

Tanya is integrally involved in the production of Lidia's public television series as an owner and executive producer of Tavola Productions, and is active in the family restaurant business. She has also led the development of the website, lidiasitaly.com, and related publications and merchandise lines of tabletop and cookware.

Together with Corrado, Tanya oversees the production and expansion of the LIDIA'S food line of all-natural pastas and sauces. Tanya has coauthored several books with her mother, including *Lidia's Mastering the Art of Italian Cuisine, Lidia's Commonsense Italian Cooking, Lidia's Favorite Recipes, Lidia's Italy, Lidia Cooks from the Heart of Italy,* and *Lidia's Italy in America.* In 2010, Tanya coauthored *Reflections of the Breast: Breast Cancer in Art Through the Ages,* a social–art historical look at breast cancer in art from ancient Egypt to today. In 2014, Tanya coauthored a book with her brother, Joe, *Healthy Pasta.* Tanya and Corrado live in New York City with their children, Lorenzo and Julia.

A Note on the Type

This book was set in Adobe Garamond. Designed for the Adobe Corporation by Robert Slimbach, the fonts are based on types first cut by Claude Garamond (c. 1480–1561). Garamond was a pupil of Geoffroy Tory and is believed to have followed the Venetian models, although he introduced a number of important differences, and it is to him that we owe the letter we now know as "old style."

Composed by North Market Street Graphics
Lancaster, Pennsylvania

Printed and bound by LSC Communications,
Crawfordsville, Indiana

Designed by M. Kristen Bearse